D0910371

Nutshell Series

of

WEST PUBLISHING COMPANY

P.O. Box 64526

St. Paul, Minnesota 55164–0526

Accounting—Law and, 1984, 377 pages, by E. McGruder Faris, Late Professor of Law, Stetson University.

Administrative Law and Process, 2nd Ed., 1981, 445 pages, by Ernest Gellhorn, Dean and Professor of Law, Case Western Reserve University and Barry B. Boyer, Professor of Law, SUNY, Buffalo.

Admiralty, 1983, 390 pages, by Frank L. Maraist, Professor of Law, Louisiana State University.

Agency-Partnership, 1977, 364 pages, by Roscoe T. Steffen, Late Professor of Law, University of Chicago.

American Indian Law, 1981, 288 pages, by William C. Canby, Jr., Adjunct Professor of Law, Arizona State University.

Antitrust Law and Economics, 2nd Ed., 1981, 425 pages, by Ernest Gellhorn, Dean and Professor of Law, Case Western Reserve University.

Appellate Advocacy, 1984, 325 pages, by Alan D. Hornstein, Professor of Law, University of Maryland.

Art Law, 1984, 335 pages, by Leonard D. DuBoff, Professor of Law, Lewis and Clark College, Northwestern School of Law.

Banking and Financial Institutions, 1984, 409 pages, by William A. Lovett, Professor of Law, Tulane University.

Church-State Relations—Law of, 1981, 305 pages, by Leonard F. Manning, Late Professor of Law, Fordham University.

Civil Procedure, 2nd Ed., 1986, 306 pages, by Mary Kay Kane, Professor of Law, University of California, Hastings College of the Law.

Civil Rights, 1978, 279 pages, by Norman Vieira, Professor of Law, Southern Illinois University.

Commercial Paper, 3rd Ed., 1982, 404 pages, by Charles M. Weber, Professor of Business Law, University of Arizona and Richard E. Speidel, Professor of Law, Northwestern University.

Community Property, 1982, 447 pages, by Robert L. Mennell, Former Professor of Law, Hamline University.

Comparative Legal Traditions, 1982, 402 pages, by Mary Ann Glendon, Professor of Law, Boston College, Michael Wallace Gordon, Professor of Law, University of Florida and Christopher Osakwe, Professor of Law, Tulane University.

Conflicts, 1982, 470 pages, by David D. Siegel, Professor of Law, St. John's University.

Constitutional Analysis, 1979, 388 pages, by Jerre S. Williams, Professor of Law Emeritus, University of Texas.

Constitutional Power—Federal and State, 1974, 411 pages, by David E. Engdahl, Professor of Law, University of Puget Sound.

Consumer Law, 2nd Ed., 1981, 418 pages, by David G. Epstein, Dean and Professor of Law, Emory University and Steve H. Nickles, Professor of Law, University of Minnesota.

Contract Remedies, 1981, 323 pages, by Jane M. Friedman, Professor of Law, Wayne State University.

Contracts, 2nd Ed., 1984, 425 pages, by Gordon D. Schaber, Dean and Professor of Law, McGeorge School of Law and Claude D. Rohwer, Professor of Law, McGeorge School of Law.

Corporations—Law of, 1980, 379 pages, by Robert W. Hamilton, Professor of Law, University of Texas.

Corrections and Prisoners' Rights—Law of, 2nd Ed., 1983, 386 pages, by Sheldon Krantz, Dean and Professor of Law, University of San Diego.

Criminal Law, 1975, 302 pages, by Arnold H. Loewy, Professor of Law, University of North Carolina.

Criminal Procedure—Constitutional Limitations, 3rd Ed., 1980, 438 pages, by Jerold H. Israel, Professor of Law, University of Michigan and Wayne R. LaFave, Professor of Law, University of Illinois.

Debtor-Creditor Law, 3rd Ed., 1986, 383 pages, by David G. Epstein, Dean and Professor of Law, Emory University.

Employment Discrimination—Federal Law of, 2nd Ed., 1981, 402 pages, by Mack A. Player, Professor of Law, University of Georgia.

Energy Law, 1981, 338 pages, by Joseph P. Tomain, Professor of Law, University of Cincinnatti.

Environmental Law, 1983, 343 pages by Roger W. Findley, Professor of Law, University of Illinois and Daniel A. Farber, Professor of Law, University of Minnesota.

Estate and Gift Taxation, Federal, 3rd Ed., 1983, 509 pages, by John K. McNulty, Professor of Law, University of California, Berkeley.

Estate Planning—Introduction to, 3rd Ed., 1983, 370 pages, by Robert J. Lynn, Professor of Law, Ohio State University.

Evidence, Federal Rules of, 1981, 429 pages, by Michael H. Graham, Professor of Law, University of Miami.

Evidence, State and Federal Rules, 2nd Ed., 1981, 514 pages, by Paul F. Rothstein, Professor of Law, Georgetown University.

Family Law, 2nd Ed., 1986, about 418 pages, by Harry D. Krause, Professor of Law, University of Illinois.

Federal Jurisdiction, 2nd Ed., 1981, 258 pages, by David P. Currie, Professor of Law, University of Chicago.

Future Interests, 1981, 361 pages, by Lawrence W. Waggoner, Professor of Law, University of Michigan.

Government Contracts, 1979, 423 pages, by W. Noel Keyes, Professor of Law, Pepperdine University.

Historical Introduction to Anglo-American Law, 2nd Ed., 1973, 280 pages, by Frederick G. Kempin, Jr., Professor of Business Law, Wharton School of Finance and Commerce, University of Pennsylvania.

Immigration Law and Procedure, 1984, 345 pages, by David Weissbrodt, Professor of Law, University of Minnesota.

Injunctions, 1974, 264 pages, by John F. Dobbyn, Professor of Law, Villanova University.

Insurance Law, 1981, 281 pages, by John F. Dobbyn, Professor of Law, Villanova University.

Intellectual Property—Patents, Trademarks and Copyright, 1983, 428 pages, by Arthur R. Miller, Professor of Law, Harvard University, and Michael H. Davis, Professor of Law, Cleveland State University, Cleveland-Marshall College of Law.

International Business Transactions, 2nd Ed., 1984, 476 pages, by Donald T. Wilson, Professor of Law, Loyola University, Los Angeles.

International Law, 1985, 262 pages, by Thomas Buergenthal, Professor of Law, Emory University and Harold G. Maier, Professor of Law, Vanderbilt University.

Introduction to the Study and Practice of Law, 1983, 418 pages, by Kenney F. Hegland, Professor of Law, University of Arizona.

Judicial Process, 1980, 292 pages, by William L. Reynolds, Professor of Law, University of Maryland.

Jurisdiction, 4th Ed., 1980, 232 pages, by Albert A. Ehrenzweig, Late Professor of Law, University of California, Berkeley, David W. Louisell, Late Professor of Law, University of California, Berkeley and Geoffrey C. Hazard, Jr., Professor of Law, Yale Law School.

Juvenile Courts, 3rd Ed., 1984, 291 pages, by Sanford J. Fox, Professor of Law, Boston College.

Labor Arbitration Law and Practice, 1979, 358 pages, by Dennis R. Nolan, Professor of Law, University of South Carolina.

Labor Law, 1986, 397 pages, by Douglas L. Leslie, Professor of Law, University of Virginia.

Land Use, 2nd Ed., 1985, 356 pages, by Robert R. Wright, Professor of Law, University of Arkansas, Little Rock and Susan Webber Wright, Professor of Law, University of Arkansas, Little Rock.

Landlord and Tenant Law, 2nd Ed., 1986, about 320 pages, by David S. Hill, Professor of Law, University of Colorado.

Law Study and Law Examinations—Introduction to, 1971, 389 pages, by Stanley V. Kinyon, Late Professor of Law, University of Minnesota.

Legal Interviewing and Counseling, 1976, 353 pages, by Thomas L. Shaffer, Professor of Law, Washington and Lee University.

Legal Research, 4th Ed., 1985, 452 pages, by Morris L. Cohen, Professor of Law and Law Librarian, Yale University.

Legal Writing, 1982, 294 pages, by Lynn B. Squires and Marjorie Dick Rombauer, Professor of Law, University of Washington.

Legislative Law and Process, 2nd Ed., 1986, about 300 pages, by Jack Davies, Professor of Law, William Mitchell College of Law.

Local Government Law, 2nd Ed., 1983, 404 pages, by David J. McCarthy, Jr., Professor of Law, Georgetown University.

Mass Communications Law, 2nd Ed., 1983, 473 pages, by Harvey L. Zuckman, Professor of Law, Catholic University and Martin J. Gaynes, Lecturer in Law, Temple University.

Medical Malpractice—The Law of, 2nd Ed., 1986, about 337 pages, by Joseph H. King, Professor of Law, University of Tennessee.

Military Law, 1980, 378 pages, by Charles A. Shanor, Professor of Law, Emory University and Timothy P. Terrell, Professor of Law, Emory University.

Oil and Gas, 1983, 443 pages, by John S. Lowe, Professor of Law, University of Tulsa.

Personal Property, 1983, 322 pages, by Barlow Burke, Jr., Professor of Law, American University.

Post-Conviction Remedies, 1978, 360 pages, by Robert Popper, Dean and Professor of Law, University of Missouri, Kansas City.

Presidential Power, 1977, 328 pages, by Arthur Selwyn Miller, Professor of Law Emeritus, George Washington University.

Products Liability, 2nd Ed., 1981, 341 pages, by Dix W. Noel, Late Professor of Law, University of Tennessee and Jerry J. Phillips, Professor of Law, University of Tennessee.

Professional Responsibility, 1980, 399 pages, by Robert H. Aronson, Professor of Law, University of Washington, and Donald T. Weckstein, Professor of Law, University of San Diego.

Real Estate Finance, 2nd Ed., 1985, 262 pages, by Jon W. Bruce, Professor of Law, Vanderbilt University.

Real Property, 2nd Ed., 1981, 448 pages, by Roger H. Bernhardt, Professor of Law, Golden Gate University.

Regulated Industries, 1982, 394 pages, by Ernest Gellhorn, Dean and Professor of Law, Case Western Reserve University, and Richard J. Pierce, Dean and Professor of Law, University of Pittsburgh.

Remedies, 2nd Ed., 1985, 320 pages, by John F. O'Connell, Professor of Law, Western State University College of Law, Fullerton.

Res Judicata, 1976, 310 pages, by Robert C. Casad, Professor of Law, University of Kansas.

Sales, 2nd Ed., 1981, 370 pages, by John M. Stockton, Professor of Business Law, Wharton School of Finance and Commerce, University of Pennsylvania.

Schools, Students and Teachers—Law of, 1984, 409 pages, by Kern Alexander, Professor of Education, University of Florida and M. David Alexander, Professor, Virginia Tech University.

Sea—Law of, 1984, 264 pages, by Louis B. Sohn, Professor of Law, University of Georgia and Kristen Gustafson.

Secured Transactions, 2nd Ed., 1981, 391 pages, by Henry J. Bailey, Professor of Law Emeritus, Willamette University.

Securities Regulation, 2nd Ed., 1982, 322 pages, by David L. Ratner, Dean and Professor of Law, University of San Francisco.

Sex Discrimination, 1982, 399 pages, by Claire Sherman Thomas, Lecturer, University of Washington, Women's Studies Department.

Taxation and Finance, State and Local, 1986, 309 pages, by M. David Gelfand, Professor of Law, Tulane University and Peter W. Salsich, Professor of Law, St. Louis University.

Taxation of Corporations and Stockholders, Federal Income, 2nd Ed., 1981, 362 pages, by Jonathan Sobeloff, Late Professor of Law, Georgetown University and Peter P. Weidenbruch, Jr., Professor of Law, Georgetown University.

Taxation of Individuals, Federal Income, 3rd Ed., 1983, 487 pages, by John K. McNulty, Professor of Law, University of California, Berkeley.

Torts—Injuries to Persons and Property, 1977, 434 pages, by Edward J. Kionka, Professor of Law, Southern Illinois University.

Torts—Injuries to Family, Social and Trade Relations, 1979, 358 pages, by Wex S. Malone, Professor of Law Emeritus, Louisiana State University.

Trial Advocacy, 1979, 402 pages, by Paul B. Bergman, Adjunct Professor of Law, University of California, Los Angeles.

Trial and Practice Skills, 1978, 346 pages, by Kenney F. Hegland, Professor of Law, University of Arizona.

Trial, The First—Where Do I Sit? What Do I Say?, 1982, 396 pages, by Steven H. Goldberg, Professor of Law, University of Minnesota.

Unfair Trade Practices, 1982, 444 pages, by Charles R. McManis, Professor of Law, Washington University.

Uniform Commercial Code, 2nd Ed., 1984, 516 pages, by Bradford Stone, Professor of Law, Detroit College of Law.

Uniform Probate Code, 1978, 425 pages, by Lawrence H. Averill, Jr., Dean and Professor of Law, University of Arkansas, Little Rock.

Water Law, 1984, 439 pages, by David H. Getches, Professor of Law, University of Colorado.

Welfare Law—Structure and Entitlement, 1979, 455 pages, by Arthur B. LaFrance, Dean and Professor of Law, Lewis and Clark College, Northwestern School of Law.

Wills and Trusts, 1979, 392 pages, by Robert L. Mennell, Former Professor of Law, Hamline University.

Workers' Compensation and Employee Protection Laws, 1984, 274 pages, by Jack B. Hood, Former Professor of Law, Cumberland School of Law, Samford University and Benjamin A. Hardy, Former Professor of Law, Cumberland School of Law, Samford University.

Hornbook Series

and

Basic Legal Texts

of

WEST PUBLISHING COMPANY

P.O. Box 64526

St. Paul, Minnesota 55164–0526

Administrative Law, Davis' Text on, 3rd Ed., 1972, 617 pages, by Kenneth Culp Davis, Professor of Law, University of San Diego.

Agency and Partnership, Reuschlein & Gregory's Hornbook on the Law of, 1979 with 1981 Pocket Part, 625 pages, by Harold Gill Reuschlein, Professor of Law Emeritus, Villanova University and William A. Gregory, Professor of Law, Georgia State University.

Antitrust, Sullivan's Hornbook on the Law of, 1977, 886 pages, by Lawrence A. Sullivan, Professor of Law, University of California, Berkeley.

Civil Procedure, Friedenthal, Kane and Miller's Hornbook on, 1985, 876 pages, by Jack H. Friedental, Professor of Law, Stanford University, Mary K. Kane, Professor of Law, University of California, Hastings College of the Law and Arthur R. Miller, Professor of Law, Harvard University.

Common Law Pleading, Koffler and Reppy's Hornbook on, 1969, 663 pages, by Joseph H. Koffler, Professor of Law, New York Law School and Alison Reppy, Late Dean and Professor of Law, New York Law School.

Conflict of Laws, Scoles and Hay's Hornbook on, 1982, 1085 pages, by Eugene F. Scoles, Professor of Law, University of Illinois and Peter Hay, Dean and Professor of Law, University of Illinois.

Constitutional Law, Nowak, Rotunda and Young's Hornbook on, 2nd Ed., 1983, 1172 pages, by John E. Nowak, Professor of Law, University of Illinois, Ronald D. Rotunda, Professor of Law, University of Illinois, and J. Nelson Young, Late Professor of Law, University of North Carolina.

Contracts, Calamari and Perillo's Hornbook on, 2nd Ed., 1977, 878 pages, by John D. Calamari, Professor of Law, Fordham University and Joseph M. Perillo, Professor of Law, Fordham University.

Contracts, Corbin's One Volume Student Ed., 1952, 1224 pages, by Arthur L. Corbin, Late Professor of Law, Yale University.

Corporations, Henn and Alexander's Hornbook on, 3rd Ed., 1983, 1371 pages, by Harry G. Henn, Professor of Law, Cornell University and John R. Alexander.

Criminal Law, LaFave and Scott's Hornbook on, 1972, 763 pages, by Wayne R. LaFave, Professor of Law, University of Illinois, and Austin Scott, Jr., Late Professor of Law, University of Colorado.

Criminal Procedure, LaFave and Israel's Hornbook on, 1985 with 1985 pocket part, 1142 pages, by Wayne R. LaFave, Professor of Law, University of Illinois and Jerold H. Israel, Professor of Law University of Michigan.

Damages, McCormick's Hornbook on, 1935, 811 pages, by Charles T. McCormick, Late Dean and Professor of Law, University of Texas.

Domestic Relations, Clark's Hornbook on, 1968, 754 pages, by Homer H. Clark, Jr., Professor of Law, University of Colorado.

Economics and Federal Antitrust Law, Hovenkamp's Hornbook on, 1985, 414 pages, by Herbert Hovenkamp, Professor of Law, University of California, Hastings College of the Law.

Environmental Law, Rodgers' Hornbook on, 1977 with 1984 Pocket Part, 956 pages, by William H. Rodgers, Jr., Professor of Law, University of Washington.

Evidence, Lilly's Introduction to, 1978, 490 pages, by Graham C. Lilly, Professor of Law, University of Virginia.

Evidence, McCormick's Hornbook on, 3rd Ed., 1984, 1156 pages, General Editor, Edward W. Cleary, Professor of Law Emeritus, Arizona State University.

Federal Courts, Wright's Hornbook on, 4th Ed., 1983, 870 pages, by Charles Alan Wright, Professor of Law, University of Texas.

Federal Income Taxation of Individuals, Posin's Hornbook on, 1983 with 1985 Pocket Part, 491 pages, by Daniel Q. Posin, Jr., Professor of Law, Southern Methodist University.

Future Interest, Simes' Hornbook on, 2nd Ed., 1966, 355 pages, by Lewis M. Simes, Late Professor of Law, University of Michigan.

Insurance, Keeton's Basic Text on, 1971, 712 pages, by Robert E. Keeton, Professor of Law Emeritus, Harvard University.

Labor Law, Gorman's Basic Text on, 1976, 914 pages, by Robert A. Gorman, Professor of Law, University of Pennsylvania.

Law Problems, Ballentine's, 5th Ed., 1975, 767 pages, General Editor, William E. Burby, Late Professor of Law, University of Southern California.

Legal Ethics, Wolfram's Hornbook on, 1986, about 1050 pages, by Charles W. Wolfram, Professor of Law, Cornell University.

Legal Writing Style, Weihofen's, 2nd Ed., 1980, 332 pages, by Henry Weihofen, Professor of Law Emeritus, University of New Mexico.

Local Government Law, Reynolds' Hornbook on, 1982, 860 pages, by Osborne M. Reynolds, Professor of Law, University of Oklahoma.

New York Estate Administration, Turano and Radigan's Hornbook on, 1986, about 575 pages, by Margaret V. Turano, Professor of Law, St. John's University and Raymond Radigan.

New York Practice, Siegel's Hornbook on, 1978 with 1985 Pocket Part, 1011 pages, by David D. Siegel, Professor of Law, St. John's University.

Oil and Gas, Hemingway's Hornbook on, 2nd Ed., 1983, 543 pages, by Richard W. Hemingway, Professor of Law, University of Oklahoma.

Poor, Law of the, LaFrance, Schroeder, Bennett and Boyd's Hornbook on, 1973, 558 pages, by Arthur B. LaFrance, Dean and Professor of Law, Lewis and Clark College, Northwestern School of Law, Milton R. Schroeder, Professor of Law, Arizona State University, Robert W. Bennett, Dean and Professor of Law, Northwestern University and William E. Boyd, Professor of Law, University of Arizona.

Property, Boyer's Survey of, 3rd Ed., 1981, 766 pages, by Ralph E. Boyer, Professor of Law, University of Miami.

Property, Law of, Cunningham, Whitman and Stoebuck's Hornbook on, 1984, 916 pages, by Roger A. Cunningham, Professor of Law, University of Michigan, Dale A. Whitman, Dean and Professor of Law, University of Missouri, Columbia and William B. Stoebuck, Professor of Law, University of Washington.

Real Estate Finance Law, Nelson and Whitman's Hornbook on, 1985, 941 pages, by Grant S. Nelson, Professor of Law, University of Missouri, Columbia and Dale A. Whitman, Dean and Professor of Law, University of Missouri, Columbia.

Real Property, Moynihan's Introduction to, 1962, 254 pages, by Cornelius J. Moynihan, Professor of Law, Suffolk University.

Remedies, Dobb's Hornbook on, 1973, 1067 pages, by Dan B. Dobbs, Professor of Law, University of Arizona.

Secured Transactions under the U.C.C., Henson's Hornbook on, 2nd Ed., 1979 with 1979 Pocket Part, 504 pages, by Ray D. Henson, Professor of Law, University of California, Hastings College of the Law.

Securities Regulation, Hazen's Hornbook on the Law of, 1985, 739 pages, by Thomas Lee Hazen, Professor of Law, University of North Carolina.

Torts, Prosser and Keeton's Hornbook on, 5th Ed., 1984, 1286 pages, by William L. Prosser, Late Dean and Professor of Law, University of California, Berkeley, Page Keeton, Professor of Law Emeritus, University of Texas, Dan B. Dobbs,

Professor of Law, University of Arizona, Robert E. Keeton, Professor of Law Emeritus, Harvard University and David G. Owen, Professor of Law, University of South Carolina.

Trial Advocacy, Jeans' Handbook on, Soft cover, 1975, 473 pages, by James W. Jeans, Professor of Law, University of Missouri, Kansas City.

Trusts, Bogert's Hornbook on, 5th Ed., 1973, 726 pages, by George G. Bogert, Late Professor of Law, University of Chicago and George T. Bogert.

Uniform Commercial Code, White and Summers' Hornbook on, 2nd Ed., 1980, 1250 pages, by James J. White, Professor of Law, University of Michigan and Robert S. Summers, Professor of Law, Cornell University.

Urban Planning and Land Development Control Law, Hagman and Juergensmeyer's Hornbook on, 2nd Ed., 1986, about 600 pages, by Donald G. Hagman, Late Professor of Law, University of California, Los Angeles and Julian C. Juergensmeyer, Professor of Law, University of Florida.

Wills, Atkinson's Hornbook on, 2nd Ed., 1953, 975 pages, by Thomas E. Atkinson, Late Professor of Law, New York University.

Advisory Board

THE LAW OF
MEDICAL MALPRACTICE
IN A NUTSHELL

by

JOSEPH H. KING, JR.
Alumni Distinguished Service Professor
University of Tennessee College of Law

SECOND EDITION

ST. PAUL, MINN.
WEST PUBLISHING CO.
1986

•

Library of Congress Cataloging in Publication Data

King, Joseph H.
  The law of medical malpractice in a nutshell.

  (Nutshell series)
  Includes index.
  1. Physicians—Malpractice—United States. I. Title.
II. Series. [DNLM: 1. Ethics, Medical. 2. Forensic
Medicine—United States. 3. Jurisprudence—United
States. 4. Malpractice—United States—legislation.
W 44 K53L]
KF2905.3.Z9K56 1986   346.7303'32   85–29579
                          347.306332
ISBN 0–314–98200–0

    King, Med.Malpractice, 2nd Ed., NS

TO
DIANE KING

*

PREFACE

The trends noted in the Preface to the first edition have continued. Although the frequency of dramatic changes in the law of medical malpractice has abated, rules elaborating the principles developed in the last two decades have continued to proliferate. New theories of liability also continue to evolve. To what extent, for example, must a physician warn a patient of the risks of refusing a recommended medical procedure? When does a physician owe a duty to prevent unintentional injuries to non-patients arising from the patient's condition?

Despite a decade of unprecedented attempts by the states to stem the rising tide of malpractice litigation through law reform, the number and size of claims continue to grow. Challenges to the constitutionality of reform legislation, although meeting with mixed success, have contributed to this continuing increase in malpractice claims. Thus, it is not clear whether the statutory reforms seen in so many states do, in fact, signal the beginning of legislative primacy in this setting, traditionally the domain of the judiciary. Moreover, the failure of reform legislation to reduce malpractice litigation—even to reverse its expansion—has reinforced the spectre of a chronic "malpractice crisis."

The substantial body of case and statutory malpractice law evokes an ambivalent reaction from the commentator. On the one hand, the sheer mass of law defies rational systematizing. Yet at the same time this mounting body of law, representing so much legal energy and potential human suffering, begs ordering. The law of medical malpractice has been an esoteric field, embracing complex concepts from two professional disciplines. Few have ventured into it with confidence. This book, by offering the reader an overview of the law, will hopefully remove some of the mystery. The book's organization and extensive use of cross-references are designed to create a framework that will facilitate understanding and foster a sense of continuity. Where difficult questions exist, an effort is made to identify and address them. But the law of medical malpractice contains few concepts that do not boast of at least two views. Given its scope, this book does not offer a comprehensive examination of the subject or the law of a specific jurisdiction. For such information, the reader should refer to the primary case and statutory law as well as to the many excellent articles in the legal literature.

Although this book was written primarily for law students and members of the legal profession, it may also be of value to others, including health care providers, insurance professionals, legislators, and others generally interested in the law of medical malpractice. A final chapter exploring possible systemic reforms is addressed not only to medical and legal practitioners and consumers, but to legislators and their constituents as well.

Various individuals have provided assistance with the second edition. A number of students provided citation help with a later draft of the book. In this regard, a special word of appreciation is due one of my students, David L. Rihtarchik. My colleague, Professor Carol Mutter, painstakingly read the final draft and shared many useful insights and impressions with me. Our professional word processing team, including Kim Whittenbarger and Jeannie Emantel, produced prompt, accurate, and polished manuscript copy. Dean Kenneth Penegar was, true to character, a source of support and encouragement. Finally, I am indebted to my wife, Diane, who managed not only to satisfy the demands of her own profession, but to assume the lion's share of responsibilities at home so that the second edition could be completed in timely fashion.

*

OUTLINE

Page

Preface --- XIX

Table of Short Citation Forms ------------- XXXIII

Table of Cases ----------------------------------- XXXV

**Chapter I. The Nature of Medical Mal-
practice** ------------------------------ 1
A. Historical Perspectives: The Emergence
of the "Malpractice Action" -------------- 1
B. Fault-Based Liability------------------------------ 5
C. Legal Theories of Malpractice: Tort or
Contract? ------------------------------------- 6

Chapter II. Liability for Negligence ------- 9
A. Elements of Negligence Action------------- 9
B. Duty—When Does It Arise and When
Does It End?---------------------------------- 9
   1. General Principles ---------------------------- 9
   2. Potential Sources for Creation of a
Duty --- 15
      a. Duty Based on a Consensual Pro-
fessional Relationship ------------ 15
      b. Duty Based on an Undertaking
to Render Medical Care-------- 16
      c. Other Sources of Duty------------- 21
      d. Multiple Health Care Providers 22

Page

B. Duty—When Does It Arise and When Does It End?—Continued

   3. Duration of the Duty and Abandonment 23

   4. Scope of the Duty—Limitations on Practice 29

   5. Non-Therapeutic Relationships and Services 30

   6. Potential Duty and Liability to Non-Patients 34

C. Nature of the Duty Owed—The Standard of Care 39

   1. Standard of Care Defined 39

     a. In General 39

     b. Professional Standards 41

   2. Nature and Effect of Professional Standards 43

     a. Acceptable or Customary Practice? 43

     b. Weight Accorded Professional Standards 47

     c. Expert Testimony Requirement 52

   3. Frames of Reference 55

     a. Time of Act or Omission 55

     b. Defendant's Situation 55

     c. Professional Frame of Reference 55

     d. Geographic Frame of Reference 58

     e. Special Rules—Peer Review and Utilization and Quality Controls 63

   4. "Respectable Minority" and "Error in Judgment" Problems 65

Page

C. Nature of the Duty Owed—The Standard of Care—Continued

    5. "Best Judgment" Rule _____ 72

    6. Average or Reasonably Competent Practitioner? _____ 75

D. Proof of Professional Negligence _____ 76

    1. Expert Testimony_____ 76

        a. Securing Expert Testimony _____ 76

        b. Testimonial Competency of Experts_____ 77

            i. Competency in General_____ 77

            ii. Professional Competency of Experts _____ 78

            iii. Geographic Competency of Experts _____ 81

    2. Potential Exceptions to Expert Witness Requirement_____ 83

        a. In General _____ 83

        b. Common Knowledge Situations__ 84

        c. Defendant's Admissions and Testimony _____ 86

        d. Manufacturers' Instructions and Information _____ 89

        e. Medical Literature_____ 98

        f. Violation of Statute, Regulation, or Ordinance _____ 102

        g. Guidelines of Professional Organizations and Institutional Rules _____ 106

        h. Court-Appointed Experts and Screening Panels _____ 110

Page

D. Proof of Professional Negligence—Continued

  3. Circumstantial Evidence and *Res Ipsa Loquitur* 111

    a. *Res Ipsa Loquitur In General* ... 111

    b. Availability of Doctrine in Medical Malpractice 112

    c. Causation and *Res Ipsa Loquitur* 113

    d. Elements of *Res Ipsa Loquitur*.. 114

      i. Elements in General 114

      ii. Inference of Negligence 116

      iii. Exclusive Control 119

      iv. Conduct of the Plaintiff 123

    e. Effect of Plaintiff's Knowledge, Pleadings, and Proof 124

    f. Procedural Effect 126

Chapter III. The Patient's Right to Self-Determination and Information 130

A. Nature of Patient's Right to Self-Determination and Information........................... 130

B. Requirement of Consent 131

  1. Forms of Consent 131

    a. Consent by the Patient 131

    b. Implied Consent 137

    c. Scope of Consent 137

    d. Substituted Consent and the Right to Refuse Treatment 143

  2. Standard for Consent 152

Page

C. Informed Consent and Decision Making 154
1. In General _____ 154
2. Battery or Negligence? _____ 155
3. Standard of Disclosure _____ 156
   a. Various Approaches_____ 156
   b. Suggested Solution_____ 163
4. Causation _____ 164
5. Privileges to Withhold Information __ 168
6. Who Must Disclose? _____ 170
7. Informed Refusal _____ 173
D. Other Informational Needs of the Patient 175
1. Subsequently-Discovered Dangers _____ 175
2. Misrepresentation, Concealment, and
   Nondisclosure_____ 175

**Chapter IV. Intentional Torts and Mis-
cellaneous Torts** _____ 179
A. Intentional Torts in Malpractice _____ 179
B. Battery and Assault _____ 180
C. False Imprisonment and Wrongful Com-
mitment_____ 181
D. Unauthorized Communications and Dis-
closures_____ 183
1. Defamation _____ 183
2. Invasion of Privacy _____ 184
3. Divulgence of Confidential Informa-
tion_____ 185
4. Privileges to Disclose _____ 188

Page

E. Intrusive Invasions of Privacy --------------- 193

F. Infliction of Mental Distress ----------------- 193

Chapter V. Causation, Damages, and Scope of Duty -------------------- 198

A. In General ----------------------------------- 198

B. Causation and Valuation ---------------------- 199

   1. Test of Causation-------------------------- 199

   2. Proof of Causation ------------------------ 200

   3. Multiple Causes --------------------------- 202

   4. Preexisting Conditions and Loss of a Chance -------------------------------------- 203

   5. Burden of Proof--------------------------- 209

C. Proximate Cause and Scope of Liability 211

   1. Nature of Proximate Cause and Scope of Duty Limitations --------------------- 211

   2. Special Problems on Scope of Liability 213

      a. Assisting in Non-Therapeutic Matters--------------------------------- 213

      b. Peer Review and Related Matters------------------------------------- 216

      c. Disposition of Dead Bodies and Human Tissue---------------------- 217

      d. Birth as an Injury ------------------ 219

         i. Nature of the Problem ------ 219

         ii. Birth of Normal Child ------- 220

         iii. Birth of Deformed or Disabled Child-------------------- 224

      e. Self-Inflicted Injury ----------------- 227

Page
D. Damages --- 229

Chapter VI. Vicarious Liability ------------- 231
A. In General -- 231
B. Liability of Physicians for Their Employ-
   ees' Torts-------------------------------------- 233
C. Liability for Torts of Other Physicians -- 234
D. Partnerships and Professional Corporations --- 236
E. Non-Employees and the "Borrowed Ser-
   vant" Rule------------------------------------- 239
   1. Theory of the Borrowed Servant------ 239
   2. Absent Physicians ---------------------- 241
   3. Physicians Present During Patient
      Care-------------------------------------- 243
      a. In General --------------------------- 243
      b. The Right to Control Standard   244
      c. Assumption or Exercise of Con-
          trol-------------------------------- 245
   4. Responsibility for Other Physicians-- 248
   5. Effect on Hospital Liability ----------- 250
   6. The Borrowed Servant: A Reap-
      praisal----------------------------------- 250

Chapter VII. Contract and Strict Liabili-
              ty Theories of Recovery 253
A. Contract Actions-------------------------------- 253
   1. In General---------------------------------- 253
   2. Contracts Promising Specific Results 254
      a. The Dilemma ----------------------- 254
      b. Possible Approaches to the Prob-
          lem----------------------------------- 256
   3. Other Uniquely Contractual Actions 259

Page

B. Strict Liability --------------------------------- 260

   1. Physicians --------------------------------- 260

   2. Hospitals ---------------------------------- 262

Chapter VIII. Defenses and Limitations on Liability -------------------- 267

A. Statutes of Limitations ------------------------ 267

   1. Limitations of Actions Generally ----- 267

   2. The Applicable Statute -------------------- 268

   3. Accrual of Cause of Action ------------ 270

      a. Traditional Rule --------------------- 270

      b. Discovery Rules --------------------- 271

         i. Pure Discovery Rule --------- 271

         ii. Hybrid Rules -------------------- 272

         iii. Nature of the Discovery Rule ----------------------------- 273

      c. Continuing Involvement or Treatment Rules ------------------ 276

   4. Possible Exceptions to General Accrual Rules ----------------------------------- 279

   5. Reform of Statute of Limitations ----- 282

B. Defenses Based on Plaintiff's Conduct --- 283

C. Releases and Related Matters -------------- 286

   1. In General --------------------------------- 286

   2. Releases of Other Tortfeasors --------- 286

   3. Exculpatory Releases Prior to Injury 289

   4. Arbitration Agreements ------------------- 290

Page

D. Possible Immunities 291
    1. In General 291
    2. Official and Statutory Immunity of
        Individuals 291
    3. Institutional Immunities 293
        a. Governmental Immunity 293
        b. Charitable Immunity 295
E. Other Potential Limitations on Liability 296

Chapter IX. Hospital Liability 298
A. In General 298
B. Vicarious Liability 299
    1. For Torts of Physicians 299
    2. For Non-Physicians 303
C. Corporate Responsibility for Patient Care 304
    1. Corporate Liability in General 304
    2. Nature of Corporate Responsibility .. 307
        a. Hospital Equipment, Supplies,
            Medication, and Food 307
        b. Hospital Environment 309
        c. Safety Procedures 310
        d. Selection and Retention of Em-
            ployees and Conferral of Staff
            Privileges 311
        e. Responsibilities for Supervision
            of Patient Care 315

Page

Chapter X. Current Perspectives and Future Prospects........................ 319

A. An Overview of Recent Statutory Changes 319
B. Need for Law Reform.............................. 324
C. Future Directions 326

Index.. 333

TABLE OF SHORT CITATION FORMS

All references to the Restatement of Torts and to the Prosser and McCormick treatises are to the Restatement (Second) and to the latest editions of the treatises, respectively. The following short citation forms are used throughout this book:

1. Restatement (Second) of Torts (1965, 1977), cited as: Restatement §_____.
2. W. Prosser & P. Keeton, The Law of Torts (5th ed. 1984), cited as: Prosser §_____.
3. McCormick on Evidence (E. Cleary, ed., 3d ed. 1984), cited as: McCormick §_____.

*

TABLE OF CASES

References are to pages

Albert v. Ertan, 214
Anderson v. Florence, 88
Anderson v. Prease, 195
Anderson v. Somberg, 122, 127

Baird v. Sickler, 244
Baldwin v. Knight, 84, 111
Barbee v. Rogers, 260
Barber v. Superior Court, 149
Barclay v. Campbell, 169
Barnes v. Schlein, 7
Bartimus v. Paxton Comm. Hosp., 80
Bass v. Barksdale, 19
Batiste v. American Home Products Corp., 261
Beaches Hosp. v. Lee, 245
Beardsley v. Wierdsma, 221
Beatty v. Morgan, 28
Bell v. Umstattd, 172
Belle Bonfils Memorial Blood Bank v. Hansen, 266
Bellotti v. Baird, 136
Berry v. Moench, 190
Berthiaume, Estate of v. Pratt, 193
Betesh v. United States, 31, 32
Bivens v. Detroit Osteopathic Hosp., 98
Blades v. DaFoe, 157
Blair v. Eblen, 42, 43, 46, 47, 61, 63
Bloskas v. Murray, 176
Boone v. Mullendore, 223
Borderlon v. Peck, 280

Bornmann v. Great S.W. Gen. Hosp., Inc., 311
Brooks v. South Broward Hosp., 218
Brown v. Colm, 78
Browning v. Norton Children's Hosp., 219
Brune v. Belinkoff, 75
Buckelew v. Grossbard, 117
Buckley v. Lovallo, 305, 307
Burns v. Hartford Hosp., 275
Burns v. Wannamaker, 258
Burton v. Brooklyn Doctor's Hosp., 73
Butler v. Louisiana St. Bd. of Ed., 58

Canterbury v. Spence, 157, 158, 159, 166, 165, 169
Caro v. Bumpus, 56
Carranza v. Tucson Med. Center, 124
Cartier v. Long Island College Hosp., 38
Cebula v. Berroit, 70
Chiero v. Chicago Osteopathic Hosp., 53
Chrestman v. Kendall, 92
Chumbler v. McClure, 66
City of (see name of city)
Cline v. Lund, 79
Cobbs v. Grant, 156
Coleman v. Garrison, 221
Conroy, Matter of, 148
Cooper v. Curry, 299
Cooper v. Sisters of Charity of Cinn., Inc., 206
Corleto v. Shore Mem. Hosp., 216, 313
Cornfeldt v. Tongen, 172
Cousins v. Henry, 124
Crouch v. Most, 168
Cucalon v. State, 105
Custody of a Minor, 145, 150

Dahlberg v. Ogle, 235
Danielson v. Roche, 138
Darling v. Charleston Comm. Mem. Hosp., 48, 108, 315, 316
Davidson v. Mobile Infirmary, 203
Davidson v. Shirley, 139

Davis v. Mangelsdorf, 36
Davis v. Tirrell, 32
Davis v. Weiskopf, 18
DeMartino v. Albert Einstein Med. Ctr. N.D., 273
Demers v. Gerety, 136
Dennis v. Allison, 261
Derrick v. Ontario Comm. Hosp., 37
Di Giovanni v. Latimer, 196
Dickinson v. Mailliard, 301
Downer v. Veilleux, 66
Dun & Bradstreet, Inc. v. Greenmoss Builders, Inc., 184
Durkin v. Equine Clinics, Inc., 93
Duvall v. Goldin, 35

Eckleberry v. Kaiser Foundation Northern Hosp., 98
Elizondo v. Tavarez, 241
Estate of (see name of estate)

Fabian v. Matzko, 14
Fall v. White, 71, 198, 285
Faulkner v. Pezeshki, 75
Ferguson v. Gonyaw, 56
Ferlito v. Cecola, 195, 257
Ferrara v. Galluchio, 194
Finn v. G.D. Searle & Co., 260
First Nat'l Bank of Chicago v. Porter, 200
Fitzmaurice v. Flynn, 80
Foil v. Ballinger, 274
Forney v. Memorial Hosp., 172
Fosgate v. Corona, 209
Fountain v. Cobb Gen. Hosp., 80, 198
Fraijo v. Hartland Hosp., 58
Frazier v. Hurd, 81
Freese v. Lemmon, 34
Fridena v. Evans, 314

Gallegor v. Fedler, 117
Gambill v. Stroud, 60
Gammill v. United States, 36, 37

TABLE OF CASES

Gertz v. Robert Welch, Inc., 184
Giallanza v. Sands, 19
Gilbert v. Campbell, 113
Gooding v. University Hosp. Bldg. Inc., 206
Grannum v. Berard, 133
Grant v. Touro Infirmary, 247
Green, In re, 145
Greenberg v. Michael Reese Hosp., 262
Greene v. Thomas, 79, 85
Griswold v. Connecticut, 220
Grubb v. Albert Einstein Med. Center, 264
Guebard v. Jabaay, 117, 142
Guerrero v. Copper Queen Hospital, 14
Guilmet v. Campbell, 256, 257

H.L. v. Matheson, 136
Hale v. Venuto, 118
Hallkey v. Birbiglia, 170
Hammer v. Rosen, 180
Harbeson v. Parke Davis, Inc., 161, 225, 227
Harnish v. Children's Hosp. Med. Ctr., 158, 162, 164, 171
Harris v. Robert C. Groth, M.D., Inc., P.S., 52, 53
Hartke v. McKelway, 164
Harvey v. Fridley Med. Center, 200
Haven v. Randolph, 167
Helling v. Carey, 49, 50, 52
Herskovits v. Group Health Co-op of Puget Sound, 206, 207
Hicks v. United States, 207
Hier, Matter of, 148
Hiser v. Randolph, 21
Hively v. Edwards, 104
Hofbauer, Matter of, 146
Hoffman v. Blackman, 35
Holbrook v. Schatten, 160
Holloway v. Hauver, 92
Holt v. Godsil, 47
Holton v. Pfingst, 162
Hood v. Phillips, 68
Hook v. Rothstein, 156, 161, 164

TABLE OF CASES

Horne v. Patton, 186
Hoven v. Kelble, 261, 262
Howard v. Mt. Sinai Hosp., 194
Humphrers v. First Interstate Bank, 186
Hynes v. Hoffman, 285

Impastato v. DeGirolamo, 235
In re (see name of party)
Incollingo v. Ewing, 46, 210

Jackovach v. Yocom, 137
Johnson v. Gamwell, 279, 312, 313, 314
Johnson v. Grant Hosp., 311
Johnson v. Misericodia Com. Hosp., 311
Johnson v. St. Bernard Hosp., 300
Johnson v. Whitehurst, 171
Johnson v. Woman's Hosp., 195, 218
Johnson v. Yeshiva Univ., 55
Joiner v. Mitchell County Hosp. Auth., 313
Jones v. Malinowski, 221
Justus v. Atchison, 197

Kaiser v. Suburban Transp. System, 34
Kapuschinsky v. United States, 310
Karrigan v. Nazareth Convent & Academy, Inc., 85
Kelly v. Carroll, 57
Kennedy v. Parrott, 7, 141, 142
Kennedy Mem. Hosp., Inc., John F. v. Bludworth, 150
Killingsworth v. Poon, 84
Kitto v. Gilbert, 244, 249, 250

Landeros v. Flood, 105
Lane v. Candura, 146
Largent v. Acuff, 201
Lausier v. Pescinski, 144
Lhotka v. Larson, 95
Little v. Arbuckle Mem. Hosp. Bd. of Control, 115
Little v. Little, 144
Logan v. Greenwich Hosp. Assn., 71, 156, 158, 171, 173

Loizzo v. St. Francis Hosp., 115, 122
Longman v. Jasieh, 24
Lopez v. Hudgeons, 36, 37, 104
Lotspench v. Chance Vought Aircraft, 31
Lyons v. Grethen, 19
Lysick v. Walcom, 54

McCarthy v. Boston City Hosp., 105
McCormack v. Lindberg, 61, 79
McCullough v. Bethany Med. Ctr., 242, 244, 288
McDermott v. Manhattan Eye, Ear & Throat Hosp., 88
McMillin v. L.D.L.R., 236
Magner v. Beth Israel Hosp., 260
Magrine v. Krasnica, 261
Mallett v. Pirkey, 162
Maltempo v. Cuthbert, 20
Marcus v. Liebman, 181
Marquis v. Battersley, 116
Marrero v. Goldsmith, 125
Marvulli v. Elshire, 248
Mastro v. Brodie, 274
Matter of (see name of party)
Maxwell v. Woman's Clinic, P.A., 87
May v. Broun, 245, 246
Mazza v. Huffaker, 181
Medina v. Figuered, 86
Mielke v. Condell Mem. Hosp., 85, 93
Miles v. Edward O. Tabor, M.D., Inc., 200
Miller v. Dore, 28
Millsaps v. Bankers Life Co., 189
Mincey v. Blando, 235
Mohr v. Williams, 138
Molien v. Kaiser Fdn. Hosp., 196, 197
Montana Deaconess Hosp. v. Gratton, 117
Morgan v. Hill, 80, 86
Moss v. Rishworth, 137
Mudd v. Dorr, 127
Mueller v. Mueller, 91, 94
Mulder v. Parke Davis & Co., 94, 95

XL

Naccash v. Burger, 242, 243
Nanke v. Napier, 221
Nelson v. Krusen, 226
Nevauex v. Park Place Hosp., Inc., 170, 263
Newhall v. Central Vt. Hosp. Inc., 305, 307
Nicholsen v. Good Samaritan Hosp., 295
Nichter v. Edmiston, 247
Nielson v. D'Angelo, 54
Nishi v. Hartwell, 169
Noland v. Freeman, 276
North Miami Gen. Hosp. v. Krakower, 310

O'Brien v. Cunard S.S. Co., 133
O'Connor v. Bloomer, 122
Ohligschlager v. Proctor Community Hosp., 93
Olsen v. Molzen, 289
Olson v. Western Airlines, Inc., 32
O'Neill v. Montefiore Hospital, 18
Overstreet v. Nickelsen, 284

Paige v. Manuzak, 198
Paintsville Hosp. Co. v. Rose, 302
Pedroza v. Bryant, 314
Peeples v. Sargent, 106
Perin v. Hayne, 117
Perna v. Pirozzi, 28, 142
Perricone, State v., 144
Pickle v. Curns, 318
Piehl v. Dalles Gen. Hosp., 250
Piller v. Kovarsky, 215
Pinky v. Winer, 86
Pisel v. Stamford Hosp., 229, 310
Pizzalotto, M.D. Ltd., Karl J. v. Wilson, 140
Planned Parenthood of Central Mo. v. Danforth, 135
Pogue v. Hospital Auth. of DeKalb County, 301
Poor Sisters of St. Francis v. Catron, 316
Poulin v. Zartman, 100
Preston v. Hubbell, 138
Procanik v. Cillo, 226

Providence Hosp. v. Truly, 263
Pry v. Jones, 85
Purcell v. Zimbelman, 311

Quinlan, Matter of, 148, 150
Quinones v. Public Adm'r of County of Kings, 286

Racer v. Utterman, 264
Rainer v. Grossman, 20
Ramey v. Fassoulas, 226
Reams v. Stutler, 52, 236
Redwine v. Baptist Gen. Con., 264
Reilly v. Straub, 125
Reinhardt v. Colton, 79, 95, 162
Revenis v. Detroit Gen. Hosp., 308
Richardson v. LaBuz, 273
Rieck v. Medical Protective Co. of Fort Wayne, Ind., 221
Roark v. Allen, 59
Roberson v. Counselmann, 207
Roe v. Wade, 220
Rogala v. Silva, 258
Rogers v. Brown, 116
Rogers v. Lumbermens Mutual Cas. Co., 139
Rosenthal v. Blum, 214
Rothe v. Hull, 138
Rule v. Cheeseman, 17

Sagmiller v. Carlsen, 189
Salazar v. Ehmann, 109
Sammons v. Smith, 115, 125
Sampson, Matter of, 145
Sanzari v. Rosenfeld, 92
Satz v. Perlmutter, 146
Schenker v. Binns, 7
Schloendorff v. Society of N.Y. Hosp., 130
Schneider v. Albert Einstein Med. Center, 249
Schroeder v. Perkel, 225
Senesac v. Associates in Obstetrics and Gynecology, 47, 53
Sesselman v. Muhlenberg Hosp., 247

TABLE OF CASES

Settoon v. St. Paul Fire & Marine Ins. Co., 235
Shilkret v. Annapolis Emergency Hosp. Ass'n, 60, 61, 62, 76, 298
Short v. Kinkade, 58
Shorter v. Drury, 289
Simmons v. St. Clair Mem. Hosp., 303
Simpson v. Davis, 58
Simpson v. Dickson, 160
Skelton v. Druid City Hosp. Bd., 264
Smith v. Karen S. Reisig, M.D., Inc., 87
Smith v. St. Francis Hosp., Inc., 301, 302
Sofo v. Frankford Hosp., 35
Somerset, City of v. Hart, 250
Spannaus v. Otolaryngology Clinic, 122
Sparger v. Worley, 244
Spring, Matter of, 150
Sprowl v. Ward, 66, 98, 101
Stahlin v. Hilton Hotels Corp., 106
Starnes v. Charlotte-Mecklenberg Hosp. Auth., 246, 308
State v. ———— (see opposing party)
Steeves v. United States, 71, 109
Stevens v. Union Mem. Hosp., 122
Stewart v. Rudner, 259
Stone v. Proctor, 109
Storar, Matter of, 149, 150
Stundon v. Stadnik, 116, 117
Sullivan v. O'Connor, 254
Superintendent of Belchertown State School v. Saikewicz, 148, 149
Sutton v. Cook, 57
Swank v. Halivopoulos, 109
Swanson v. Chatterton, 78

Talbot v. Dr. W.H. Groves' Latter-Day Saints Hosp., 122
Tarasoff v. Regents of U. Cal., 38
Taylor v. Hill, 58, 61, 79
Thomas v. St. Joseph Hosp., 263
Thompson v. County of Alameda, 38
Thompson v. Presbyterian Hosp., Inc., 248
Thompson v. Sun City Community Hosp., 208

XLIII

TABLE OF CASES

Tittle v. Hurlbutt, 105
Tomer v. American Home Products Corp., 55
Toppino v. Herhahn, 84, 85
Toth v. Community Hosp. at Glen Cove, 72, 74, 75
Tresemer v. Barke, 175
Trujillo v. Puro, 215
Truman v. Thomas, 165, 174, 175
Tucson Med. Ctr., Inc. v. Misevch, 317

University of Ariz. v. Superior Ct., 222

Vaillancourt v. Medical Center Hosp. of Vt., Inc., 196
Van Steensburg v. Lawrence & Mem. Hospitals, 108
Van Zee v. Sioux Valley Hosp., 113, 202
Variety Children's Hosp., Inc. v. Perkins, 242
Vassos v. Roussalis, 22, 47, 53, 61, 201, 236
Vistica v. Presbyterian Hosp. & Med. Center of San Francisco,
    Inc., 123

Wall v. Stout, 59
Weinstock v. Ott, 284
Whetham v. Bismark Hosp., 197
Wiles v. Myerly, 84, 122, 127
Williams v. St. Claire Med. Center, 108
Willoughby v. Kenneth W. Wilkins, M.D.P.A., 301, 302
Winchester v. Meads, 243
Winkjer v. Herr, 92
Witherell v. Weimer, 279

Ybarra v. Spangard, 120, 121, 122
Young v. Caspers, 127
Young v. Cerniak, 108
Younts v. St. Francis Hosp. and School of Nursing, Inc., 134

Zoski v. Gaines, 134

MEDICAL MALPRACTICE
IN A NUTSHELL

*

CHAPTER I

THE NATURE OF MEDICAL MALPRACTICE

A. HISTORICAL PERSPECTIVES: THE EMERGENCE OF THE "MALPRACTICE ACTION"

Medicine is the science of preventing, palliating, and healing illness. The practice of the healing arts can be traced back to the origins of Middle Eastern and Oriental civilizations. Perhaps as early as 2000 B.C. the Code of Hammurabi evidenced concern for the quality of medical practice. The Oath of Hippocrates, written in the fourth century, B.C., is still a part of the tradition of the medical profession. Yet, it has only been in the last century that modern medicine has blossomed. The historical "schools" of the healing arts, with their varied philosophies, have now largely been subsumed into a single unified field of medical science. The level of education and access to information and facilities now afforded medical practitioners is unprecedented. What was a guild of artisans or craftsmen is today a learned profession. Moreover, scientific advances such as the development of antibiotics, chemotherapy, antiseptic surgical techniques, immunizations, X-ray diagnosis and therapy, definitive diagnostic tests, and complex team surgery have only recently given the medical prac-

1

titioner the means of preventing and curing illness on a broad scale.

The methods chosen by society to deal with what it regards as substandard performance by medical practitioners has also undergone marked change. Under early English common law, physicians were regarded almost as members of a public calling, much the same as innkeepers, with their liability defined accordingly. With the rise of commercialism, the physician's role became more a creation of contract law, with individual rights and liabilities established by the parties. This was followed by the emergence of traditional torts precepts, especially negligence law with its notion of the "reasonable person," as the dominant theory of liability. Torts principles have now largely supplanted the law of contracts as the animating doctrine that defines professional medical liability. Current legal concepts governing the professional liability of medical practitioners reflect a new awareness of the potentials of modern medicine and the heightened public expectations they inspire. They are also based on the assumption that reasonable medical skill can make a difference in human wellbeing, and that the judicial system, aided by experts from the medical profession, is capable of distinguishing acceptable from unacceptable levels of professional performance. Not all agree, however, on the continuing validity of this latter assumption given the increasing technical complexity of modern medicine.

Tort law continues to be the dominant legal theory in this area. There has been, however, growing recognition that the matters relating to the control of the quality of medical services and to allocation of losses for medical accidents may, to some extent, be *sui generis,* calling for particularized legal solutions.

The term "medical malpractice," as it is used here, embraces all liability-producing conduct arising from the rendition of professional medical services. The phrase "malpractice" is retained here for several reasons. First, despite its sometimes negative connotation, it is an almost universally recognized expression. Second, use of the more comprehensive concept of malpractice underscores the fact that negligent medical care does not exhaust all potential sources of professional liability. Liability may also result, for example, from intentional misconduct, breaches of contracts guaranteeing a specific therapeutic result, defamation, divulgence of confidential information, unauthorized postmortem procedures, and failures to prevent injuries to certain non-patients. In addition, given the unique features of malpractice litigation, traditional torts and negligence principles may not always be suitable in the medical malpractice context. The law of medical malpractice has not only developed syncretically, borrowing and adapting rules from the law of torts and contracts, it has also spawned a host of singular legal concepts reflecting its unique aspects.

Because physicians are the health care providers primarily responsible for patient care, most malpractice claims are asserted against them. For this reason, primary attention will be focused on malpractice litigation involving physicians. Nevertheless, it is important to note that other health care providers, especially hospitals and nurses, are increasingly becoming the objects of malpractice claims. Many of the legal principles governing actions against physicians may apply with equal force to malpractice claims asserted against other health care providers such as hospitals, dentists, nurses, psychologists, and veterinarians. There may, however, be aspects of patient care that are unique to these other providers. While some of the unique legal issues relating to hospitals have been examined in a separate chapter, it was not possible to address here the legal issues peculiar to other health care providers.

In evaluating the legal principles that govern malpractice cases, it is useful to bear in mind that there are three interested groups. First, there are the aggrieved patients who seek redress for what they believe were needless injuries resulting from allegedly unsound medical practices that may have left them maimed and disabled. Second, there are the health care providers, who declare their innocence and whose professional conduct is challenged *sub judice.* For them a malpractice action holds forth the presentiment of years of haunting self-recrimination and time-consuming legal proceedings. There is also the possibility of an adverse judgment that might result in higher liability insurance premiums or cancellation of insurance. There is even the possibility of a financially devastating judgment in excess of insurance coverage. Finally, the members of the public have an interest. They must finance, through taxes and higher medical charges, the costs of this loss-shifting apparatus known as the malpractice action. They will also be the ones who must be treated by physicians who are preoccupied with the spectre of liability, practice defensive medicine, and fear their patients, and as a result bring less than their full concentration and expertise to bear on the ultimate objective of healing.

B. FAULT–BASED LIABILITY

Medical malpractice law is a system of loss allocation that for the most part* is based on the "fault" of the defendant. To be sure, liability based on a breach of a contract guaranteeing a specific result, a master-servant relationship, *res ipsa loquitur,* a lack of informed consent, and perhaps other doctrines all have aspects that may smack of liability without fault. Yet even with many of these doctrines there is usually some unacceptable conduct by the defendant or by some-

---

* As will be discussed more fully later, some cases have extended strict liability principles to some health care providers, such as hospitals, for harm caused by defective items or substances used in patient care. And even here, there is a sharp division of authority. *See generally VII,* B.

one for whom the defendant bears responsibility. For the vast majority of malpractice cases, liability will depend upon evidence that the defendant's conduct fell below the level of care that society allows with impunity. Thus, the mere fact that a patient suffered a health-impairing experience during the course of a medical procedure will not, without more, ordinarily render one who provided the medical services that caused the harm liable for malpractice.

The question whether the existing system of liability based on fault can be justified or should be preserved is examined in Chapter X. Aside from this, the primary emphasis of the treatise will be upon the manner in which the current fault system operates to redistribute losses from medical accidents.

C. LEGAL THEORIES OF MALPRACTICE: TORT OR CONTRACT?

As will be seen (*see* II, B, 2), a physician-patient relationship may be based upon a contract between the parties (a contract basis), an undertaking to perform (a tort basis), or both. Given this dual source of the physician-patient relationship, a question sometimes arises whether tort or contract law governs the rights and liabilities of the parties. Malpractice actions fall into two basic categories with respect to this issue.

In the great majority of cases plaintiff alleges that the physician has in some way failed to perform in accordance with the required standard of care. Regardless of whether the physician-patient relationship is based on a contract or on an undertaking, the duty of care in such cases will usually be the same. A health care provider is required to conform to the applicable standard of care not only when he impliedly agreed to do so, but also because the law requires it once he undertakes to render care. There are also other aspects of such cases in which the question of the applicable law may be significant. For example, the statute of limitations or the measure of damages may be affected by the applicable theory of recovery. When it is alleged essentially that defendant failed to exercise the requisite degree of care, the decided trend has been to hold that tort law rather than contract law provides the rule of law with respect to such matters. *See* Barnes v. Schlein, 192 Conn. 732, 473 A.2d 1221 (1984) (statute of limitations); VII, A, 4. *See also* Schenker v. Binns, 18 Mass.App. 404, 466 N.E.2d 131 (1984) (applicability of public employee immunity provision of statute). As one court observed, for the purposes of personal injury the usual consensual arrangement reached by the parties more aptly "creates a status or relation rather than a contract." Kennedy v. Parrott, 243 N.C. 355, 360, 90 S.E.2d 754, 757 (1956). This preference for tort law in the "due care" cases not only indicates an aversion to theory shopping, but also reflects the traditional predominance of tort law in the area of personal injury litigation.

A second category of cases consists of situations in which a plaintiff relies upon a contractual theory of recovery that may have no analogue in tort law. Perhaps in addition to or instead of charging a want of due care, plaintiff might assert, for example, that defendant had breached an express guarantee that he would achieve a specific therapeutic result. Such claims are generally decided on contract principles, unless otherwise required by a special malpractice legislation. *See* VII, A, 2.

CHAPTER II

LIABILITY FOR NEGLIGENCE

A. ELEMENTS OF NEGLIGENCE ACTION

In medical malpractice litigation, negligence is the predominant theory of liability. Negligence has been defined as "conduct which falls below the standard established by law for the protection of others against unreasonable risk of harm." Restatement (Second) of Torts § 282 (1965) (hereinafter cited as the Restatement). In order to recover for negligent malpractice, the plaintiff must establish the following elements: (1) that a *duty* of care was owed by the physician to the patient; (2) that the physician violated the applicable *standard of care*; (3) that the plaintiff suffered a *compensable injury*; and, (4) that such injury was *caused in fact* and *proximately caused* by the substandard conduct. Subject to a few exceptions, the burden of proving these elements is on the plaintiff.

B. DUTY—WHEN DOES IT ARISE AND WHEN DOES IT END?

1. General Principles

An essential element in any malpractice claim is the existence of a duty owed by the defendant to the injured party. The concept of duty may involve two inquiries. First, there may be a question whether one had a *duty to act* at all for the benefit of another. And, second, once a duty has arisen, there remains the question of the *nature* of that duty. The first question relates to the *existence* of a duty and is discussed in subsection B. The matter of the nature of the duty, more particularly the standard of care, is addressed in subsections C and D.

When a person affirmatively acts in a way that creates a risk of harm to another, a duty of care arises requiring the actor to exercise reasonable care to protect that other person. This duty arises irrespective of any prior relationship between the parties. This principle applies in both medical and non-medical settings. Thus, both the commuting doctor and the truck driver owe a duty to operate their vehicles in a manner that does not unreasonably threaten pedestrians even though they are strangers. In the medical context, a doctor must not injure another by his affirmative acts, such as by carelessly manipulating a patient's neck during a physical examination, irrespective of whether or not there would otherwise be a duty owed to the examinee.

The foregoing aspect of the duty question involves misfeasance. The more difficult matter of when a physician has a duty to act involves nonfeasance. A physician who has not agreed or under-taken to render care to a patient and who is not otherwise subject to the orders of others regarding acceptance of patients generally owes no duty to enter into a professional relationship. He would therefore not be required to treat another individual under such circumstances. This rule can be traced back to the common law distinction between misfeasance (active misconduct) and nonfeasance (passive inaction). Traditionally, liability would be imposed for the former, where a duty of care was imposed by law requiring that an actor avoid inflicting an unreasonable injury upon another. On the other hand, absent some existing relationship or some other basis to support a duty *to act,* there was generally held to be no duty owed by one individual to come to the aid of another and no liability was imposed for a failure to do so.

Some have defended the "no duty" rule observing that a party who has simply failed to do anything has at least not altered the status quo and is therefore less blameworthy than an active wrongdoer. A more credible explanation is that any other rule might have been inconsistent with the highly individualistic notions of independence that characterized much of the nation's history. The courts shrank from abrogating the right of an individual in a free society to say "no." Moreover, the medical practitioner was for the most part a participant in an essentially private enterprise. Abolition of the "no duty" rule raised the spectre of forcing free delivery of what had traditionally been a marketable service.

Physicians have seldom withheld emergency care because of the identity of the person in jeopardy. Moreover, governmental financing and private insurance have helped to pay for medical costs, thereby reducing the class of patients who might be refused treatment solely for economic reasons. "Good Samaritan" statutes limiting the liability of various persons rendering care at emergencies may also have encouraged emergency assistance. *See* VIII, E. Courts have also shown increased willingness to seize on the slightest association or actions as evidence that the physician has undertaken to care for a patient, thereby creating a duty of care.

Given the vast public financial support of medical education and services, the governmental involvement in the licensing of physicians, and the general interest of society in the well-being of its members, perhaps it would not be unjust to require that physicians take reasonable steps to render emergency care to those in need of it. Imposition of such a duty should, however, be in the form of legislation, accompanied by provisions for reimbursement from the state for emergency service to insolvent patients and, perhaps, limitations on liability.

Historically, hospitals were free to determine whom they would admit and the circumstances under which such admissions would be made. Today, however, this principle is riddled with qualifications and exceptions. *See generally* 2 Hosp. Law

Manual, *Admitting and Discharge* §§ 1–2 (1980). Even in *non-emergency situations*, a hospital's discretion in terms of whom to admit is becoming increasingly circumscribed. Neither public nor private hospitals may discriminate, for example, on the basis of race, color, national origin, or handicap in connection with programs receiving federal assistance. Discrimination by public hospitals may also be prohibited and possibly other limitations placed on their admission practices on the basis of statutory and Constitutional protections. Some states have also enacted anti-discrimination legislation. Moreover, there is a qualification to the receipt of federal construction funds by any hospital under various statutes that may require that a certain volume of services be provided to persons who are unable to pay. Some charters and statutes creating public hospitals as well as hospitals' own admission criteria often reflect a commitment to render medical care to the indigent. When a right of action can be implied from a statute or regulation, or they are held to create a duty upon which common law liability may rest, a hospital may be liable for unjustified failure to treat or admit an individual in violation of the prescribed standards.

Subject to applicable statutes and regulations, the right of hospitals, especially private ones, to establish admission criteria on non-discriminatory grounds, at least in the absence of an emergency situation, continues to be recognized as a general rule. *See* Fabian v. Matzko, 236 Pa.Super. 267, 344 A.2d 569 (1975). When, however, any hospital, public or private, actually undertakes to render medical care, a hospital-patient relationship may be created with its accompanying duties.

Even when none of the foregoing statutory or regulatory rules create a duty on the part of a hospital, a number of courts and legislatures have shown a marked willingness to require that any hospital (public or private) maintaining emergency facilities render care to those in need of *emergency treatment.* Some courts have relied upon public policy as evidenced by licensing statutes and health regulations to justify imposition of a duty to treat emergency patients. *See* Guerrero v. Copper Queen Hosp., 112 Ariz. 104, 537 P.2d 1329 (1975). Other courts have found a duty when the custom of a hospital to render emergency care to members of the public is relied upon by an individual requiring emergency treatment. A number of states have enacted legislation that expressly or impliedly requires all or some (depending on the statute) hospitals, especially with emergency departments, to render emergency services consistent with their capabilities to anyone in need of such care. *See* Cal.Health & Safety Code § 1317 (West 1979). Hospitals receiving federal construction funds may be prohibited from refusing emergency care to certain residents (and certain others) because of inability to pay.

In the future one would anticipate wide acceptance of the principle that all hospitals with emergency facilities should be required to render emergency services. Even as things presently stand, any hospital that refuses to provide available emergency services to one who reasonably appears in need of such services probably does so at its peril.

2. Potential Sources for Creation of a Duty

a. *Duty Based on a Consensual Professional Relationship*

The most common way in which a duty arises is when the physician (or other provider) and patient voluntarily enter into a physician-patient relationship. In most malpractice cases, the plaintiff is the patient—the individual who received or should have received medical care—or his survivor or legal representative. Occasionally, however, a physician may be sued by a non-patient to whom a duty was owed. *See* II, B, 6. Nevertheless, even such duties to non-patients generally emanate from a physician-patient relationship with someone or from a special contract with the plaintiff.

The most common basis for the creation of a physician-patient relationship is a simple contract. When a physician agrees that in exchange for a fee he will treat an individual, an express contract may be created. An implied contract may also be created—one that the courts will infer from circumstances such as the commencement of treatment with the consent of the patient and with the expectation of compensation for the physician.

Because an express or implied agreement between the physician and the patient often gives rise to their professional relationship, the duty owed by a physician to his patient is sometimes perceived as one based on a service contract. This, however, is an overly restricted view. Although most physician-patient relationships do involve the mutual assent of the parties and are therefore usually creatures of at least an implied contract, this may not always be the case. *See* II, B, 2, b. Moreover, once a physician-patient relationship arises, the duty of care ordinarily demanded of the health care provider is usually imposed by society through its tort law rather than as an incident of any existing contract between the parties. *See* I, C. For this reason, the physician's duty should be viewed as one broadly based on a professional medical relationship, a relationship that may arise in several ways and that may give rise to rights and obligations independent of any agreement by the parties. Of course, the parties may ordinarily agree to enlarge the scope of a physician's duty (such as by guaranteeing a specific therapeutic result) or to limit the scope of the professional relationship. *See* II, B, 4. *But cf.* VIII, C, 3. But in the absence of such a special agreement, the underlying contract is important primarily as one source for creation of a professional relationship from which the physician's duty is created.

b. Duty Based on an Undertaking to Render Medical Care

There are some situations that may not fit neatly into the traditional contract mold. For example, a physician may render gratuitous services to a patient without any promise or expectation of receiving a fee. A more workable theoretical basis for creating a physician-patient relationship in such situations is the rule that holds that a physician who undertakes to render care to another thereby creates a professional relationship with a corresponding duty of care to the recipient.*

The physician's duty of care may arise as a result of his undertaking to render treatment even when the services are gratuitous and not based on a contract, and there is no expectation of payment. Under the "undertaking" theory, neither the existence of the physician-patient relationship nor the underlying duty it creates is dependent upon payment for the physician's services. *See* Rule v. Cheeseman, 181 Kan. 957, 317 P.2d 472 (1957). When there has been some overt conduct by the physician, courts have usually had little trouble in finding a sufficient undertaking to create a physi-

---

* *See* Restatement § 323 (liability may result from substandard care when one undertakes to render services which he should recognize are necessary to protect the safety of another, and his failure to exercise due care increases the other's risk of harm or the harm is suffered because the other relied upon the undertaking). *See also id.* at § 324 (recognizing that one who takes charge of another who is helpless may be liable for bodily harm caused by failure to exercise reasonable care to secure the other's safety while in the actor's charge or by leaving the other in a worse position than before by discontinuing aid). The Restatement expresses a caveat as to whether liability might also result in other situations in which there has been an undertaking to perform even though the actor's conduct has induced no reliance and has in no way increased the risk.

King, Med.Malpractice, 2nd Ed., NS—3

cian-patient relationship. The clearest example is
when the physician actually begins to administer
treatment.

Perhaps the most extreme examples of a physician-patient relationship based upon an undertaking theory have arisen out of telephone conversa-
tions. In one case, plaintiff's decedent awoke at
5:00 a.m. with possible symptoms of a heart attack
including severe chest pains. With the help of his
wife, decedent walked to a nearby hospital. A
nurse telephoned one of the doctors assigned to
treat members of the hospital insurance plan to
which the decedent was a subscriber. The doctor
inquired in some detail about decedent's symptoms,
history and prior electrocardiograms. The doctor
maintained that he had offered to come to the
emergency room but the decedent had declined his
offer. Plaintiff, on the other hand, contended that
decedent had been instructed to go home and to
return in the morning. After the telephone conversation and after examination and treatment
were allegedly refused by hospital personnel, decedent walked home and died. In a malpractice suit,
the court held, *inter alia*, that the jury could have
concluded that the doctor undertook to diagnose
the condition of the deceased. O'Neill v. Montefiore Hospital, 11 A.D.2d 132, 202 N.Y.S.2d 436
(1960). *See also* Davis v. Weiskopf, 108 Ill.App.3d
505, 64 Ill.Dec. 131, 439 N.E.2d 60 (1982) (accepting
referral of and making appointment with a new
patient may create duty to inform him of possible

serious illness known to the physician after the physician allegedly declines to see the patient after being advised that patient would be late for a rescheduled appointment); Lyons v. Grethen, 218 Va. 630, 239 S.E.2d 103 (1977) (making an appointment with a new patient to treat a specific condition created a professional relationship and corresponding duty).

In Giallanza v. Sands, 316 So.2d 77 (Fla.App. 1975), the evidence indicated that a physician had agreed as a favor to allow his name to be used to have a patient admitted to a hospital for emergency care by the staff. He had written the information furnished to him on the patient's chart and had, according to his testimony, advised hospital physicians that he would not be handling the case. At no time had the doctor met the patient, diagnosed her condition, or had any contact with the patient or her family. The court held that a triable issue of fact existed whether a physician-patient relationship had been created. Conversely, another case held that the mere fact that a physician signed a prescription on behalf of another physician with the notation "per telephone order [of other physician]," did not create a physician-patient relationship. Bass v. Barksdale, 671 S.W.2d 476 (Tenn.Ct.App.1984).

In the case of hospitals, courts have been even more willing to find the necessary undertaking to support the creation of a hospital-patient relationship. *See* II, B, 1.

Although the trend has been in the direction of an increasing willingness to find a sufficient undertaking to support a duty, there are limits. In one case, a patient sued a medical school professor who, at a professional conference, had offered an opinion that surgery was indicated after hearing the patient's history. In upholding dismissal of the malpractice case, the appellate court held that there had been no physician-patient relationship between the professor and the patient. The court noted that the defendant had no right to control the patient's treating physicians and that the imposition of liability might stifle efforts aimed at disseminating medical knowledge. Rainer v. Grossman, 31 Cal.App.3d 539, 107 Cal.Rptr. 469 (1973).

When there has been merely a gratuitous promise to render services, the general rule has been to impose no tort liability* on the promisor for nonperformance, even when the promisee relied on the promise to his detriment. However, the courts have tended to seize upon almost any act beyond a mere promise in order to find a sufficient undertaking that would support a duty.**

* The doctrine of promissory estoppel and related contract principles may, however, afford a remedy for breach of contract in some situations. See Restatement (Second) Contract § 90 (1979).

** Moreover, a promise by a patient or third party to pay for future services promised by a physician should be adequate consideration to support a contract that would create a duty. In Maltempo v. Cuthbert, 504 F.2d 325 (5th Cir. 1974), a physician's promise to parents to look into reports of the deteri-

c. Other Sources of Duty

A duty may be based on a contractual obligation with a third party. The most obvious situation is when parents pay for treatment of their child. The duty owed to the child might be explained under third party beneficiary contract principles or on a torts undertaking theory if the physicians conduct proceeded far enough to constitute an undertaking to perform.

A duty based on a physician's contract with a non-patient sometimes arises in other circumstances. In one case defendant, along with other doctors, took turns manning the emergency room on an "on call" basis and were paid for each shift. Plaintiff arrived at the hospital in a semi-comatose acute diabetic condition. She was clearly entitled to emergency room care, and indeed had been treated at the emergency room the preceding day. The defendant allegedly refused to attend her and by the time another doctor arrived, 40 minutes had elapsed. The patient died the next morning. On appeal, the court held that the doctor's contract with the hospital created a duty to the patient unless some reasonable justification could be shown. Hiser v. Randolph, 126 Ariz. 608, 617 P.2d 774 (1980).

orating condition of their imprisoned diabetic son (presumably in exchange for the parents' at least implied promise to pay for his services) apparently created a duty. Although there was evidence that the physician had undertaken to perform by calling the jail, the court did rely on this basis for the duty.

d. Multiple Health Care Providers

A patient will often be attended by a number of health care professionals, including physicians (such as a surgeon and anesthesiologist), nurses, and medical technicians. As a result, a number of health care providers may simultaneously owe a duty of care to the patient. If one physician simply covers the primary physician's patient on a temporary basis, the respective duties of both physicians would be commensurate with their involvement with the patient. The real problem arises when multiple physicians assume *continuing* responsibility for primary care.

Recent decisions have taken the position that multiple physicians concurrently attending a patient may owe a duty to the patient even though one physician has paramount authority. In Vassos v. Roussalis, 658 P.2d 1284 (Wyo.1983), both the surgeon and the patient's regular physician attended the patient for post-operative peritonitis following surgical removal of a ruptured appendix. Although the surgeon was, according to the testimony, primarily responsible for the patient's post-operative care, the court held that the regular physician who also continued to actively attend the patient also owed the patient a duty of care. The court held that the jury could have found from the evidence that the regular physician should have determined that the post-operative treatment of the patient was substandard, should have confronted the surgeon, and if necessary, should have called in another surgeon.

3. Duration of the Duty and Abandonment

Unless the patient has discharged the physician or otherwise terminated the relationship, or some emergency or other circumstance occurs that justifies a failure to attend the patient, the physician is not entitled to terminate the relationship or fail to attend the patient unless he first gives reasonable advance notice. What constitutes reasonable notice will depend on the condition of the patient and the availability of other suitable medical care. Thus, if the patient reasonably appears to require additional medical care, the notice should be sufficiently far in advance to afford the patient a reasonable opportunity to come under the effective management of another suitable physician. In order for the notice to be reasonable, it must not only be sufficiently far in advance of termination, but it should also reasonably apprise the patient of his medical status and the type of future medical care required, including specialized care.

If reasonable notice under the circumstances is not possible, a physician may owe a duty to continue to attend the patient through the course of an acute illness. In one case, the court held that a dentist specializing in oral surgery owed a duty to attend the patient through her post-operative complications. When complications developed following oral surgery, the dentist referred the patient to her family physician, whose treatment was unsuccessful in arresting the post-operative infection. The dentist was held liable for the post-operative complications that would likely have been avoided had the patient been seen promptly by an oral surgeon. *See* Longman v. Jasieh, 91 Ill.App. 3283, 46 Ill.Dec. 636, 414 N.E.2d 520 (1980). Although the court did not clarify this, the notice may have been unreasonable because the patient was not referred to another suitable specialist, and in any event, her condition may have been too acute to warrant a delay in treatment while plaintiff sought another specialist. Thus, there is implicit in *Longman* the suggestion that a physician may be liable when the plaintiff was not clearly afforded both the time *and* guidance to obtain other suitably specialized care.

Under some circumstances, a physician may not be completely free to terminate the relationship even with reasonable advance notice. For example, when a physician agrees to perform surgery on the patient and then decides not to do so, the patient may have an action for breach of contract. Damages might include costs of repeating pre-operative laboratory studies as well as loss of time attributable to the cancellation of the surgery. And, of course, if reasonable notice were not given, a tort action might lie if the patient's health suffered as a result.

The reasonableness of the notice and termination of the professional relationship may also be affected by the way in which that relationship was created in the first place. The expectations of the parties would be especially important. Thus, a physician who renders emergency care at the scene of an accident should not ordinarily be required to attend the patient once his care has been entrusted to hospital emergency personnel or to the patient's family physician, and this fact has been communicated to the patient or his surrogate.*

When the physician-patient relationship is unilaterally terminated by the physician without rea-

---

* It has been suggested that one whose duty is based exclusively upon an undertaking may terminate his services at will as long as his action has not left the patient in a worse position by increasing the risk of harm to the patient or by inducing the patient to forego other opportunities for assistance. Restatement § 323, comment c. *See also id.* at § 324 (recognizing, inter alia, potential liability of one who, after taking charge of a helpless person, leaves him in a "worse position" than before by discontinuing aid to him). Nevertheless, a court would probably find, on one theory or another, that a continuing duty was owed to an endangered patient until he was out of danger or entrusted to the care of another competent physician, or until the patient released the physician. A court might, for example, reason under comment c that the patient's position was in fact worsened by the physician's intervention or by the fact that others did not intervene, relying on the physician. Or, an implied contract might be found to have arisen between the parties. Or, a court might simply reject the limited view of comment c outright. In this connection, the Restatement leaves open the question of potential liability for withdrawing from an undertaking that leaves one in unreasonable danger even though the actor's conduct has induced no reliance and has in no way increased the risk. *See id.* at § 323, comment e, § 324, caveat. On the other hand, it must be borne in mind that the imposition of too onerous a duty upon Good Samaritans might discourage them from offering any aid to those in jeopardy.

sonable notice or justification or unreasonably interrupted by a failure to attend the patient, it is said that the physician *abandoned* the patient. The concept of abandonment has been the subject of some confusion because courts have sometimes lumped together situations involving intentional termination of the relationship with those involving negligent failure to attend a patient. If the physician prematurely terminates the relationship, conscious of the patient's continuing need for care, he may be liable for intentional abandonment (and perhaps for breach of contract). If, on the other hand, the physician negligently discharges the patient or fails to attend him as reasonably required, he would be subject to liability for negligent abandonment. The latter situation is better addressed as simply a negligence matter (*see* II, C), reserving the "abandonment" nomenclature for terminations involving a conscious absence of reasonable notice. The practical effect of this distinction is that when negligence is alleged, expert testimony as to the standard of care will usually be required. In the conscious abandonment cases, on the other hand, the mere fact of termination of the relationship may establish the defendant's fault, although expert testimony may still be needed to prove the patient's continuing need for treatment and the unreasonableness of the notice.

A number of circumstances have, with varying degrees of success, been relied upon in attempts to excuse what might otherwise be actionable terminations of physician-patient relationships. Generally, incapacity of the physician that was not reasonably anticipated and that prevents the physician from giving further care or timely notice to the patient should prevent liability. However, when the patient merely fails to pay or does not cooperate in the treatment, such actions probably will not relieve a physician who, without reasonable notice, abandons or negligently fails to attend the patient. At least this is true when the patient's conduct does not become so obstinate as to defeat the efficacy of the treatment, constitute a withholding of consent to treatment, or become tantamount to termination by the patient.

Since a physician frequently may have to be absent for personal or professional reasons, arrangements are often made to have a substitute physician serve in his absence. The rotation of "on call" physicians is a common example. Unless the physician has agreed to attend the patient for a specific medical procedure or on a specific occasion, the use of such substitutes should not constitute abandonment when such arrangements are commonly known or are explained to the patient in advance. *See generally* II, B, 4. Sometimes a physician will also designate another to perform on a specific occasion in the event of the first physician's absence. One obstetrician might arrange with another obstetrician to deliver the plaintiff's child if the patient goes into labor while the first doctor was, for example, home sleeping after a full day. If this arrangement is fully explained and agreed to by the patient at the outset or reasonably far in advance, such conduct should not constitute abandonment. But, the patient should be informed of the substitution in advance and his consent obtained even if the substitute is in the original physician's medical group. *See* Perna v. Pirozzi, 92 N.J. 446, 457 A.2d 431 (1983).

Selection of a competent substitute physician without justification to care for a patient may not prevent liability for harm proximately resulting from the substitution, if notice is not given in sufficient time to enable the patient to engage a physician of her choice. *See* Miller v. Dore, 154 Me. 363, 148 A.2d 692 (1959). The same is true when another physician, even a competent one, substitutes for the physician agreed to by the patient without justification and without the patient's knowledge. *See* Perna, *supra*. A few cases, however, suggest that *either* giving reasonable notice *or* providing a competent substitute (presumably without any notice) is sufficient. *See* Beatty v. Morgan, 170 Ga.App. 661, 317 S.E.2d 662 (Ga.App. 1984).

If the patient is injured by a competent substitute physician without sufficient advance notice, a question arises as to what the damages should be. Clearly, the patient should be entitled to reimbursement for the costs and harm resulting from any medical procedures that had to be repeated because of the substitution of physicians. But what if harm also results because the original physician would have followed a different course that would likely have averted the harm, but the course actually followed was not negligent? The abandonment did in fact cause the injury. On the other hand, should non-negligent harm at the hands of a fully competent substitute physician be one of the risks compensated in an abandonment case? Perhaps such damages should be awarded against the original physician* at least when he intentionally refused to attend the patient knowing that the patient was in need of care and that insufficient time was available for the patient to select a suitable substitute of his own choice, and the patient had chosen the original physician in reliance upon his use of a technique or approach different than the method employed by the substitute.

When a patient is referred by one physician to another apparently competent physician, there should generally be no abandonment when the patient's condition reasonably appears to warrant such a referral and advance notice is afforded the patient where reasonably possible.

4. Scope of the Duty—Limitations on Practice

Since the physician-patient relationship is normally consensual, the physician is usually free to limit its scope. When a physician is also an em-

* The substituting physician might also be liable if the patient did not consent to the substitution and consent was feasible.

ployee of a third party such as a hospital, his freedom to limit his practice would be subject to the orders of his employer. Moreover, there are probably certain minimum requirements that society would impose as a matter of public policy that the physician could not disregard even if a patient ostensibly agreed. *See* VIII, C, 3.

A private practitioner may choose to limit the conduct of his practice with respect to such matters as office hours, house calls, and after hours telephone answering policies. A physician may also limit his type of practice. Thus, a dermatologist can obviously refuse to perform an appendectomy when other suitable physicians are available. Unless, however, the limitations on one's practice are already known or reasonably to be expected, the physician should inform his patients of them in advance. Furthermore, the limitations should not be so unreasonable as to endanger ones patients in a way that violates public policy.

5. Non-Therapeutic Relationships and Services

As previously noted, a physician may still owe a duty of care to someone even though the physician contracts with or is paid by someone else. This duty may be explained by either a contractual third party beneficiary theory or, if the physician has undertaken to perform, by a tort undertaking theory. *See* II, B, 2. When the purpose of the services is therapeutic—to medically benefit the recipient—it is clear that the physician owes the recipient a duty of care. A more complex question arises when services that are paid for by a third party were not intended to serve a therapeutic purpose.

There are numerous examples of situations involving at least arguably non-therapeutic examinations. Examples include examinations of insurance applicants; of claimants for personal injury, disability, and medical benefits; of applicants for employment; and of prospective employees. There are two possible types of injuries in such cases. The first involves physical harm to the examinee. Virtually every court would agree that a physician whose negligent conduct *actively* injures a non-therapeutic examinee would be liable regardless of who paid for the examination. Thus, a physician who negligently ruptures an examinee's spleen while palpating his abdomen during an examination would be liable. The more difficult question in these non-therapeutic cases is whether the physician might be liable to the examinee for negligent *omissions*—his failure to diagnose a disease or to notify the examinee of a potentially dangerous condition. The traditional rule had been that there was no physician-patient relationship and therefore no duty owed to the examinee in such situations. In recent years, however, the courts have been divided on the question. *Compare* Lotspench v. Chance Vought Aircraft, 369 S.W.2d 705 (Tex.Civ.App.1963) (no duty) *with* Betesh v. U.S., 400 F.Supp. 238 (D.D.C.1974) (duty). One case, for example, found a duty to notify a person receiving a preinduction physical of signs suggestive of cancer. *See* Betesh, *supra.* There is even language in some cases suggesting a duty not only to notify the examinee of dangerous conditions actually discovered but to exercise reasonable care *to discover* the condition.

The second type of injury involves economic loss that does not arise out of physical injury. An example would be a case in which a physician negligently and incorrectly reported that a job applicant suffered from a serious disease and as a result the applicant was denied employment. There is a division of authority on whether a physician hired by one other than the examinee* might be liable to examinees undergoing non-therapeutic examinations in situations involving economic losses unrelated to physical harm. *Compare* Davis v. Tirrell, 110 Misc.2d 889, 443 N.Y.S.2d 136 (1981) (no duty), *with* Olson v. Western Airlines, Inc., 143 Cal.App.3d 1, 191 Cal.Rptr. 502 (1983) (duty).

Until the law becomes more settled in this area, the following approach may be worth considering. At the time of a non-therapeutic examination, the

---

* A physician would also owe a duty to the person who hired him to perform the examination. For example, a physician who negligently failed to interpret correctly the x-rays of an insurance applicant might be liable to the insurance company that improvidently approved the application. Potential liability to that person would depend not only on the degree of care exercised, but the nature of the parties' contractual obligations.

physician should explain the non-therapeutic nature of the examination to the examinee. He should obtain consent to report the results to the individual that ordered the examination. *See* IV, D, 3. He should also explain the fact that the examination may be of limited scope and not intended to take the place of care by the examinee's personal physician. *See also* II, B, 4. The examinee should designate a private physician and consent to forwarding significant findings or test results to him. Then, if the examining physician actually discovers abnormalities that indicate a need for follow-up, he should be required to send a report to the examinee's private physician and a note to the examinee urging him to contact his private physician.

The examining physician should also be required to exercise reasonable care with respect to accuracy of any tests and findings actually communicated to the examinee. Moreover, if he actually undertakes to care for the patient or fails to explain the non-therapeutic nature of the examination, a duty of care should probably arise to notify the examinee not only of conditions actually discovered, but also to discover and report conditions that should reasonably have been discovered given the scope of the examination. Absent any of the preceding circumstances, the better rule would be to impose no liability on a physician hired by one other than the examinee to conduct a non-therapeutic examination for a failure to discover dangerous conditions or to properly evaluate the examinee's condition.

When an examination serves both therapeutic and non-therapeutic objectives, a normal duty of care should be owed by the physician to his examinee. For example, a preparticipation physical examination of an athlete may serve both objectives. What's more, such a duty should not be affected by the fact that the examination was paid for by a third party or was even free.

6. Potential Duty and Liability to Non-Patients

An increasingly important issue in the law of professional liability is to what extent a physician may owe a duty to take reasonable steps to protect non-patients. The issue may arise in a variety of situations. For example, a physician may negligently misdiagnose a patient's condition, and as a result a third party is injured by the unintentional acts of the patient. Although the courts are divided on the question, a clear trend favors holding the physician liable. For example, a physician might be liable if he negligently failed to diagnose epilepsy and to warn the patient of possible fainting, and the patient thereafter lost control of his automobile and injured the pedestrian-plaintiff. *See* Freese v. Lemmon, 210 N.W.2d 576 (Iowa 1973). There is also a duty to protect others by warning the patient about the effects of prescribed medication on his ability to operate a motor vehicle. *See* Kaiser v. Suburban Transp. System, 65 Wn.2d

461, 398 P.2d 14, amended 65 Wn.2d 461, 401 P.2d 350 (1965); *see also* Duvall v. Goldin, 139 Mich. App. 342, 362 N.W.2d 275 (1984) (potential liability to third person for alleged negligence in discontinuing anticonvulsive medication and failing to warn patient of dangers of driving without medication).

Some cases have held that the physician may be liable to relatives of a patient who contracts a contagious disease such as tuberculosis from the patient, if his condition was negligently misdiagnosed. *See* Hoffman v. Blackman, 241 So.2d 752 (Fla.App.1970). On the other hand, one court has refused to find a duty to the husband of a patient when the physician allegedly misdiagnosed his wife's condition as a drug overdose when it actually resulted from carbon monoxide inhalation from a defective gas heater. The non-patient husband later died from a carbon monoxide poisoning from the same heater. *See* Sofo v. Frankford Hosp., 478 F.Supp. 1134 (E.D.Pa.1979). This case may be distinguishable from the preceding ones in that the plaintiff neither contracted a disease from the patient nor suffered harm from him.

A recent Arizona case imposed limits on how far the court would extend a duty to non-patients. The plaintiff was injured when a former patient of the defendant suffered an epileptic seizure and lost control of his automobile. Seventeen years earlier the defendant doctor had discontinued the patient's anti-convulsive medication. The former patient had last seen the defendant-doctor 15 years prior to the accident. The court held as a matter of law that no duty was owed by the doctor to the accident victim. Although the court stated that a duty might arguably have existed for a reasonable period of time, it did not last for the 15–17 years during which the doctor was unaware of the former patient's condition. Davis v. Mangelsdorf, 138 Ariz. 207, 673 P. 2d 951 (App.1983).

A question that has received little attention is whether a physician who determines that the patient's condition poses a significant risk of unintentional harm to another should be under a duty to notify persons *in addition to the patient?* One court has implied that when a statute requires notification of state officials of the diagnosis that a patient is subject to loss of consciousness, and someone is injured because a physician failed to notify the officials so that his license could be withdrawn or restricted, a physician might be liable to the person injured by the patient if the physician negligently failed to fulfill his statutory duty. *See* Lopez v. Hudgeons, 115 Cal.App.3d 673, 171 Cal.Rptr. 527 (1981) (dicta; but finding for defendants under facts of the instant case).

Another question is whether failure to satisfy statutory requirements for giving notice to public officials regarding communicable diseases might subject the physicians or other health care providers to civil liability to persons who contract the disease. The few cases appear somewhat divided on the question. *Compare* Gammill v. U.S., 727

F.2d 950 (10th Cir.1984) (no duty or liability based on disease reporting statute, but there may be a duty independent of the statute), *with* Derrick v. Ontario Comm. Hosp., 47 Cal.App.3d 145, 120 Cal. Rptr. 566 (1977) (duty owed and potential liability for failure to report to public officials in accordance with statute).

It is unclear whether the preceding statutory duties would apply only to the physician (or other health care providers) making the initial diagnosis, or also to other treating physicians and providers who knew of the condition. *See* Lopez, *supra.* Moreover, the legal effect of a violation of statute on civil liability may vary from state to state. *See* II, D, 2, f.

There is also a question whether a physician owes a duty independent of statute to notify the close contacts of the patient of the dangers of contracting the disease. Here, too, the courts are divided. *Compare Gammill, supra* (dictum suggesting a duty to notify close relatives and others known likely to have been exposed) *with Derrick, supra* (no duty, at least of hospital, to notify non-patients). Similarly, there is also a question whether there may be a duty, independent of statute, to notify others (such as operator licensing authorities, employers, or family) in addition to the patient of a danger posed by a patient's non-communicable condition, such as the fact that his vision is impaired by glaucoma. In one case, a pedestrian struck by an automobile sued a hospital and physicians who treated the driver for alcoholism at the hospital's outpatient clinic. The court held that the defendants owed no duty to the general public, apart from warning the patient, to have the patient's license revoked or otherwise to prevent him from driving. *See* Cartier v. Long Island College Hosp., 490 N.Y.S.2d 602 (A.D.1985). There is also an issue whether such duties, if recognized at all, would apply to physicians other than those who make the initial diagnosis.

A psychotherapist may also have a duty to exercise reasonable care to protect non-patients from *intentionally-inflicted* injuries by patients. In a landmark California case, the court held that a psychotherapist owes a duty to take reasonable steps to protect a non-patient when he discovers or reasonably should have discovered that the patient poses a danger to that non-patient. Tarasoff v. Regents of U. Cal., 17 Cal.3d 425, 131 Cal.Rptr. 14, 551 P.2d 334 (1976). Although a few courts have recognized a broader rule, most courts seem to limit such a duty to situations in which there was a specific readily identifiable victim. *See* Thompson v. County of Alameda, 27 Cal.3d 741, 167 Cal. Rptr. 70, 614 P.2d 728 (1980). This line of cases raises troubling questions. How does one predict dangerousness? Will we really save more lives by forcing the therapist to warn the victim or take other steps than we would if he were encouraged to simply continue the therapeutic relationship, at least in the absence of an unmistakable threat?

And what about the shattered therapist-patient relationships that may ensue when therapists, perhaps erring on the side of caution, warn potential victims in situations in which nothing would ever have happened in any event?

If a duty requires a communication to someone other than the patient, a privilege to make communications to non-patients to satisfy that duty should also be clearly established. *See* IV, D, 4.

Another question is whether a non-patient, such as a close relative, can recover for mental distress resulting from the fact that the patient was negligently harmed by the physician. This question is examined in a later chapter. *See* IV, F.

C. NATURE OF THE DUTY OWED— THE STANDARD OF CARE

1. Standard of Care Defined

a. *In General*

Negligence law in general presupposes some uniform standard of behavior by which a defendant's conduct is to be evaluated. W. Prosser and P. Keeton, Law of Torts 173 (5th ed. 1984) (hereinafter cited as Prosser). Conduct is judged by objective criteria. Thus, it may not be sufficient that the actor has performed at full potential with the utmost good faith. Rather, he must have conformed to the standard of a reasonable person under like circumstances. Restatement § 283. Although the standard of care of the medical profession is also an objective one, it traditionally has departed from the reasonable person paradigm in several respects. First, as members of learned professions, physicians and other health care providers have been expected to possess and exercise skill and knowledge in the practice of their professions beyond that of ordinary individuals. Second, as to matters involving professional skills and knowledge, the conduct of such defendants has been largely evaluated in terms of professional standards determined by their profession. Thus, except in situations in which the alleged negligence is comprehensible to laymen (*see* II, D, 2, b) or to some extent in informed consent cases in some jurisdictions (*see* III, C, 3), the existence of negligent malpractice usually must be proven by expert testimony or by an acceptable substitute for it. *See* II, D, 2.

The language used by the courts to articulate the standard of care has become overgrown with shibboleths and superfluous phraseology. It is often said, for example, that a physician must both possess and exercise the requisite level of skill and knowledge. This appears redundant. Either a defendant exercised the required degree of care or he did not. Whether in such circumstances he possessed such skill and knowledge would be subsumed by the question whether the requisite care was actually employed. A few courts have also said that there is a presumption that a physician exercised due care. Given the fact that the plaintiff normally bears the burden of proof, the added gloss of a presumption in defendant's favor would not appear to have much practical significance.

The formulation and nature of the standard of care* is examined in the subsections that follow.

b. Professional Standards

There has been a good deal of variation in judicial and, more recently, legislative pronouncements of the standard of care for medical malpractice. To facilitate analysis, the following questions should be considered in any thorough examination of the standard of care:

a. How should one *define* professional standards of conduct? Should they be equated with customary practice of other members of the medical profession? If not custom, then what professional referent should be used to identify professional standards of conduct? *See* II, C, 2, a.

b. Should professional standards normally be accorded *conclusive weight* in identifying the standard of care in a malpractice case? *See* II, C, 2, b.

c. Should *expert testimony* normally be required to establish the appropriate standard of care, regardless of the weight to be accorded professional standards? *See* II, C, 2, c; II, D.

* Some of the analysis of professional negligence was derived in part from King, *In Search of a Standard of Care for the Medical Profession: The "Accepted Practice" Formula,* 28 Vand. L.Rev. 1213 (1975).

d. What if there is *disagreement* within the profession generally as to how a medical condition should be treated? *See* II, C, 4.

e. To what standard should a physician be held who possesses skill or knowledge *in excess* of that of an ordinary physician practicing in the same type of practice or specialty? *See* II, C, 5.

f. Should a practitioner be held to the degree of care and skill expected of an "*averag* e" practitioner or that of a "*reasonably competent*" practitioner? *See* II, C, 6.

g. To what extent should the *specialty or school* and *geographic location* in which one practices, affect the applicable standard of care? *See* II, C, 3.

One well-articulated statement of the standard of care is set forth in Blair v. Eblen, 461 S.W.2d 370, 373 (Ky.1970):

[A physician is] under a duty to use that degree of care and skill which is expected of a reasonably competent practitioner in the same class to which he belongs, acting in the same or similar circumstances.

.   .   . [L]ocality is merely one factor to be taken into account in applying general professional standards.   .   .   . [T]he standard should be established by the medical profession itself and not by lay courts.   .   .   .

.   .   . [T]he evidence may include the elements of locality, availability of facilities, specialization or general practice, proximity of specialists and special facilities as well as other relevant considerations.

While virtually every significant aspect of the *Blair* formulation is subject to disagreement, it nevertheless serves as a useful reference point for the analysis that follows.

2. Nature and Effect of Professional Standards

a. Acceptable or Customary Practice?

The language of the *Blair* formulation, above, equates the professional standard with that level of performance "expected" of a competent physician. This represents somewhat of a departure from the traditional rule in malpractice cases. Historically, the professional standard has been articulated in terms of the customary or usual practice of members of the profession, emphasizing their typical conduct. Thus, while the *Blair* formulation focuses on what is expected of the practitioner by his profession, the customary practice rule looks to those practices actually employed by members of the profession.

The customary practice formulation at one time had substantial support. The rule has, however, met with some criticism in recent years. The strongest objections have been leveled at the geographic limitations on the standard—those defining the standard not merely in terms of custom, but the custom within a particular locality or type of locality. *See* II, C, 3, d. A number of courts and commentators have also rejected the more fundamental notion of conclusively equating the standard of care with any custom. Criticism of the customary practice rule has been based primarily upon a fear that a substandard custom, especially a local one, might become enshrined and immune from challenge. Incentive to adopt better practices might also be lost if the customary practice were deemed conclusive evidence of the standard of care.

One alternative to the customary practice approach might be to define the professional standard in terms of *acceptable* rather than the customary practice. Medical practices approved by the profession and expected of its members would be controlling. This "acceptable practice" standard would not depend exclusively on the historical conduct of the profession, or on what its members customarily did, but on what a reasonably competent member of the profession practicing in the same specialty as the defendant would be expected to do in order to conform to acceptable professional practice. The reasonable expectations and collective sense of members of the profession as to what constitutes sound medicine would be the controlling inquiry.

Under an acceptable practice formulation, especially when coupled with an abandonment of geographic limitations on the standard of care, a dangerous substandard custom would not automatically be insulated from challenge. Since acceptable practice would reflect the collective expectations of the profession, it would be more reflective of the true costs and benefits involved in various therapeutic techniques and approaches. The acceptable practice model would also afford a more satisfactory analytical standard for unprecedented medical situations and would better accommodate the dynamic milieu of new technologies, innovative therapies, and new scientific information.

In most instances there would be little significant difference between customary and acceptable practices. When medical practitioners are plying their art in a manner that members of the profession collectively would expect, the custom would also represent the professionally accepted practice. Nevertheless, there may be differences. Although proof of both the customary and the acceptable medical practices would normally require expert testimony, in ascertaining the acceptable practice, the expert would not rely exclusively upon medical custom. He would also draw upon his own educational and practical background, the medical thinking in general as manifested by the relevant literature and available educational resources and information, and the general sense of other competent practitioners as to the parameters of sound medical practice. The acceptable practice formula would not depend on impossible head counts among practitioners, but would rely instead upon the expert's sense of what was, at the time of the alleged negligence, reasonably expected of medical practitioners by their profession.

The potential difference between acceptable and customary practices is illustrated in Incollingo v. Ewing, 444 Pa. 263, 282 A.2d 206 (1971). An osteopathic physician was sued for authorizing refills of a Chloromycetin prescription (written by another physician) without first examining or apparently monitoring the patient. The repeated use of the antibiotic was alleged to have caused aplastic anemia and ultimately the death of the patient. Neither the purported widespread indiscriminate use of the antibiotic in the community nor the absence of testimony suggesting that defendant had violated the customary practice exculpated the defendant. The court noted that there had been expert testimony critical of defendant's conduct, and did not require proof of a violation of the customary practices. The court required that physicians give due regard to the advanced state of the profession and use reasonable care in the exercise of their medical skill and knowledge. Although the court in *Incollingo* did not expressly adopt an acceptable practice formula, by emphasizing both the experts' disapproval of defendant's conduct and the advanced state of the profession, it came close to the spirit of such a rule.

Language clearly supporting an acceptable professional practice version of the professional standard can be found in a growing number of judicial and legislative formulations. *See* Blair v. Eblen,

461 S.W.2d 370 (Ky.1970); Tenn.Code Ann. § 29–26–115(a)(1) (1980). One recent decision described the standard in terms of "the recognized standards of the medical profession." Vassos v. Raussalis, 658 P.2d 1284, 1289 (Wyo.1983). The court also held:

> The skill, diligence, knowledge, means and methods are not those "ordinarily" or "generally" or "customarily" exercised or applied, but are those that are "reasonably" exercised or applied. Negligence cannot be excused on the grounds that others practice the same kind of negligence.

Id. at 1288.

b. *Weight Accorded Professional Standards*

A central question in connection with the standard of care in medical malpractice cases is whether conformity to the professional standard should conclusively establish the defendant's due care, or should simply constitute evidence of due care which the finder of fact may accept or reject. Surprisingly few decisions have adequately addressed this fundamental issue. Most courts seem to treat professional standards as conclusively establishing the standard of care for negligence. *See* Holt v. Godsil, 447 So.2d 191 (Ala.1984); Senesac v. Associates in Obstetrics and Gynecology, 141 Conn. 310, 449 A.2d 900 (1982). Thus, in Blair v. Eblen, 461 S.W.2d 370, 373 (Ky.1970), the court unequivocally stated that it would "leave determination of the standard to the medical profession and not the lay courts." This deference in malpractice cases is in contrast to the rule in negligence cases in many other fields outside the medical setting, in which conformity to a particular industry's standard, at least when defined in terms of customary practice, is rarely given conclusive weight, though it is usually considered evidence of due care. Professional standards have also been made controlling by numerous statutes adopting a professional standard of care in medical malpractice cases. *See* Tenn. Code Ann. § 29–26–115(a)(1) (1980); Vt.Stat.Ann. tit. 12 § 1908(1) (1984).

A few courts have purported to reject the conclusiveness of the professional standard, holding that conformity to that standard constitutes only evidence of due care. The attitude of some of these courts to the question may have been affected by the way in which such professional standards are defined. When examined closely some of these cases appear to be concerned mostly with a particular version of the professional standard. In Darling v. Charleston Comm. Mem. Hosp., 33 Ill.2d 326, 331, 211 N.E.2d 253, 257 (1965), *cert. denied* 383 U.S. 946 (1966), the court held that "custom" was relevant in determining the standard of care of hospitals, but that it "should never be conclusive." Some other cases ostensibly rejecting the conclusiveness of professional standards were probably actually attacking various geographic limitations on the professional standard rather than the validity of the standard generally. Other cases appear to have involved allegations of negligence so patent that they were "common knowledge" cases (*see* II, D, 2, b) for which no expert testimony (conclusive, probative, or otherwise) was even necessary.

At least one important case has squarely rejected the conclusiveness of the professional standard however defined, at least under the facts presented. In Helling v. Carey, 83 Wn.2d 514, 519 P.2d 981 (1974), the patient sued defendant ophthalmologists for failing to diagnose glaucoma in time to prevent serious impairment of her vision. Defendants had treated plaintiff for nearsightedness for a number of years. Since there was no indication that plaintiff's symptoms called for a glaucoma test significantly sooner than the date on which it was finally administered (she was tested about a month after the onset of relevant symptoms), the issue was whether the physicians should have *routinely* tested plaintiff's intraocular eye pressure years earlier. The expert testimony established that the standards of ophthalmology did not then require *routine* glaucoma testing for persons under forty years of age, for whom the incidence of glaucoma was estimated at one in 25,000. A verdict and judgment were rendered for the defendants. On appeal, the Washington Supreme Court reversed, holding that defendants were negligent as a matter of law for not having routinely administered the glaucoma test to this plaintiff at an earlier stage, presumably years earlier. The court based its decision on its perception of the relative cost, safety, simplicity, and definitiveness of the pressure test as compared with the gravity of the untreated disease. Thus, it rejected the conclusiveness of the standard of the profession as applied to the facts of this case. The *Helling* case not only rejected the conclusiveness of professional standards, but found negligence as a matter of law, rather than simply leaving that question to the jury. Apparently, the court believed that the unreasonableness of defendants' conduct was so clear that reasonable minds could not even differ on the question.

Credible arguments can be made on both sides of the question whether the profession's standards should conclusively establish the standard of care. Those criticizing the conclusiveness of professional standards—especially those based on the customary rather than acceptable practice—have expressed the fear that dangerous, ineffective, or even venal medical customs might go unchecked if customary practice were conclusively equated with due care. Moreover, even if professional standards were no longer conclusive, the jury might still have the benefit of expert testimony, but it would presumably focus on the feasibility of alternatives rather than merely on identifying the professional standards.

Arguments favoring the contrary view—that would accord professional standards conclusive weight—are perhaps even more compelling. It is not merely that lay jurors and judges are not equipped to decide whether a course of diagnosis or treatment was acceptable. This observation, without more, may be an oversimplification. Judges and juries have always been confronted with difficult, complex questions. Also, even if the conclusiveness of the professional standards were rejected, that does not mean that triers of fact would be without expert guidance. Expert testimony on the feasibility of alternatives would still usually be required. The real issue is thus not whether the medical matter in controversy can be made comprehensible to laymen. Rather, it is the more fundamental question of the proper allocation of medical decision-making responsibility. Should medical decisions that are not a matter of common knowledge be evaluated by the *ad hoc* judgment of lay jurors aided by hindsight and often unrealistic expectations, or should deference to the collective judgment of the medical profession be required? The latter view appears more defensible. The evolving and time-tested standards of the medical profession are more reliable than the conclusions of lay triers of fact even if enlightened by a few hours of technical medical testimony by experts. If professional standards can no longer be confidently relied upon, one would anticipate a proliferation of defensive medicine with its inherent costs and a paralysis of professional judgment. Moreover, the threat of unpredictable or arbitrary factual determinations in the future might seriously skew the allocation of medical resources. Furthermore, when a defendant's only wrong was to adher faithfully to the teachings of his profession, the ravaging impact of malpractice liability seems grossly disproportionate to the quality of the conduct challenged. Finally, the argument that a whole industry might be adhering to unreasonable practices appears less convincing when applied to the medical professions. More importantly, use of an acceptable rather than a customary practice formulation should eliminate the possibility that isolated instances of unreasonably dangerous procedures might be insulated from liability.

The trend, while sometimes not readily discernible from the cases and statutes, appears to be in the direction of affording greater weight, probably even conclusive weight, to professional standards.*

c. *Expert Testimony Requirement*

Unless an exception applies (*see* II, D, 2), expert testimony is required to establish defendant's pro-

---

* The question is far from settled. In Washington, for example, following the *Helling* case, the legislature enacted statutes addressing the standard of care. One provision adopts a standard based on "that degree of care, skill, and learning expected of a reasonably prudent health care provider in the profession or class to which he belongs, in the state of Washington . . . " Wash.Rev.Code Ann. § 7.70.040(1) (Supp.1985); *See also id.* § 4–24–290. The court has apparently been unwilling, however, to interpret this formulation as according conclusive weight to a professional standard based on practices expected by the medical profession. *See* Harris v. Robt. C. Groth, M.D., Inc., P.S., 99 Wn.2d 438, 663 P.2d 113 (1983). Other courts, however, seem more inclined to construe similar language as adopting a professional ("good and accepted medical . . . practice") standard. *See* Reams v. Stutler, 642 S.W.2d 586, 588 (Ky.1982) (construing judicial language).

fessional negligence. Senesac v. Assoc. in Ob-Gyn., 141 Vt. 310, 449 A.2d 900 (1982); Vassos v. Roussalis, 658 P.2d 1284 (Wyo.1983). Such testimony must establish the applicable professional standards and that the defendant's alleged conduct departed from them. It is not enough for the expert merely to testify as to what he personally would have done. The requirement of expert testimony is based on the fact that laymen are normally not capable of evaluating the quality of care exercised by professional medical personnel without expert guidance.

The expert testimony requirement would generally apply regardless of the conclusiveness or weight accorded professional standards. When the professional standards are accorded conclusive weight, as they usually are, expert testimony would be required to delineate what those professional standards are and establish that they have not been satisfied. Even when a court holds that professional standards are not conclusive, expert testimony would still usually be needed to demonstrate the technical feasibility of the course that plaintiff alleges was not, but should have been, followed. *See* Chiero v. Chicago Osteopathic Hosp., 74 Ill.App.3d 166, 29 Ill.Dec. 646, 392 N.E.2d 203 (1979); Harris v. Robt. C. Groth, M.D., Inc., P.S., 99 Wn.2d 438, 663 P.2d 113 (1983).

Whether an expert is competent to testify is a matter for the court. *See* II, D, 1, b. The weight of the testimony of a competent expert witness is a matter for the jury or other trier of fact. The expert's demeanor, background, qualifications, and general persuasiveness all may be relevant to the trier of fact in evaluating his opinion.

The courts are divided on the issue of the conclusiveness of uncontradicted expert testimony. Given the role of the trier of facts as the primary evaluator of a witness' demeanor and the probativeness of his testimony, the sounder view is that even uncontradicted expert testimony is not necessarily conclusive. *See* Nielson v. D'Angelo, 1 Conn. App. 239, 471 A.2d 965 (1984). *But cf.* Lysick v. Walcom, 258 Cal.App.2d 136, 65 Cal.Rptr. 406 (1968). Thus, under the better approach, while professional standards *once established* may be conclusive (*see* II, C, 2, b), the expert testimony introduced to establish such standards and their violation need not necessarily be believed or accepted by the trier of fact. This rule would have little practical effect in most cases when an uncontradicted expert testified on behalf of the defendant. In such cases, if plaintiff (who normally has the burden of proof) introduced no expert testimony and did not rely on an exception to the expert testimony requirement (perhaps in conjunction with *res ipsa loquitur*), a judgment in defendant's favor would be compelled even if defendant had called no experts at all. When, however, the plaintiff introduced uncontradicted expert testimony, the question of its conclusiveness could be significant.

3. Frames of Reference

a. *Time of Act or Omission*

For the purposes of negligence, a defendant's conduct is to be evaluated in terms of the professional standards and state of medical science as they existed at the time of the allegedly wrongful conduct. *See* Tomer v. Amer. Home Products Corp., 170 Conn. 681, 368 A.2d 35 (1976); Johnson v. Yeshiva Univ., 42 N.Y.2d 818, 396 N.Y.S.2d 647, 364 N.E.2d 1340 (1977). To judge a defendant's conduct in light of later scientific advances would be unfair and would fly in the face of traditional notions of fault-based liability.

b. *Defendant's Situation*

Defendant's professional status and the geographic area in which he practiced at the time of the alleged negligence may be relevant in malpractice cases in two ways. First, they may affect the level of care against which the defendant's conduct is to be measured. Second, they may affect the competency of expert witnesses to testify regarding the standard of care. The following subsections discuss the relevance of the defendant's professional and geographic status to the applicable standard of care. The competency of experts is examined in connection with proof of negligence. *See* II, D, 1, b.

c. *Professional Frame of Reference*

Historically the healing arts were fragmented into different "schools" or "systems" which represented different philosophical approaches to diagnosis and treatment. In more recent times, most of the various schools have given way to what has been termed "the regular practice of medicine." McCoid, *Care Required of Medical Practitioners*, 12 Vand.L.Rev. 549, 562 (1959). Nevertheless, a number of separate schools have survived in various locations. They include osteopathy, chiropractic, and Christian Science, to name the more common.

It has been repeatedly held that a practitioner in a specific school should be judged in accordance with the standards of that school. This principle has frequently been invoked in the case of osteopaths and chiropractors. *See* Caro v. Bumpus, 30 Colo.App. 144, 491 P.2d 606 (1971); Ferguson v. Gonyaw, 64 Mich.App. 685, 236 N.W.2d 543 (1975). Apart from osteopaths and chiropractors, the "same school" standard has lost much of its practical significance. States may prescribe prerequisites and qualifications for the practice of medicine. As a result, the freedom to practice non-traditional types of medicine has been narrowly circumscribed by the legislatures. When the legislature has been silent, some courts have also refused to recognize the legitimacy of some schools.

Even when other schools have apparently been recognized, some courts have held their practitioners to the standards of the regular medical profession or to certain minimum standards when practitioners in such schools undertook to treat conditions for which there was a generally recognized course of treatment in the regular practice of medicine. This has especially been true if these practitioners attempted to treat ailments outside of their field. *See* Kelly v. Carroll, 36 Wn.2d 482, 219 P.2d 79, *cert. denied* 340 U.S. 892 (1950) (drugless healer); Restatement § 299A, comment f (requiring minimum skill and knowledge). Other courts have, however, recognized the right of practitioners in the more common fields such as chiropractic to have their conduct tested by the standards of their school even if the regular medical profession would have used a different method, at least as long as such practitioners did not step outside the bounds of his competency. *See* Sutton v. Cook, 254 Or. 116, 458 P.2d 402 (1969). When courts have recognized the right of practitioners to have their conduct tested by the standards of their school they have also been careful to narrowly define the types of therapy such practitioners are legally qualified to practice and to have evaluated by the standards of their school. Such practitioners have been held to the standards of medical doctors when they stepped outside the parameters of their field.

Within the regular practice of medicine there are a number of recognized specialties. In addition, a number of allied health care fields have flourished. These include psychology, dentistry, nursing, and others. Courts have generally held such specialists or practitioners in allied health care fields to the professional standards of other similarly-situated members of the specialty or field in which they practice. *See* Fraijo v. Hartland Hosp., 99 Cal.App.3d 331, 160 Cal.Rptr. 246 (1979) (nurse); Taylor v. Hill, 464 A.2d 938 (Me.1983) (surgeon). Moreover, when one holds himself out as a specialist or undertakes to perform procedures normally requiring the expertise of a specialist, he may also be held to the professional standards of that specialty even though he may not have been certified in the speciality in question. *See* Simpson v. Davis, 219 Kan. 584, 549 P.2d 950 (1976) (dentist who undertook to do endodontic work should be held to standard of specialist); Butler v. Louisiana St. Bd. of Ed., 331 So.2d 192 (La.Ct.App.1976) (biology professor supervising project involving the taking of blood samples held to level of care of physician); Restatement § 299A, comment d.*

d. *Geographic Frame of Reference*

Historically, the courts defined the standard of care of the medical profession with reference to the practice in a limited geographical setting. The most narrow formulation was in terms of the practice in defendant's locality. This so-called "strict locality rule" is now followed in only a small number of jurisdictions. *See* Del.Code Ann. 18 § 6801(7) (Supp.1984). There were probably justifications for the strict locality rule when it originat-

---

* A recent case stated that one could be held to a specialized standard even though the procedure performed was not part of a formally recognized specialty if the defendant was performing a procedure that involved heightened knowledge and training. *See* Short v. Kinkade, 685 P.2d 210 (Colo.App.1984) (dentist performing occlusal equilibration procedure).

ed a century ago. There were marked geographic differences in opportunities for primary and continuing medical education, and in access to modern facilities and information. Moreover, certain diseases were often concentrated in specific geographical areas, thus fostering regional differences in emphasis in medical practices.

The strict locality rule proved objectionable because of its potential effect of insulating pockets of substandard practice and of limiting the pool of available expert witnesses. Furthermore, this balkanization of the medical profession was inconsistent with increasing uniformity in the practice of medicine. The latest medical information is now widely disseminated by professional journals, continuing education, and other means. Access to modern channels of transportation and communication have further eroded regional differences in medical care.

The most common successor to the strict locality rule has been simply a variation on the former theme. Many courts and legislatures hold that the standard of care should be based on the practice in the "same or similar locality." *See* Wall v. Stout, 310 N.C. 184, 311 S.E.2d 571 (1984); Roark v. Allen, 633 S.W.2d 804 (Tex.1982); Tenn.Code Ann. § 29–26–115 (1980). Some courts adhering to the "same or similar" variation have qualified the rule somewhat by adding that regard must also be given to the state of medical science at the time of the incident.

Retention of the same or similar locality rule has been defended on several grounds. Some courts and legislatures are still not convinced that parity among communities exists with respect to access to medical information and facilities. It is also argued that the rule as enlarged to include similar localities prevents serious local abuses. There has also been concern that a broader rule might deter practitioners from entering small or rural communities.

There has been some uncertainty as to what factors should render two communities "similar" for the purpose of the rule. Under the prevailing view, similarity depends not on population or area, but rather upon similarity of medical facilities and practices. Gambill v. Stroud, 258 Ark. 766, 531 S.W.2d 945 (1976). Other courts have focused on different factors, such as geographic proximity between communities, or demographic factors such as population, economy, size of city, and income of inhabitants. *See* Shilkret v. Annapolis Emergency Hosp. Ass'n, 276 Md. 187, 196 n. 5, 349 A.2d 245, 250 n. 5 (1975) (summarizing various definitions of "similar" but rejecting locality rules generally).

Several other rules containing a spatial limitation on the standard of care have been adopted in place of the strict locality rule. Some states, for example, have adopted a state-wide standard. *See* Ariz.Rev.Stat.Ann. § 12–563(1) (1982).

The locality rules have been subjected to a wide range of attacks. Some cases have eroded them in piecemeal fashion. Some courts have found, for example that with respect to certain medical procedures, no regional differences should be tolerated.*

A growing number of courts have attacked the locality rules directly. Many have held that there should be no geographic limitation on the standard of care for specialists, who should be held to the level of care of members of the same specialty generally. *See* Taylor v. Hill, 464 A.2d 938 (Me. 1983); McCormack v. Lindberg, 352 N.W.2d 30 (Minn.App.1984). These courts have relied on the standardization of the practice, education, and board certification of particular specialties, as well as on the opportunities for staying abreast of the current state of the art through specialty journals and continuing education.

An increasing number of courts have gone further and abrogated the locality rules for all physicians, general practitioners as well as specialists. *See* Blair v. Eblen, 461 S.W.2d 370 (Ky.1970); Shilkret v. Annapolis Emergency Hosp. Ass'n, 276 Md. 187, 349 A.2d 245 (1975); Vassos v. Roussalis, 658 P.2d 1284 (Wyo.1983). Some courts have added that one's locality is not conclusive but merely one factor to be taken into account. *See* Blair,

---

* Other courts have occasionally held that when there is a standard procedure or a medical technique uniformly accepted throughout the country, the physician may be held to that standard even when some locality rule otherwise applies. For criticism of this analysis as applied to the competency of experts, see II, D, 1, b, iii.

supra, at 373. It is also said that courts should consider the "advances in the profession, availability of facilities, specialization or general practice, proximity of specialists and special facilities, together with all other relevant considerations. . . ." Shilkret, *supra* at 253.

Generally, the abandonment of the locality rules has been a positive development, especially when the courts have held that geographic factors may continue to be relevant though not necessarily conclusive. By potentially insulating substandard practices from judicial challenge, geographic limitations on the standard of care are not only unfair to claimants, but they may also perpetuate substandard medical care. Locality rules, especially the archaic "same" locality rule, could also prove unfair to physicians as well. A physician working assiduously to apply the latest medical techniques could conceivably be found negligent under the locality rules for departing from the more backward locality standard, especially under a narrowly conceived professional standard.

As the quality of medical care continues to improve nationally and access to information and facilities grows, the ultimate demise of all locality rules is likely. It may, however, be inhibited at least for a time by a tendency of some legislatures to re-affirm some version of the locality rule. *See, e.g.,* Ark.Stat.Ann. § 34–2614(A)(1) (Supp.1983) (same or similar locality).

It should be noted that geographic limitations on the standard of care are to some extent tied to the basic question of the weight to be accorded the professional standards. *See* II, C, 2, b. Rejection of the conclusiveness of professional standards would also largely nullify the conclusiveness of any geographic limitations (although geographic limitations might still be imposed on the competency of expert witnesses). The converse, however, is not necessarily true. Abrogation of the geographic limitation on the standard should not mean that professional standards are no longer conclusive, but only that those professional standards are more broadly defined. *See* Blair, *supra,* at 373 (rejecting the locality rules but retaining the professional standard).

e. *Special Rules—Peer Review and Utilization and Quality Controls*

In 1972 Congress enacted the Professional Standard Review Organization (PSRO) Amendment to the Social Security Act and in 1982 replaced it with a similar set of provisions for creation of Peer Review Organizations. *See* 42 U.S.C.A. §§ 1320c et seq. (1983). The legislation contemplates the creation of area Peer Review Organizations (PRO's) throughout the nation and the establishment of prescribed norms of diagnosis and treatment to guide health care providers in patient care in connection with certain federally sponsored programs. The statute, among other things, confers civil immunity on physicians and others providing services under federally sponsored programs for certain actions taken in compliance with applicable norms. *See Id.* § 1320c–6(c).

The grant of immunity is qualified (and confused) by a proviso making it available to a defendant "only if [*inter alia*] he exercised due care in all professional conduct . . . reasonably related to, and resulting from the actions taken in compliance with or reliance upon such professionally accepted norms of care and treatment." *Id.* It is unclear whether this "due care" qualification applies both to the decision to rely upon applicable PRO norms as well as to actions related and incidental thereto, or only to the latter. It would seem that the due care proviso should not be applied to the threshold decision to rely upon applicable norms if the immunity provision is to fulfill its function of encouraging conformity to the norms.

There are also questions about the reach of the immunity provision. Matters involving professional discretion as well as many complex, non-routine procedures may not be amenable to the kind of explicit classification envisaged by the norms. Delays in the creation and revision of norms might also render them incompatible with medical matters involving an especially fluid state of the art. Thus far, the immunity provision has seldom if ever been invoked in reported cases, reflecting perhaps delays in developing applicable norms. There is also a question of the legal effect, if any, of a failure to conform to applicable PRO norms.

Congress has also considered other legislative proposals creating an alternative liability system for federal health care programs. *See generally* X.

In 1983, a new fee system for Medicare patients was introduced whereby payment to most hospitals for inpatient care would be set in advance under a prospective pricing system based on the Diagnosis Related Groups (DRG's) into which a patient fell. Except for situations involving conformity to PRO norms (discussed above), the fact that a therapeutic decision was motivated by or conformed to a DRG may not necessarily preclude a finding of negligence. Rather, liability for DRG-motivated decisions would probably depend on the extent to which DRG's reflected professional standards, which might in turn depend on how such professional standards are defined (*see* II, C, 2, a) and the normative influence DRG's have on their development.

4. "Respectable Minority" and "Error in Judgment" Problems

In a field as complex as medicine, there will seldom be complete agreement on the proper therapeutic approach for a particular medical condition. Although this pluralism sometimes may reflect regional variations in practice, more often it transcends geographic differences in medical practice. The courts have recognized that they ordinarily are in no position to decide among competing regimens of treatment and diagnosis. Most courts would agree that a practitioner should not be penalized for following a course approved by at least a respectable segment of his profession.

In response to this need to accommodate differing medical viewpoints, the courts developed the so-called "respectable minority" rule. It holds that "a physician does not incur liability merely by electing to pursue one of several recognized courses of treatment." Downer v. Veilleux, 322 A.2d 82, 87 (Me.1974); Sprowl v. Ward, 441 So.2d 898, 900 (Ala.1983) ("The decision to use one method of treatment as opposed to others, where there is reasonable doubt as to the proper course, is not a breach of duty."). In Chumbler v. McClure, 505 F.2d 489, 492 (6th Cir.1974), the court noted that "[t]he test for malpractice . . . is not to be determined solely by a plebiscite."

The courts have yet to adequately resolve the question of what constitutes a "respectable minority" or acceptable support for a particular technique or approach. It is not clear whether the answer should depend on sheer numbers endorsing a specific practice, or upon some other criteria such as the professional standing of those supporting such a technique. Probably both factors should be weighed. Moreover, the existence of a legally relevant respectable alternative approach for the purpose of the standard of care might also depend on the geographic frame of reference applied in a particular jurisdiction. *See* II, C, 3, d. While the narrower locality rules have been perceived as advantageous to physicians, this would not be true in the context of the respectable minority rule. The broader and more universal the geographic frame of reference, the more likely it would become that there would exist other respectable approaches to a medical problem. Thus, one effect of abrogating or eroding the locality rules would possibly be to broaden the number of respectable approaches that might be relied upon by the physician without incurring liability.

A difficult question concerns innovative or less recognized medical procedures. On the one hand, if there is to be medical progress, professional standards must be defined broadly enough to accommodate sound innovation. On the other hand, patients deserve protection against ill-considered untested procedures, especially when traditional acceptable therapies are available.

Some authorities, especially older ones, have advocated liability for any departure from established practices. Some have intimated that a physician should be held strictly liable for employing so-called "experimental" procedures. Analysis of the problem is obscured by the failure to distinguish experimentation motivated primarily for research from therapeutic innovation motivated primarily by the patient's welfare. *See generally* J. Waltz & F. Inbau, Medical Jurisprudence 179–202 (1971). As to the former research-motivated procedures, an argument can be made that some provision should be made, if not for strict liability, then for providing insurance against adverse effects of the experiment. And, as with all medical treatment, fully informed consent should be obtained and governmental regulations followed.

With respect to therapeutic innovation, the problem is more complicated. A rule that required conformity to a narrowly defined professional standard or even to an approach sanctioned by at least a respectable minority might well impose liability for any departure from the medical mainstream or its respectable tributaries. Such a result might be based on an application of negligence principles and would not even need to invoke strict liability. While there are courts that would follow such a course, a more flexible approach seems preferable. Thus, the fact that one's diagnostic or therapeutic approach did not fall within either the prevailing medical practice or within a respectable minority should not automatically result in liability. Instead, liability for one's choice of medical procedure should depend more on whether the defendant undertook a form of treatment that "a reasonable and prudent member of the . . . profession would undertake under. . . similar circumstance." Hood v. Phillips, 554 S.W.2d 160, 165 (Tex.1977). Factors to consider might include the availability, effectiveness, and relative safety of more traditional alternatives; the level of the patient's understanding of the risks, benefits, and alternatives to the procedure; and, the extent and quality of research that preceded the employment of the procedure in question. Thus, while professional standards should be accorded conclusive weight when the defendant conformed to them, the defendant who departed from the usual practices should be allowed to prove that such a decision was reasonable. Perhaps it could be said that reasonable innovation might, under appropriate circumstances, be consistent with acceptable medical practice, especially under a liberal application of the respectable minority rule.

Another concept that was born of the inherrent uncertainty of much of medical science has been termed the "error in judgment" or "medical judgment" rule. This facile doctrine has been the source of much confusion. Stated simply, the doctrine holds that a medical professional who otherwise follows the applicable professional standards should not be found liable merely because his decision turns out to have been the wrong one.

The "error in judgment" doctrine represents a particularized reaffirmation of three related malpractice concepts. First, it underscores the fundamental requirement that before a physician can be held liable plaintiff must prove that the defendant's conduct was negligent—that it did not conform to the applicable standard of care. Second, it reemphasizes the basic premise of fault-based liability that a physician should not, without evidence of negligence, be held liable merely because there was an unfavorable result from the therapy. Third, the doctrine reaffirms the respectable minority rule protecting a physician's right to choose among reasonably acceptable therapeutic approaches even though in retrospect the choice turns out to have been the less beneficial one, or in other words, an error in judgment.

As a practical matter, the "error in judgment" rule rarely is automatically outcome determinative of a case. Generally, it is simply included in the instructions to the jury. Correctly understood, it does not change the basic inquiry into whether the defendant was negligent. Rather, it serves to elaborate the nature of such negligence and its proof. When the concept is ostensibly relied upon to support a decision in favor of the defendant as a matter of law, such a result can usually be explained in terms of a failure of plaintiff to introduce sufficient proof of malpractice to even present a jury question. Thus, for example, one appellate court relied upon the medical judgment concept in upholding a directed verdict for a surgeon who decided not to reenter the patient's chest wall during surgery to search for a needle fragment. The surgeon weighed the dangers of disrupting the prior incisions and of increasing the risk of infection against the small risks from this particular needle fragment. The true basis for the court's decision was simply that no negligence had been proven—plaintiff failed to introduce expert testimony to establish that the surgeon had violated the applicable standard of care. *See* Cebula v. Berroit, 652 S.W.2d 304 (Mo.App.1983).

Loose language in a few cases, if taken literally, might be read to support the view that once a medical decision somehow becomes judgmental, it is no longer subject to judicial scrutiny regardless of the quality of that judgment. Such a view is clearly a misapplication of the error in judgment principle. Recent cases make it clear that it is only *non-negligent* errors in judgment that will not result in liability. As one court observed, "[e]rrors in judgment which occur with the best intentions constitute negligence if they result from a failure to use reasonable care." Logan v. Greewich Hosp. Assn., 191 Conn. 282, 299, 465 A.2d 294, 303 (1983). Other courts achieve essentially the same result by conditioning the rule on the exercise of reasonable care. *See* Fall v. White, 449 N.E.2d 628, 635 (Ind.App.1983) ("[A] doctor will not be negligent *if* he exercises such reasonable care and ordinary skill even though he mistakes a diagnosis, makes an error in judgment or fails to appreciate the seriousness of the patient's problem."). Thus, for example, when a physician fails to conduct the required tests or appropriate examinations, secure an adequate factual basis for his decision, or complete the necessary preparation in order to formulate a sound and timely judgment, the error in judgment concept should afford no protection. *See* Steeves v. United States, 294 F.Supp. 446 (D.S.C.1968) (failure to diagnose appendicitis because of allegedly negligent failure to keep patient hospitalized for observation or to perform appropriate tests). Even if the necessary information is gathered, liability might still be imposed if the medical decision reached was not consistent with at least one reasonable decision or course that accorded with acceptable professional standards.

5. "Best Judgment" Rule

It is sometimes suggested that not only must a doctor comply with the requisite professional standard of conduct, but he must also exercise his best judgment when he knows that the prevailing medical practice is unreasonably dangerous. In the leading case expounding this rule, the court observed: "If a physician fails to employ his expertise or best judgment . . ., he should not automatically be freed from liability because in fact he adhered to acceptable practice. . . . [A] physician should use his best judgment and whatever superior knowledge, skill and intelligence he has." Toth v. Comm. Hosp. at Glen Cove, 22 N.Y.2d 255, 263 & n. 2, 292 N.Y.S.2d 440, 447–48 & n. 2, 239 N.E.2d 368, 373 & n. 2 (1968).

A recent New York decision serves as a useful illustration. A premature infant was placed under the care of a physician, a pediatric resident, who ordered the oxygen dosage reduced based on his knowledge that oxygen had been implicated in retrolental fibroplasia, a disease that may cause blindness. Two days later, however, another physician who was an instructor in pediatrics allegedly countermanded the resident's order and ordered an increase in oxygen, without examining the infant and despite an awareness of the danger of increased oxygen. This was allegedly part of a study on the effects of increased oxygen in which some babies were given a higher dose of oxygen than others. The court held that the instructor was charged with knowledge that the child was progressing well in the previously ordered curtailed oxygen environment. In upholding the imposition of liability on the staff physician-instructor and hospital, the court observed:

> Although the conventional medical wisdom at the time believed that increased oxygen was essential to the survival of premature babies, the hospital and Dr. Engle cannot avail themselves of the shield of acceptable medical practice when a number of studies, including their own, had already indicated that increased oxygen was both unnecessary and dangerous, particularly for an otherwise healthy baby, and especially when the attending physician, who had primary responsibility for the patient's health, had recommended a decrease.

Burton v. Brooklyn Doctor's Hosp., 88 A.D.2d 217, 223, 452 N.Y.S.2d 875, 879–80 (1982).

The "best judgment" rule presents little difficulty when the exercise of one's best judgment merely enhances the safety of the patient with no appreciable added risk. Thus, for example, if a physician knew that a relatively safe innoculation should be performed more frequently than traditional practice indicated, he should be required to proceed in accordance with his best judgment. A more difficult situation arises when the exercise of one's best judgment does not merely add an additional measure of safety, but conflicts with the traditional practice and entails other risks. In such a case, a physician choosing to follow his best judgment might conceivably be subject to liability for violating the applicable professional standard. A partial solution to this dilemma might be to adopt an acceptable practice formulation of the professional standard to allow for greater individual flexibility than would the traditional customary practice formula. *See* II, C, 2, a. Liberal application of the respectable minority and error in judgment doctrines and a broadly defined professional standard permitting room for reasonable therapeutic innovation might afford additional protection to the practitioner. *See* II, C, 4; *Toth, supra* N.E.2d at 373 n. 2. Nevertheless a potential conflict between the requirements that a practitioner adhere to the recognized professional standards and the "best judgment" principle remains a possibility. Courts should therefore be cautious in requiring one to exercise his best judgment when it would not only conflict with a professional practice but would involve other potential risks or an unproven or untested procedure. The requirement that a physician exercise his best judgment should probably be limited to circumstances in which the indicated course either added no appreciable risk or was at least approved by a respectable segment of the profession.

A corollary to the *Toth* rule followed by some courts holds:

Where a physician sets his own standard of professional competence and testifies that he measured up to that standard, but the jury finds from other evidence that the physician failed to do that which he himself considers proper and necessary, the physician cannot complain that the plaintiff has not proved negligence.

Faulkner v. Pezeshki, 44 Ohio App.2d 186, 195, 337 N.E.2d 158, 165 (1975).

6. Average or Reasonably Competent Practitioner?

Some courts have defined the professional standard in terms of an *average* practitioner in the professional class to which defendant belonged. *See* Brune v. Belinkoff, 354 Mass. 102, 235 N.E.2d 793 (1968). Other courts have eschewed use of the "average" model, preferring instead to use as a guide the more sensible* "reasonably competent"

---

* The fallacy in the "average" formulation has been explained as follows:

[The standard] is not that of the most highly skilled, nor is it that of the average members of the profession . . . since those who have less than . . . average skill may still be competent and qualified. Half of the physicians of America do not automatically become negligent in practicing medicine . . . merely because their skill is less than the professional average. . . . [The standard] is that common to those who are recognized in the profession . . . itself as qualified, and competent to engage in it.

Restatement, § 299A, comment e.

physician. *See* Shilkret v. Annapolis Emergency Hosp. Ass'n, 276 Md. 187, 349 A.2d 245 (1975).

D. PROOF OF PROFESSIONAL NEGLIGENCE

1. Expert Testimony

a. *Securing Expert Testimony*

Absent an applicable exception (*see* II, D, 2), expert testimony is required to establish the appropriate standard of care and its violation. *See* II, C, 2, c. As a practical matter, defendants in most instances encounter little difficulty in obtaining expert witnesses. Besides colleagues who are usually willing to testify, the defendant himself can often offer an expert opinion. Furthermore, since the burden of proof is usually on the plaintiff, a failure of defendant to produce expert testimony may not necessarily be fatal to defendant's case.

In contrast, plaintiffs must usually overcome a marked reluctance on the part of medical professionals, especially local practitioners in smaller cities and towns, to testify against each other. This tendency sometimes referred to as a "conspiracy of silence," may be attributable to a number of factors. Preparation for and appearance in legal proceedings is time-consuming and diverts time away from one's practice. Some physicians fear retaliation by insurers or colleagues if they testify. There is concern about loss of referrals or staff privileges and about a willingness of the other physician to testify against the expert if he is ever sued. Others decline to testify out of sense of a professional loyalty. Matters are further complicated where locality rules limit the pool of available experts. Despite all of this, there are signs of increasing willingness of some physicians to serve as plaintiffs' experts.

Expert testimony is usually also necessary to establish a causal connection between the alleged negligence and the injury (*see* V, B, 2) and often to prove the extent of plaintiff's injury. Generally, however, a more rigorous test will be applied to determine the competency of an expert for standard of care purposes since it may be limited by professional and sometimes geographic factors. *See* II, D, 1, b. On the other hand, the basic facts of human physiology are universal, thus making the competency of experts on causation and damages issues, absent some special statutory limitations, less subject to challenge. The discussion that follows focuses on the use of expert testimony to establish the standard of care and its violation.

b. *Testimonial Competency of Experts*

i. Competency in General. Before a witness can offer an expert opinion, he must be "competent" to do so. The competency of expert witnesses is usually addressed to the sound discretion of the trial judge subject to specific parameters set by statutory and case law. The weight to be accorded the witnesses' testimony, on the other hand, is usually left to the jury. In evaluating the competency of

an expert for purposes of proving negligent malpractice, an expert witness should ordinarily be
required to show adequate familiarity with (1) the
medical procedures (at least when such techniques
are established and accepted ones) and medical
condition involved; and (2) the applicable professional standards at the time of the conduct in
question in the relevant geographic area or type of
area to the extent that geographic limitations have
been imposed on the standard of care. An expert
may also have to satisfy various special statutory
requirements for competency.

ii. Professional Competency of Experts. An expert witness must generally be reasonably knowl-
edgeable about the particular medical techniques
(at least when they are well established or accepted
ones)* and the medical condition in question, and
the applicable professional standards at the time of
the alleged negligence. *See* Swanson v. Chatterton, 281 Minn. 129, 160 N.W.2d 662 (1968). Although some courts have traditionally held that
the source of such familiarity must come from
occupational experience, the trend is against such
an inflexible requirement. *See* Brown v. Colm, 11
Cal.3d 639, 114 Cal.Rptr. 128, 522 P.2d 688 (1974)
(expert witness who was experienced generally and

---

* When the defendant has employed an uncommon or innovative technique or approach (*see* II, C, 4), it may be unrealistic to
expect an expert to be familiar with such techniques. In such
circumstances, it should be enough if the expert is familiar with
other more traditional techniques and has made a reasonable
effort to learn about the defendant's methodologies.

had made an exhaustive study of the standards applicable to a 1949 operation was competent to testify even though he had not been admitted to practice in 1949); Cline v. Lund, 31 Cal.App.3d 755, 107 Cal.Rptr. 629 (1973). The Federal Rules of Evidence speak in broad terms of an expert qualified by "knowledge, skill, experience, training, or education. . . ." Fed.R.Evid. 702. Other courts, however, have adhered to a requirement that an expert testifying on the standard of care possess sufficient "occupational experience," at least when the technique in question was not a rare one. *See* Reinhardt v. Colton, 337 N.W.2d 88 (Minn.1983). Even these courts, however, may not require practical experience with the specific medical procedure if the physician possesses sufficient experience with the general area of practice as well as sufficient basic education and training generally. *See* McCormack v. Lindberg, 352 N.W.2d 30 (Minn.Ct.App.1984).

Under the prevailing and preferred view, most courts hold that the testimony of an otherwise competent physician will not *automatically* be excluded in an action against a specialist simply because the witness is a general practitioner or a member of another specialty (or vice versa), if the witness is otherwise sufficiently familiar with the applicable standards. *See* Greene v. Thomas, 662 P.2d 491 (Colo.App.1982) (dicta); Taylor v. Hill, 464 A.2d 938 (Me.1983). Once the witness is held sufficiently familiar with the medical standards in question to render hlm competent to testify, the quality of his training and specialization has been held to go to the weight of the testimony rather than to its admissibility. As one court observed, "[i]t is the scope of the witness' knowledge and not the artificial classification by title that should govern the threshold question of admissibility." Fitzmaurice v. Flynn, 167 Conn. 609, 618, 356 A.2d 887, 892 (1975). Although, under majority view, an expert will not automatically be disqualified because he is not a member of defendant's specialty, that fact may obviously be relevant in deciding whether he possesses sufficient familiarity with the procedure and the standards of that specialty to be competent to testify.

Courts have shown greater disagreement on whether to allow a member of one "school" of medicine (*see* II, C, 3, c) or one profession to testify against a member of another. *Compare* Morgan v. Hill, 663 S.W.2d 232 (Ky.App.1984) (physician may not testify as to standard of care of chiropractor), *with* Bartimus v. Paxton Comm. Hosp., 120 Ill. App.3d 1060, 76 Ill.Dec. 418, 458 N.E.2d 1072 (1983) (physician may, if sufficiently familiar with the standards, be qualified to testify against osteopath). Some courts are especially cautious about allowing a member of a profession with more limitations on the scope of its practice to testify against a physician engaged in the regular practice of medicine. *See* Fountain v. Cobb Gen. Hosp., 167 Ga.App. 36, 306 S.E.2d 37 (1983) (nurse not competent to testify as to standard of care of physicians performing Caesarean section). When standards of two schools of practice are or should be the same, courts have been more willing to find a witness competent to testify against a defendant from a different school. *See* Frazier v. Hurd, 380 Mich. 291, 157 N.W.2d 249 (1968). When a practitioner from one school or profession practices beyond the scope of his profession, he may be held to a level of care of the profession whose members would have been qualified to handle the condition. In such circumstances, a member of the latter profession would ordinarily be qualified to testify as to the standards of that profession.

Some statutes impose special requirements to render an expert competent to testify. These have included requirements, sometimes subject to exception, that an expert have been engaged in active practice during a specified period, sometimes within certain geographic parameters, and sometimes within the defendant's or a relevant profession or specialty.

iii. Geographic Competency of Experts. The issue of the competency of experts may also arise in connection with geographic considerations. Generally, when the standard of care is defined with reference to a particular locality, similar locality or other type of geographical setting, the expert witness must be familiar with the standard of care in that geographical frame of reference.

In order to ameliorate the perceived harshness of the locality rules (*see* II, C, 3, d), some decisions have held that an expert may be competent to testify about the standards in the same or similar localities or other geographic region (depending on which type of locality rule is applied) in effect at the time of the conduct in question even though he has not practiced there, as long as he is familiar with such standards. The fact that the expert had never personally practiced in the applicable geographic settings is said to go to the weight of his testimony but not to his competency as an expert. Some states, however, have taken a somewhat more stringent approach, adding further requirements. *See* Tenn.Code Ann. § 29–26–115(b) (1980) (requiring that the expert must actually have been "licensed to practice in the state or a contiguous bordering state a profession or specialty which would make his expert testimony relevant . . . and had practiced this profession or specialty in one of these states during the year preceding the date that the alleged injury or wrongful act occurred," a requirement that the court may waive when it determines that the appropriate witnesses would not otherwise be available).*

---

* Some courts have suggested that when a witness is familiar with a standard that he states is uniform throughout the nation, he would almost by definition be familiar with the standards in the relevant geographic area. A witness who is familiar with standards throughout the nation could arguably show that he would necessarily be familiar with similar communities so as to render him competent to testify un-

2. Potential Exceptions to Expert Witness Requirement

a. In General

The unwillingness of competent experts to testify against other practitioners coupled with the expense of retaining an expert, have motivated parties (especially plaintiffs) to seek other ways of establishing the applicable standard of care. A number of techniques have been tried with varying degrees of success to circumvent the expert witness requirement. The following discussion will focus primarily on expert proof of the standard of care. Given the usual requirements for expert testimony on the issues of causation and perhaps damages, some of the rules discussed below may offer potential avenues for avoiding the expert witness requirement as to those matters as well.

In the discussion that follows, it should be borne in mind that a number of states have enacted statutes that purport to codify an expert witness requirement, often with special requirements for competency. It remains to be seen to what extent

der a same or similar rule. Reliance on one's familiarity with a supposed uniform nation-wide medical standard to prove familiarity with the standards in a single specific geographic setting to satisfy a "same" locality or a state-wide standard is probably specious or redundant. Unless the witness was actually familiar with the standards within the applicable locality, he could not really know that there was in fact a truly uniform nation-wide professional standard. And, if he were actually familiar with the applicable locality, he would usually be deemed competent for that reason and it would be unnecessary to add that the same practice was followed nationwide.

various potential exceptions to the expert witness requirement that might have otherwise been available will be permitted under the statutorily-imposed expert witness requirements. Hopefully, such statutes will be construed broadly enough to accommodate such exceptions. *See* Baldwin v. Knight, 569 S.W.2d 450 (Tenn.1978) (approving a "common knowledge" exception to the statute).

b. *Common Knowledge Situations*

The most important exception to the expert witness requirement is the so-called "common knowledge" doctrine. It holds that when the alleged negligence is comprehensible to laymen without the guidance of expert evidence, expert testimony will not be required to prove a violation of the standard of care. The finders of fact are allowed to rely on their common knowledge to evaluate the defendant's conduct, and arrive at the appropriate standard of care. *See* Toppino v. Herhahn, 100 N.M. 564, 673 P.2d 1297 (1983).

While the common knowledge doctrine frequently operates with the doctrine of *res ipsa loquitur* (*see* II, D, 3), the common knowledge rule is also applied in situations in which the events are fully known and *res ipsa* is not applied. Common knowledge cases typically have involved fairly perspicuous fact situations. *See* Killingsworth v. Poon, 167 Ga.App. 653, 307 S.E.2d 123 (1983) (whether an injection into shoulder that resulted in punctured lung constituted negligence); Wiles v. Myerly, 210 N.W.2d 619 (Iowa 1973) (burns discov-

ered on patient's buttocks following vascular surgery involving another part of patient's body);
Karrigan v. Nazareth Convent & Academy, Inc.,
212 Kan. 44, 510 P.2d 190 (1973) (whether a post-
operative patient's acute condition required notification of patient's attending physician). There has
been a tendency by some courts in recent years to
enlarge the scope of the common knowledge exception. Thus, in Pry v. Jones, 253 Ark. 534, 487
S.W.2d 606 (1973), expert testimony was not required to establish the applicable standard of care
when a patient's ureter was allegedly severed during a hysterectomy, even though this surgery was
complex and required an incision near the ureter.
In another case the court held that notwithstanding the absence of expect testimony that the defendant had deviated from the standard of care, "[t]he
repeated misplacement of [a breast] implant, later-
ally and vertically, the miscalculation as to its
proper size, and the successful results obtained by
another surgeon after only one surgical procedure
. . . are facts that, while not conclusive, raise
inferences of negligence that should properly be
resolved by a jury." Toppino, *supra.*

There are, however, limits. Thus, the extent of
an incision required to remove a skin neurofibroma
was held not a matter of common knowledge.
Greene v. Thomas, 662 P.2d 491 (Colo.App.1982).
Nor is the standard of care for a hospital pharmacy
in a complex case involving the pharmacological
effects of a drug within common knowledge. Miel-

ke v. Condell Mem. Hosp., 124 Ill.App.3d 42, 79 Ill.Dec. 78, 463 N.E.2d 216 (1984). *See also* Medina v. Figuered, 3 Haw.App. 186, 647 P.2d 292 (1982) (standard of care with respect to constructing and fitting dentures not within common knowledge).

A defendant sometimes responds to an allegation based on a purported common knowledge situation by introducing evidence of compliance with a professional standard. The courts are divided on whether the professional standard should be conclusive in such a case. If the alleged negligence is truly a matter of common knowledge, there is no reason why conformity to professional standards should be conclusive. Indeed, it is debatable whether such evidence should even be admissible in such a case.

c. *Defendant's Admissions and Testimony*

A plaintiff may establish a sufficient case to reach the jury on the basis of the defendant's own statements alone if they are sufficiently probative. Such evidence may be in the form of extrajudicial statements, pleadings, pre-trial discovery, or testimony at trial. Thus, for example, when the defendant-chiropractor testified that the plaintiff's cervical spine injury required "gentle" manipulations, and plaintiff testified that the manipulations were anything but gentle, plaintiff made a submissible case for the jury. Morgan v. Hill, 663 S.W.2d 232 (Ky.App.1984). *See also* Pinky v. Winer, 674 S.W.2d 158 (Mo.App.1984) (defendant's deposition provided sufficient evidence to entitle plaintiff to reach jury). Defendant's out-of-court statements may also support a jury verdict. When a defendant's statements are established by the testimony of others who heard the statements, they may constitute exceptions to the hearsay rule. *See* McCormick §§ 262 et seq.

Statements by the defendant must establish a violation of the standard of care. Thus, a statement in post-operative notes that the defendant caused a harmful result by an "inadvertent entry of the bladder" during a hysterectomy was not sufficient to satisfy the expert testimony requirements to entitle the plaintiff to reach the jury. *See* Smith v. Karen S. Reisig, M.D., Inc., 686 P.2d 285 (Okla.1984). Nor was the "inadvertent" characterization sufficiently indicative of substandard conduct. *See also* Maxwell v. Woman's Clinic, P.A., 102 Idaho 53, 625 P.2d 407 (1981) (alleged statement that defendant "obviously messed up" not sufficient). *But see also id.* (Bristline, J., dissenting, summarizing more lenient view).

The courts are divided on the question of the conclusiveness of pleadings, discovery, and testimony, which may depend on the procedural rules of the jurisdiction in question and the form of the statement. *See* McCormick §§ 265, 266. To what extent may the defendant successfully repudiate such statements by later testimony or other evidence? Some statements, such as those in the effective pleadings and in formal responses to requests for admissions may, unless properly amended, be conclusive on the issues they address. *See id.* § 265. There is less agreement on the conclusiveness of defendant's statements made during discovery or in testimony at trial. *See id.* § 266. The better-reasoned view would allow such statements to be used as evidence, but not accord them conclusive weight. Extrajudicial statements are generally not accorded conclusive weight, but rather are subject to contradiction or explanation. *See id.* § 262.

Statutes in many jurisdictions provide that one party may call an opposing party as an adverse witness, may interrogate him by leading questions, and may contradict and (under the more sensible view) impeach his testimony. A question arises whether a defendant called by plaintiff (as upon cross) or cross-examined by plaintiff may be compelled to testify regarding the applicable standard of care. The early cases often limited the scope of examination of adverse parties to factual matters and did not require the witness to give an expert opinion. However, the modern trend has recognized plaintiff's right to compel the defendant-physician to respond to questions calling for an expert opinion. *See* McDermott v. Manhattan Eye, Ear & Throat Hosp., 15 N.Y.2d 20, 255 N.Y.S.2d 65, 203 N.E.2d 469 (1946). Any claim of unfairness or loss of a property right in one's expert opinion will usually be outweighed by the policy of maximizing the disclosure of relevant matters. *See* Anderson v. Florence, 288 Minn. 351, 181 N.W.2d

873 (1970) (pre-trial discovery). Moreover, some statutes permit courts to award a fee to a witness examined as an expert.

For obvious reasons, plaintiff's counsel should try not to rely exclusively upon the admissions or testimony of the defendant-doctor to prove his case. Defendants can be expected to vigorously resist efforts by plaintiff to elicit and make use of their admissions.

d. *Manufacturer's Instructions and Information*

Diagnosis and treatment are increasingly dependent on drugs and medical devices and materials. These items are invariably prepared with instructions, warnings, indications and contraindications for use, and other information prepared by the manufacturer. This has led to the important question of the relevance of this manufacturers' information in a malpractice claim, particularly regarding the standard of care.

The role of manufacturers' information has probably reached its furthest development in the area of pharmaceuticals. New drugs must, unless subject to an exemption, be approved by the Food and Drug Administration before they may be introduced into interstate commerce or, under some state statutes, administered to patients. *See* 21 U.S.C.A. § 355 (West Supp.1985). One of the requirements for initial and continuing approval of a drug is adequate labeling, a matter subject to detailed regulation. *See id.* ; 21 C.F.R. §§ 201.1 et seq. (1985). The manufacturer's information for prescription pharmaceuticals is contained in the package inserts and labels that accompany the products. Much of this information is incorporated into the Physician's Desk Reference (PDR), a privately printed publication published annually, with supplements published during the year.

There are two potential questions regarding the use of manufacturer's recommendations and information in malpractice cases. First, there is the question of its admissibility in light of the prohibition against hearsay evidence. Hearsay has been defined as "a statement other than one made by the declarant while testifying at the trial or hearing, offered in evidence to prove the truth of the matter asserted." Fed.R.Evid. 801.

If one classifies manufacture's literature such as package inserts and the PDR with learned writings, such information would usually be held inadmissible when offered to prove the truth of the assertions of the statements (rather than to impeach a witness on cross-examination). *See* II, D, 2, e, *infra.* There are, however, a number of possible arguments against excluding such information under the hearsay rule. First, such information may be admissible in those jurisdictions that admit learned writings in general. Second, an extension of some other exception to the hearsay rule, such as the exception for public records and reports, might support admission. *See* McCormick §§ 315 et seq. Third, such information may be admissible as non-hearsay when it is introduced for some purpose other than proving the truth of the statement, such as proving information that defendant knew or should have known. And finally, a strong argument can be made that even if one generally excludes medical literature as hearsay, an exception should be made for manufacturer's information. *See* Mueller v. Mueller, 88 S.D. 446, 221 N.W.2d 39 (1974). This argument is especially compelling in the case of package inserts (or the PDR), for which many of the traditional objections to hearsay seem less persuasive. *See generally* McCormick § 321.*

If a court decides to admit manufacturer's recommendations, the second question relates to the legal effect of such evidence. A number of courts have held that package inserts (or PDR) may be used in conjunction with the common knowledge rule to establish negligence in situations cognizable to laymen. Some courts have held that the manufacturer's information may be used to show what

---

* Fear that information might be out of date and not reflect the standards at the time of treatment loses its force when one considers the manufacturer's duty to keep information of its approved drugs current. Concern that the manufacturer's information might be taken out of context or confuse the jury seems exaggerated in the case of package inserts, which are typically only a few pages in length at most. Moreover, the defendant could and should be afforded an opportunity to explain any deviation from the manufacturer's recommendations. The unavailability of the author of the manufacturer's information for cross-examination would to some extent be offset by the ongoing scrutiny of the information by the FDA and the manufacturer itself.

the defendant knew or should have known regarding the possible dangers of the drug. Thus, in Sanzari v. Rosenfeld, 34 N.J. 128, 167 A.2d 625 (1961), the court held that the brochure was admissible to prove what defendant knew or should have known regarding the possible dangers of a vasoconstricting drug to hypertensive patients. The references from the brochure, when combined with the common knowledge doctrine, were then held sufficent to avoid a dismissal. Other courts allowing use of the manufacturer's information when combined with the common knowledge rule seem to confer broader relevance on the information. Thus, one court implied that information could be considered in showing not only what the defendant should have known but also what he should have done. *See* Winkjer v. Herr, 277 N.W.2d 579, 585 (N.D.1979).

Some courts have held that package inserts may be considered as evidence of the applicable standard of care as long as there is competent expert testimony or admissions by the defendant that such information reflects the applicable standard of care. *See* Chrestman v. Kendall, 247 Ark. 802, 448 S.W.2d 22 (1969). In Holloway v. Hauver, 22 Md.App. 303, 322 A.2d 890 (1974), the patient was burned by a flash allegedly caused when an electro-cautery device was used in the presence of flammable Merthiolate in disregard of the operators' manual. The appellate court held that a directed verdict for the defendant was improper when defendant admitted that a paragraph from the manual introduced into evidence represented the applicable standard of care.

Cases upholding use of package inserts in conjunction with the common knowledge doctrine or with expert testimony do not represent a significant departure from the traditional requirements of expert proof in malpractice litigation. There remains, however, the question whether manufacturer's recommendations should ever be sufficient to entitle the plaintiff to reach the jury in cases not falling within the common knowledge rule nor supported by expert testimony. There has been little clear case law on this question. Some cases have held that manufacturer's instructions could be evidence of the standard of care, but failed to mention whether other supporting evidence was present or required. *See* Durkin v. Equine Clinics, Inc., 313 Pa.Super. 75, 459 A.2d 417 (1983) (veterinarian allegedly prescribed drug for a horse in excess of recommended dosage).

A few cases have suggested that the manufacturer's recommendations might alone be sufficient to entitle plaintiff to reach the jury. *See* Ohligschlager v. Proctor Community Hosp., 55 Ill.2d 411, 303 N.E.2d 392 (1973). *But cf.* Mielke v. Condell Mem. Hosp., 124 Ill.App.3d 42, 79 Ill.Dec. 78, 463 N.E.2d 216 (1984) (not sufficient evidence alone on standard of care of hospitals and narrowly contrued *Ohligschlager* rule as to physicians). The force of some of these cases is often weakened by

the fact that there was probative expert testimony
to support plaintiff's case or the facts were within
the common knowledge of laymen, thus making
any suggestion that the manufacturer's recommendations were alone sufficient to support a finding
of negligence nearly dicta. *See* Mulder v. Parke
Davis & Co., 288 Minn. 332, 181 N.W.2d 882 (1970);
Mueller v. Mueller, 88 S.D. 446, 221 N.W.2d 39
(1974). For example, in *Mulder,* the court held:

> Where a drug manufacturer recommends to
> the medical profession (1) the conditions under
> which its drug should be prescribed; (2) the
> disorders it is designed to relieve; (3) the precau-
> tionary measures which should be observed; and
> (4) warns of the dangers that are inherent in its
> use, a doctor's deviation from such recommenda-
> tions is prima facie evidence of negligence if
> there is competent medical testimony that his
> patient's injury or death resulted from the doc-
> tor's failure to adhere to the recommendations.

> Under such circumstances, it is incumbent on
> the doctor to disclose his reasons for departing
> from the procedures recommended by the manu-
> facturer.

181 N.W.2d at 887. Although the court expressly
relied upon the package inserts in reversing a
directed verdict, plaintiff had also introduced competent expert testimony.

Even among courts accepting in principle that
manufacturer's recommendations may be sufficient
to entitle the plaintiff to reach the jury, the rule

has often been qualified. Thus, in Lhotka v. Larson, 307 Minn. 121, 238 N.W.2d 870 (1976), the court held that before such evidence could be sufficient it must be "clear and unambiguous." And, of course, plaintiff must also establish the other elements of his case, including causation. _See_ Reinhardt v. Colton, 337 N.W.2d 88 (Minn.1983). Moreover, the recommendations are ordinarily not accorded conclusive weight. Rather, the physician's reasons for deviating from those recommendations may, if accepted by the jury, exculpate him. _See Mulder, supra._

The questions of the admissibility and substantive effect of manufacturers' information and recommendations is subject to competing considerations. Favoring greater use and effect is the fact that the information is clearly an important factor in guiding the treatment decisions of physicians. Moreover, since a defendant's conduct is evaluated in terms of the professional standards prevailing at the time of the alleged conduct, the manufacturer's information or PDR at the time of treatment provides a valuable source of information on the drug. Finally, the unavailability of medical experts militates in favor of liberal rules regarding manufacturers' information.

Conversely, the choice and timing of therapeutic approaches often reflects a complex appraisal of the patient's condition and balancing of risks and benefits. Lay jurors usually lack the background and perspective needed to evaluate a physician's performance in this regard. Moreover, it is safe to say that many manufacturers err on the side of overinclusiveness of warnings. Giving their warnings and instructions too much significance in malpractice cases may inhibit physicians from exercising independent professional judgment.

One possible approach might consist of the following. Manufacturers' information and recommendations should be admissible when relevant. They should also be sufficient evidence of the standard of care to entitle the plaintiff to reach the jury on that issue: (1) when competent expert testimony or an admission by defendant indicates that the manufacturers' information reflects the applicable standard of care; (2) when the alleged malpractice, when considered along with the relevant manufacturers' information or warnings, is within the common knowledge of laymen; or, (3) when manufacturer's recommendations in question are unequivocal, clearly appear applicable, and constitute mandatory precautions or contraindications, and the plaintiff has after reasonable efforts been unable to secure the services of a competent medical expert. The manufacturer's recommendations should, when admissible, be deemed evidence of the standard of care which the jury may accept or reject based on all the evidence. The defendant should also be free to to explain his departure from the manufacturer's recommendations or to show why such recommendations are not applicable or should not preclude a finding that he followed an

acceptable course of action. Such proof might include evidence that defendant's actions were consistent with at least a course approved by a respectable segment of the relevant profession. *See*
II, C, 4.

The preceding analysis has for the most part
focused on the situation in which the use of a drug
or device was approved by the federal government
for some purposes, but was allegedly used in a
dosage or manner or for a condition that was
neither within that approval nor recommended by
the manufacturer. Unless such use violated some
state or specific federal statutory or regulatory
prohibition, deviation from the manufacturer's recommendations or the absence of express approval
for the use in question should at most be considered as evidence of negligence, but should not be
conclusive. In some situations, however, a physician may use a drug or device that has not yet
been approved at all for any use despite a requirement for approval. Unless such use was authorized under some special procedure such as that governing use of investigational drugs or devices and
was within the scope of that authorization, use of
an unapproved drug or device might conceivably be
deemed negligence *per se* based on a violation of
federal statutory prohibitions, such as those
against introducing such items into interstate commerce, or possibly on a violation of state statutory
or regulatory prohibitions. *See generally* Kaban &

Gibbs, *The Impact on Medical Malpractice Cases of FDA Regulation,* 20 Forum 418 (1985); II, D, 2, f.

The rules governing the various uses of professional literature for cross-examining and impeaching expert witnesses (rather than direct evidence) should probably apply to similar uses of manufacturer's information, although there does not appear to be much law directly on point. *See generally* McCormick § 321.

e. Medical Literature

As with manufacturer's information, there are two questions regarding the use of medical treatises and other medical literature in malpractice actions—whether it is admissible and if so, whether it may satisfy the expert witness requirement.

Under the prevailing rule of evidence, medical literature is hearsay and not admissible as *direct evidence* to prove the statements it contains (as opposed to its use for impeachment). *See* Bivens v. Detroit Osteopathic Hosp.,   403 Mich. 820, 282 N.W.2d 926 (1978); Eckleberry v. Kaiser Foundation Northern Hosp.,   226 Or. 616, 359 P.2d 1090 (1961); Annot.,   84 A.L.R.2d 1338 (1962; Supp. 1979, 1984); McCormick § 321. The rule has, however, been changed by statute or case law in a few jurisdictions. *See* Mass.Gen. Laws Ann. ch. 233, § 79C (West Supp.1985) (relevant material by recognized expert); Sprowl v. Ward, 441 So.2d 898 (Ala.1983). The Federal Rules of Evidence as well as quite a few states' rules recognize an exception to the hearsay rule for medical literature that is established as reliable authority when an expert relies on the literature during direct examination or it is properly called to his attention upon cross-examination. *See* Fed.R.Evid. 803 (18); 4 J. Weinstein & M. Berger, Weinstein's Evidence ¶ 8.03(18) [01–03] (1985).

Persuasive arguments can be made on both sides of the question. Opponents of the admissibility of medical treatises have raised various objections. The author may not be present to be sworn or to have his demeanor observed. There is no opportunity for cross-examination. The finders of fact might accord undue deference to treatises. The treatises might be confusing to a jury or taken out of context. A treatise might not reflect medical practices at the time of the alleged negligence. Treatises are not necessary when competent expert witnesses are available. The requirement for testimony by an expert witness helps prevent unmeritorious claims. Since there may be a divurgence of opinion on a subject, the admission of medical literature invites abuse through selection of literature favorable to one's position. There are also arguments supporting the admissibility of treatises. The fact that a witness is under oath or present to be observed does not insure veracity. Moreover, a general treatise by a disinterested scholar may be less biased than the testimony of a hired expert. Cross-examination is not essential when other experts (or treatises) are available to qualify and explain the treatise in question. The finders of fact are as likely to accord undue weight to an expert witness as to a treatise. The state of the art does not evolve so rapidly as to render obsolete current treatises and recent periodicals. Moreover, the literature may serve as an important source of information about the medical standards prevailing at the time of the alleged malpractice when it has occurred years ago. The "conspiracy of silence" and the high costs of retaining medical experts also militate in favor of the admissiblity of medical literature. *See generally* Poulin v. Zartman, 542 P.2d 251 (Alaska 1975) (identifying some of the foregoing arguments).

On balance, the approach represented by the Federal rules appears to be a sound compromise, especially if it is remembered that the mere fact that a piece of medical literature is admitted over a hearsay objection does not resolve the remaining question whether such evidence will alone be sufficient to entitle the plaintiff to reach the jury.

Most courts do admit medical literature during cross-examination of an expert witness for the purpose of impeaching the witness or challenging his testimony. Some courts require that the witness have relied on the authority in forming his opinion, others that he relied upon authorities generally, others that he acknowledge that the material is a recognized authority, and still others that it merely be established by proof or judicial notice that the literature in question is reliable. *See*

Annot., 60 A.L.R.2d 77 (1958; Supp.1984); McCormick § 321. It is often held, however, that the effect of such evidence is limited to the credibility of the witness. *See id.*

When the literature has been admitted under some exception to the hearsay rule as substantive evidence (rather than merely for impeachment purposes), the question arises whether that evidence may alone be sufficient to entitle the plaintiff to reach the jury. There are few recent cases on point. In Sprowl v. Ward, 441 So.2d 898 (Ala. 1983), defendant sought to excuse his failure to use a rubber dam to prevent swallowing of foreign objects because of the risk that the dam might damage the patient's teeth. A portion of a text on endodontics, established as a leading authority, that listed alternative ways of using a rubber dam with less risk of damage to teeth was held sufficient evidence on the standard of care to warrant submission of the case to the jury.

The following is a suggested approach. Relevant medical literature, shown to be reliable, should be admissible as direct evidence of the standard of care (and not merely for impeachment) notwithstanding the hearsay rule when relied upon by an expert on direct examination or when called to his attention during cross-examination. Such evidence should not, however, be sufficient to entitle the plaintiff to reach the jury *unless* expert testimony (or admissions by the defendant) confirmed that those statements reflected the applicable standard of care at the time of the alleged negligence, and it was clear from the literature that any departure from those standards or at least that defendant's conduct was unacceptable.* There are several reasons for this limited approach. First, the abundance of medical literature invites biased selective use. Second, statements in the medical literature may be much more extensive than manufacturer's recommendations, and thus more confusing and of debatable relevance. Finally, some statements in the literature may represent only one of a number of acceptable therapeutic alternatives (*see generally* II, C, 4 *supra*), and thus not really prove, even if believed, that the defendant's conduct departed from all acceptable courses of action.

f. Violation of Statute, Regulation, or Ordinance

The fact that a defendant has violated a criminal or civil statute, regulation, or ordinance may support a finding of negligence even absent other proof of the applicable standard of care and its violation. The effect that such a violation has depends on two questions: first, whether the statute (or other codification) is *applicable* to the case; and second, assuming its applicability, what *procedural effect* the court gives its violation.

---

* It is commonly held that expert testimony must not only establish the standard of care, but also that the defendant violated it. Therefore, unless the medical literature suggested either that *any* departure from the stated standard or that defendant's conduct was unacceptable, there would have to be expert testimony to that effect.

Some statutes expressly provide for civil liability for harm caused by their violation. Under these statutes, the matters of applicability and effect are specifically spelled out in the statute itself. Most criminal statutes, however, expressly address only criminal penalties. Nevertheless, courts have frequently adopted the standards expressed in criminal statutes as the controlling standards for a civil torts claim based on the conduct that violated the statute. Before a court adopts the standards expressed in the criminal statute—in other words, holds the statute *applicable*—several determinations must be made. First, it must appear that the statute was designed to protect a class of persons of which plaintiff is a member. Second, the harm must have been a materialization of a risk the statute was designed to prevent. *See generally* Restatement §§ 286–88. Some courts also inquire whether adoption of the standard of the criminal statute would be *appropriate* in civil cases.

A plaintiff may also assert, independent of any violation of statute, that the defendant was negligent under common law concepts of reasonableness. Thus, the fact that a statute is not applicable to a case does not necessarily mean that the plaintiff will not prevail. It only means that the standard of care and its violation will have to be established by traditional means independent of the statute.

Once a codification is found to apply, it must be determined what effect its violation should have.

The courts have not always agreed. Occasionally, a court will hold that a violation conclusively establishes negligence and recognize no excuse. Most courts, however, hold that only unexcused violations constitute negligence *per se* conclusively establishing a violation of the standard of care without further proof by the plaintiff. *See* Prosser, at 230. Some courts hold that a violation creates a rebuttable presumption of negligence. Under either the negligence *per se* or rebuttable presumption approach, the plaintiff not only usually avoids a directed verdict, but will prevail if the defendant fails to offer proof of an acceptable excuse (or to rebut the presumption under that approach).* Quite a few courts hold that violation of an applicable statute merely constitutes evidence of negligence that the jury may accept or reject based on all the evidence. *See id.* A similar diversity of opinion exists with respect to violations of governmental regulations or ordinances.

Liability may not be based upon violation of a codification unless such violation was the cause in fact and proximate cause of the harm in question. *See* Hively v. Edwards, 278 Ark. 435, 646 S.W.2d 688 (1983).

---

* Generally, the trend appears to be in the direction of a more permissive attitude toward excuses or rebuttals. Thus, in Lopez v. Hudgeons, 115 Cal.App.3d 673, 171 Cal.Rptr. 527 (1981), the court held that alleged negligence in failing to comply with statute requiring a report to health authorities that patient was subject to lapses of consciousness could be rebutted by evidence that the physician acted as a reasonable person would act who desired to comply with the law.

There have been an increasing number of cases in which a violation of statute or other codification has been invoked by the plaintiff. In Landeros v. Flood, 17 Cal.3d 399, 131 Cal.Rptr. 69, 551 P.2d 389 (1976), a child sued a physician and hospital for alleged negligence in failing to report the battered child syndrome, allegedly resulting in further injury to the child. The court held that expert testimony was not mandatory to prove a duty on the part of one who diagnoses the battered child syndrome to report it when statutory provisions require that such reports be made. In Cucalon v. State, 103 Misc.2d 808, 427 N.Y.S.2d 149 (Ct.Cl. 1980), liability was based on a psychiatric hospital's failure to conform to a statutory requirement requiring that a female patient being transferred from one part of a facility to another be accompanied by another female. As a result of this violation, patient was allegedly raped by a male employee of the hospital.

A number of cases have involved alleged violation of a licensing statute. The weight of authority holds that a competent practitioner will not be found negligent solely because he was not currently licensed to practice in the state in question. Some courts have held that when a practitioner is otherwise qualified, the mere lack of a license is simply not probative of a lack of skill and therefore not an appropriate standard. *See* Tittle v. Hurlbutt, 53 Hawaii 526, 497 P.2d 1354 (1972) (alternative holding). In McCarthy v. Boston City

Hosp., 358 Mass. 639, 266 N.E.2d 292 (1971), the court held that in the absence of evidence that the lapse of the registration contributed to the quality of the patient's care, the fact that defendant was not licensed was not a proximate cause of the injury. What these cases really seem to be saying is simply that for the purposes of tort liability the risk the statute was designed to alleviate was practice by incompetent individuals, not by those who had simply failed to apply for or maintain a valid license. When, however, the defendant is not qualified to practice, the violation of statute rule is more likely to be applied if the harm would not have occurred had the patient been treated by a qualified practitioner. *See* Stahlin v. Hilton Hotels Corp., 484 F.2d 580 (7th Cir.1973) (nurse unlicensed in violation of the Nursing Act who apparently did not possess the qualifications required of nurses).

While an unexcused violation of a statute may help to establish negligence, the mere fact that one complied with a statute does not, unless it so provides, relieve the actor of the duty of conforming to the common law requirements of due care. *See* Peeples v. Sargent, 77 Wis.2d 612, 253 N.W.2d 459 (1977).

g. *Guidelines of Professional Organizations and Institutional Rules*

Institutions such as hospitals, and professional boards, societies, and organizations often adopt rules and guidelines relating to medical services.

When these rules and guidelines relate to the conduct challenged as malpractice, the issues of the admissibility, relevance, and weight of these materials for the purpose of the standard of care arise.

Despite the fact that both institutional rules and the guidelines of professional organizations might arguably constitute hearsay when offered as direct proof of the standard of care, the trend of recent cases holds that such materials generally are admissible as direct evidence. *See generally* Annot., 50 A.L.R.2d 16 (1956; Supp.1978; 1984); Annot., 58 A.L.R.3d 148 (1974; Supp.1984). Although few cases have been decided in the medical setting, they generally follow the trend in favor of admitting such evidence when relevant. The admissibility of hospital rules might be sometimes explained by an extension of the hearsay exception governing admissions by a party opponent. *See* McCormick § 262. Even the guidelines of professional organizations might arguably be deemed admissions of members of that organization for the purpose of the hearsay rule. Federal Rule of Evidence 801 includes among admissions of a party opponent "a statement of which he has manifested his adoption or belief in its truth" as well as "a statement by a person authorized by him to make a statement concerning the subject." Although one may have to stretch the preceding definitions to construe guidelines of professional organizations as admissions by its members, there are other good reasons to admit the guidelines. They may represent collective expressions by the defendant's profession of the applicable standards of performance, and thus clearly be relevant.

Assuming that institutional rules and professional guidelines are admissible, it must be determined what weight to accord them. Most courts have held that they may be *evidence* of the standard of care, but not conclusive. *See* Darling v. Charleston Comm. Mem. Hosp., 33 Ill.2d 326, 211 N.E.2d 253 (1965) (American Hospital Association Standards for Accreditation and the hospital's own bylaws were admissible as evidence of the standard of care for the hospital defendant, but not conclusive). Numerous other cases have recognized that hospital bylaws and rules are evidence of the standard of care. *See* Van Steensburg v. Lawrence & Mem. Hospitals, 194 Conn. 500, 481 A.2d 750 (1984); Williams v. St. Claire Med. Center, 657 S.W.2d 590 (Ky.App.1983).*

Courts have also held that standards sponsored by professional nongovernmental organizations are admissible on the issue of the standard of care for physicians. Thus, standards for electroshock treatment prepared by the American Psychiatric Association (to which defendant-psychiatrist belonged), admittedly applicable in defendant's region, were admissible as evidence of the standard of care in

* An interesting question is whether such hospital policies may be admitted against physicians performing medical services in the hospital but not employed by it. *Compare* Young v. Cerniak, 126 Ill.App.3d 952, 81 Ill.Dec. 923, 467 N.E.2d 1045, (1984), *with* Van Steensburg, *supra.*

Stone v. Proctor, 259 N.C. 633, 131 S.E.2d 297 (1963). *See also* Steeves v. United States, 294 F.Supp. 446 (D.S.C.1968) (AMA Principles of Medical Ethics and AHA Standards for Hospital Accreditation); Salazar v. Ehmann, 505 P.2d 387 (Colo. App.1972) (the Chiropractic Oath). Other courts, however, have followed a less flexible approach. Thus, Standards and Recommendations of the American Academy of Pediatrics have been held inadmissible as evidence of the applicable standard of care. *See* Swank v. Halivopoulos, 108 N.J.Super. 120, 260 A.2d 240 (1969).

Most courts have agreed that institutional rules and professional organizations guidelines may be evidence of the standard of care, but not necessarily conclusive. The question remains whether such materials, while not given conclusive weight, might nevertheless be sufficient to allow plaintiff to reach the jury even in the absence of expert testimony (or its equivalent) on the standard of care. In most cases admitting institutional rules and professional guidelines as evidence, there was also expert testimony on the standard of care. A few cases seem to at least imply that the institutional rules or guidelines, in some cases, might alone be sufficient evidence on the standard of care issue to make a submissible case, assuming that there is also sufficient evidence on the other elements (*see* II, A, *supra*) of the case.*

---

* *See Stone, supra.* In *Stone,* although the defendant admitted that the standards of the American Psychiatric Association "could" have been followed in his case, such a statement was

Clearly, the institutional rules and professional guidelines should be admissible when relevant, but should ordinarily not be given conclusive weight. When, however, such rules and guidelines are clear and unequivocal with respect to the challenged conduct, and plaintiff has been unable to secure an expert, the sensible approach would be to hold that such rules and regulations are sufficient to make a submissible issue for the jury as far as the standard of care was concerned.

h. *Court-Appointed Experts and Screening Panels*

The Federal Rules of Evidence and some state statutes provide for appointment of impartial experts. Fed.R.Evid. 706. The impetus behind this Rule lies in the parties' difficulty in obtaining expert witnesses and in concerns about biased testimony of witnesses retained by the parties. Although court-appointed experts have rarely been employed in malpractice cases, the approval of such a procedure in Rule 706 may encourage its greater use.

Some state statutes have created screening panels or review boards that review those malpractice cases subject to the statute prior to the regular trial. While the results of such deliberations are generally not conclusive, they are sometimes admissible as

probably not specific enough to constitute an admission by the defendant that the Association standards stated the standard of care. The court nevertheless held that those standards, as such, were sufficient to make a jury question on the standard of care issue.

evidence at the subsequent trial. There appears to be a split of authority on the question whether the findings of the panel or board, where admissible, might be sufficient to allow the plaintiff to reach the jury on the standard of care issue without introducing expert testimony at trial. *Compare* Del. Code Ann. 18 § 6853 (Supp.1984) (sufficient), *with* Baldwin v. Knight, 569 S.W.2d 450 (Tenn.1978) (not sufficient under former review board provisions). One statute even creates a presumption that the findings of the panel are correct and shifts the burden of proof to the party rejecting them to refute such findings at trial. *See* Ann.Code Md., Cts. & Jud.Proc. § 3–2A–06(d) (1984). The most sensible view would be to hold that favorable findings are sufficient to make a submissible case for the jury when a competent expert sat on the panel or board or testified at the hearing.

3.   Circumstantial Evidence and *Res Ipsa Loquitur*

a.   Res Ipsa Loquitur *in General*

Negligent malpractice can be proved in two ways. Plaintiff may introduce *direct evidence* that delineates the injury-producing transaction and explains the ways in which it was negligent. Plaintiff may also prove negligence indirectly with *circumstantial evidence.* This manner of establishing negligence is often referred to as the doctrine of *res ipsa loquitur,* which literally means "the thing speaks for itself." Negligence may be inferred from the fact of an unexplained injury of a type that normally does not occur in the absence of negligence. Although direct evidence of precisely how the injury occurred is lacking, the nature of the injury itself may so strongly suggest wrongful conduct that nothing more is necessary to allow plaintiff to reach the jury on the question of the violation of the standard of care. *Res ipsa* has two dimensions: first, is the doctrine *applicable* to the factual situation presented; and second, if so, what *procedural effect* does its application have?

b. Availability of Doctrine in Medical Malpractice

Judicial response to the doctrine of *res ipsa loquitur* in the medical setting has been understandably ambivalent. On the one hand, the remedial effects of the doctrine are particularly compelling here. The patient has entrusted his well-being into the hands of a physician, and, often, a hospital. He may have been unconscious or otherwise incapable of fully knowing what caused his injury. Because of the physician's training and position, he is normally in a better position to explain how the injury occurred.

Reservations about the doctrine are similar to those that underlie the basic principle that a physician does not impliedly guarantee the success of the therapy and should not, without more, be found negligent merely because an unfavorable result occurs. The practice of medicine is an inexact science. Modern medical procedures and medication carry inherent risks. The doctrine of *res ipsa loquitur* sometimes threatens to impose malpractice liability for unexplained occurrences that may have had an innocent origin.

The weight of authority holds that *res ipsa loquitur* is available under appropriate circumstances, in medical malpractice cases. *See* Van Zee v. Sioux Valley Hosp.,   315 N.W.2d 489 (S.D.1982). Some jurisdictions limit the doctrine to specific types of situations. *See* Del.Code Ann. 18 § 6853 (Supp.1984). Some courts that ostensibly refuse to recognize the doctrine in malpractice cases reach a similar result by invoking related doctrines such as a rule recognizing the probative force of circumstantial evidence or one holding that certain facts constitute negligence *per se.*   There are, nevertheless, courts that apparently have rejected the doctrine in malpractice cases, at least in actions against physicians. *See* Gilbert v. Campbell, 440 So.2d 1048 (Ala.1983).

c. *Causation and* Res Ipsa Loquitur

Technically speaking, the concept of *res ipsa loquitur* applies to the element of fault—that there has been substandard care—and does not obviate the requirement that causation also be established. However, the same circumstantial evidence that supports application of *res ipsa loquitur* may also support a finding of at least some aspects of the causation inquiry. *See generally* V, A, *infra.* Thus, the fact that a dental drill bit is discovered on X-ray to have perforated patient's large intestine, may, depending on all the facts, support a dual inference that the dentist who filled the patient's tooth earlier in the week was *negligent* and that his negligence *caused* the injury, or at least caused the presence of the foreign object that other evidence demonstrates caused the harm.

Moreover, considerations of causation are in some ways inextricably involved in the doctrine of *res ipsa*. When a possible force other than the alleged negligence is a more or equally likely cause of the injury, or when another force is in fact shown to have caused the injury, the doctrine of *res ipsa loquitur* will not apply. Causation is also the animus underlying the other two *res ipsa* elements—the requirements that the defendant was in exclusive control and that plaintiff not have caused his own injury. Although some courts have attempted to separate the concepts of *res ipsa* and causation, causation will often be to some extent subsumed in the three traditional requirements of *res ipsa*.

d. *Elements of* Res Ipsa Loquitur

i. Elements in General. There are three elements that generally must be satisfied in order for *res ipsa loquitur* to apply. The injury must have:

(1) resulted from an occurrence which does not ordinarily occur in the absence of negligence, (2) [been] caused by an instrumentality or agency under the exclusive management or control of the defendant, and (3) occurred under circumstances indicating the injury was not due to any

voluntary act or negligence on the part of the plaintiff.

Loizzo v. St. Francis Hosp.,   121 Ill.App.3d 172, 76 Ill.Dec. 677, 459 N.E.2d 314, 317 (1984).

A question on which there has been a dearth of clear judicial analysis is who decides whether the elements of *res ipsa* have been satisfied. Under the most sensible view, the court decides whether there is sufficient evidence* so that reasonable minds could at least differ on whether the elements of *res ipsa* have been satisfied. If so, it would then be for the jury to decide whether the elements are in fact satisfied. *See* Sammons v. Smith, 353 N.W.2d 380 (Iowa 1984); Little v. Arbuckle Mem. Hosp. Bd. of Control, 665 P.2d 1227 (Okla.App.1983). Under this view, once the court decides that reasonable minds could differ on whether the elements are satisfied and the jury decides that they are satisfied, the jury must then decide based on all of the evidence and the procedural effect of the doctrine (*see* II, D, 3, f, *infra*) whether negligence has been established. Some courts, following a second approach, suggest that whether the elements have been satisfied in order to render the doctrine applicable is for the court to decide, with the jury's role presumably limited to

---

* In this connection, the court would also have to decide whether expert testimony was required to support a finding of negligence. If so, the plaintiff would be entitled to rely on *res ipsa* only if the jurisdiction permitted use of *res ipsa* in conjunction with expert testimony and if such testimony were presented.

applying the procedural effect of the doctrine employed in that jurisdiction. *See* Rogers v. Brown, 416 So.2d 624 (La.Ct.App.1982).

ii. Inference of Negligence. The most crucial element of *res ipsa loquitur* requires that the injury be of a type that does not normally occur in the absence of negligence. In other words, the injury must be such that one could reasonably conclude that negligence by this defendant was more likely than not its cause.

A question that has divided the courts is whether plaintiff may rely on expert testimony to help support an inference of negligence. Traditionally, quite a few courts held that *res ipsa* could not apply unless the inference of negligence could be based entirely on the common knowledge of laymen. *See* Marquis v. Battersley, 443 N.E.2d 1202 (Ind.App.1982); Stundon v. Stadnik, 469 P.2d 16 (Wyo.1970). This limitation on the doctrine appears in part to have an historical explanation. *Res ipsa loquitur* evolved in the malpractice setting largely in "common knowledge" situations in which no expert testimony was needed to establish the standard of care. *See* II, D, 2, b. As a result, some courts probably came to regard *res ipsa* as simply one variation of the common knowledge principle.

A number of jurisdictions have significantly broadened the applicability of *res ipsa,* holding that it may be invoked not only when the inference of negligence is comprehensible to laymen, but also when the inference can be and is supported by expert testimony. *See* Buckelew v. Grossbard, 87 N.J. 512, 435 A.2d 1150 (1981); Gallegor v. Fedler, 329 Pa.Super. 204, 478 A.2d 34 (1984); Restatement § 328D, comment d. There would appear to be little justification for limiting the doctrine exclusively to common knowledge situations. *Res ipsa loquitur* is not simply an extension of the common knowledge principle; it is a rule of circumstantial evidence. As such, reference should be permitted to any competent fund of knowledge and experience that supports an inference of negligence, including expert testimony.

Res ipsa loquitur does not automatically become applicable merely because the treatment was unsuccessful or produced an unsatisfactory result. *See* Montana Deaconess Hosp. v. Gratton, 169 Mont. 185, 545 P.2d 670 (1976); Stundon v. Stadnik, 469 P.2d 16 (Wyo.1970). There must not only have been an untoward result, but also a rational basis in experience for concluding that such results do not normally occur in the absence of negligence. Generally, it must appear that the injury more probably than not resulted from the defendant's negligence. *See* Guebard v. Jabaay, 177 Ill.App.3d 1, 72 Ill.Dec. 498, 452 N.E.2d 751 (1983). An inference of negligence cannot ordinarily be based solely on the fact that a rare or unusual result occurred. *Id.*; *See* Perin v. Hayne, 210 N.W.2d 609 (Iowa 1973). A few courts have, however, indicated that the doctrine may apply when there is both a low incidence of such accidents when due care is used and there is some proof of specific acts of negligence of a type which could have caused the injury. *See* Hale v. Venuto, 137 Cal.App.3d 910, 187 Cal.Rptr. 357 (1982).

Perhaps the most common factual pattern in which plaintiff has sought to rely on *res ipsa* involves allegations that a surgical sponge, laparotomy pad, surgical instrument, or other medical device was left in an incision following surgery. Courts have reached different conclusions as to the applicability of *res ipsa* when a medical instrument breaks while being used on the patient. *Res ipsa* has also been applied when a patient falls while under the control of medical personnel.

The unnecessary removal of or injury to healthy tissue has also provided fertile ground for *res ipsa*. *See* Annot., 37 A.L.R.2d 464 (1971, Supp.1984). Courts have generally been quite willing to apply the doctrine to cases involving burns or traumatic injuries to parts of the patient's body not in the immediate field of the operation or procedure. When the injury involves healthy tissue within the general anatomical site of the surgery, courts have been more circumspect and divided in invoking the doctrine.

Infections following a medical procedure have also sometimes been relied upon by patients to support an inference of negligence, especially when nonsterile instruments were a suspected cause.

The courts, however, remain divided in applying *res ipsa* to infection cases.

Courts have generally been reluctant to apply *res ipsa* when the thrust of plaintiff's case is that defendant selected the wrong course of treatment or misdiagnosed plaintiff's condition. Some errors of professional judgment may simply not have been negligent. *See generally* III, C, 4. Moreover, circumstantial inferences should seldom even be necessary since the negligence, if any, in a particular exercise of professional discretion should be more susceptible to direct rather than circumstantial proof.

The refusal of some courts to apply *res ipsa* in some circumstances may have been because such matters were deemed beyond the common knowledge of laymen and either no expert testimony was offered to support the inference of negligence or the applicability of the doctrine in the jurisdiction was limited to common knowledge situations. Thus, it is difficult to generalize about when a particular injury will sufficiently suggest negligence to warrant application of *res ipsa*. Such questions are best determined on an *ad hoc* basis. As a minimum, there must be some basis for concluding that, in light of past experience, the nature of the injury makes it more likely the result of the alleged negligence than of some other cause.

iii. Exclusive Control. It is commonly said that *res ipsa loquitur* will not apply unless defendant was in "exclusive control" of the patient or the injurious instrumentality at the time of the alleged negligence. It is not enough for the plaintiff to prove that the injury was probably produced by someone's negligence. It must ordinarily appear that the defendant was probably a cause of the harm.

In many situations, more than one person may have exercised control over the patient or the instrumentality that injured him. The traditional rule in non-malpractice *res ipsa* cases has been that plaintiff fails in his burden of proof against multiple defendants when he can only show that the negligence of one of them probably caused his injury, but is unable to specify which one.* Some courts, however, have taken a more liberal approach. In Ybarra v. Spangard, 25 Cal.2d 486, 154 P.2d 687 (1944), the patient suffered an unexplained traumatic shoulder injury during or shortly before or after an appendectomy. In reversing a directed verdict for the defendants, the California Supreme Court held that *res ipsa loquitur* applied to all of the defendant medical personnel who had been involved in the surgery or post-operative care of the patient. It was virtually impossible for all of the defendant physicians and nurses to have caused plaintiff's injury. Further, neither the hospital nor any one defendant could have been vicariously liable for all of the others. Nevertheless, the

---

* Of course, when a defendant is vicariously liable for others, and it is more likely than not that his negligence or the negligence of those for whose acts he is vicariously liable caused the harm, this element would be satisfied.

court held that "[w]here a plaintiff receives unusual injuries while unconscious and in the course
of medical treatment, all those defendants who had
any control over his body or the instrumentalities
which might have caused the injuries, may properly be called upon to meet the inference of negligence by giving an explanation of their conduct."
154 P.2d at 691.

The *Ybarra* case has been criticized as an unde-
sirable extension of the doctrine of *res ipsa.* In the
typical *res ipsa* case, there is always the risk that
the inference of negligence, though apparently reasonable, may be wrong, imposing liability on an
innocent party. In the multiple defendant situation, however, there is not only a risk but a good
possibility and sometimes even a likelihood that at
least some of the defendants may be held responsible despite their innocence. On the other hand,
the patient being unconscious, is in no position to
account for the events that preceded his injury.
This especially vulnerable position of the patient
may justify a duty on members of the medical
profession at least to look after the patient careful-
ly enough to be able to explain the source of
unusual injuries. The fact that some members of
the profession have sometimes been perceived as
not merely ignorant of the causes of patients' injuries, but as concealing their involvement or knowledge of the cause, has also likely figured in some of
the multiple-defendant cases. Application of *res
ipsa* to multiple defendants has been accepted by a

number of decisions. *See* Wiles v. Myerly, 210 N.W.2d 619 (Iowa 1973); Anderson v. Somberg, 67 N.J. 291, 338 A.2d 1 (1975). Others refuse to apply it in such circumstances. Stevens v. Union Mem. Hosp., 47 Md.App. 627, 424 A.2d 1118 (1981); Talbot v. Dr. W.H. Groves' Latter-Day Saints Hosp., 21 Utah 2d 73, 440 P.2d 872 (1968).

Some cases applying the *Ybarra* rule have required that the plaintiff have sued all potential defendants who controlled possible causes of the injury. Spannaus v. Otolaryngology Clinic, 308 Minn. 334, 242 N.W.2d 594 (1976). Other cases, however, have said that this requirement should be construed reasonably and have not mandated that every imaginable defendant be joined. *See* Anderson, *supra.* The *Ybarra* approach was held not to apply when the potential sources of the injurious catheter left in the patient's body may have encompassed different treatment by different entities at different times spanning a number of years in different locations. *See* Loizzo v. St. Francis Hosp., 121 Ill.App.3d 172, 76 Ill.Dec. 677, 459 N.E.2d 314 (1984). Moreover, the mere fact that a defendant was involved in the treatment of the patient generally would not justify application of the doctrine to him if it were established that he had absolutely no responsibility in connection with any potential cause or source of the injury. *See* O'Connor v. Bloomer, 116 Cal.App.3d 391, 172 Cal.Rptr. 128 (1981) (uncontradicted testimony that duties of assistant surgeon did not include insuring that the proper prosthetic valve was available prior to aortic valve replacement).

iv. Conduct of the Plaintiff. It is often said that the injury must not have been caused by the acts of the plaintiff. This formulation, as such, is confusing and perhaps misleading. The mere fact that the plaintiff's actions contributed to the injury should not operate to exclude *res ipsa* unless the causal actions of the plaintiff and an inference of causal negligence by the defendant were mutually exclusive. The reason is that both plaintiff and defendant may have caused the harm since there may be more than one cause of an injury. *See* V, B. Thus, for example, although a mental patient's suicidal acts was a cause of the patient's death, such causal acts would not preclude an inference that the death was also caused by the alleged negligence by the hosptial in not protecting the patient from her own self-destructive impulses. *See* Vistica v. Presbyterian Hosp. & Med. Center of San Francisco, Inc., 67 Cal.2d 465, 62 Cal.Rptr. 577, 432 P.2d 193 (1967).

This element of *res ipsa* could more rationally be addressed by the first element—requiring an inference that the alleged negligence was more likely than not a cause of the injury—and other rules. Thus, the fact that the patient's contribution to his own injury tended to exclude the defendant's negligence as a cause could be decisive to the first element. Moreover, plaintiff's conduct might also be relevant to the question of contributory negligence and, in rare instances, proximate cause. *See generally* VIII, B; V, C, 1.

e. Effect of Plaintiff's Knowledge, Pleadings, and Proof

It is sometimes stated as an additional element of *res ipsa* that evidence regarding the injury must have been more accessible to the defendant than to the plaintiff. *See* Prosser at 254. This consideration appears to be as much a policy justification for the doctrine as an indispensable precondition. It has also been held that the plaintiff must not be in a position to show the particular circumstances of how the offending agency or instrumentality operated to cause the injury. *See* Carranza v. Tucson Med. Center, 135 Ariz. 490, 662 P.2d 455 (1983). When the three primary elements are satisfied, one would seldom expect a court to refuse to apply *res ipsa loquitur* because of the comparative ignorance of the parties, assuming that no clear explanation of the occurrence was available to the plaintiff or forthcoming. When the "access to the evidence" factor has been relied on to preclude *res ipsa,* at least one other element has often also been missing. *See* Cousins v. Henry, 332 So.2d 506 (La. App.1976).

A question also arises with respect to the effect, if any, on the availability of *res ipsa* of pleadings and proof of specific acts of negligence. Traditionally, courts have followed a variety of approaches to the pleadings question. The most enlightened approach holds that plaintiff may plead both specific acts of negligence (or under some views, general allegations of negligence) and *res ipsa* in the alternative and rely on *res ipsa* without restriction. Some courts limit the scope of *res ipsa* to establishing the specific allegations when plaintiff pleads specific allegations of negligence, especially when he pleads neither general allegations of negligence nor *res ipsa*. Finally, some cases suggest that mere allegations of specific acts of negligence preclude resort to *res ipsa* for any purpose, presumably even in the presence of a general allegation of negligence or of *res ipsa*. Obviously, to the extent that the evidence clearly establishes specifically how the injury occurred, the need for *res ipsa* should disappear. Short of this there appears to be no good reason why a plaintiff should not be permitted, to the extent allowed under the applicable rules of civil procedure, to plead in the alternative and rely upon both specific acts of negligence as well as on *res ipsa loquitur*. *See* Reilly v. Straub, 282 N.W.2d 688 (Iowa 1979).

When the evidence conclusively establishes how the injury occurred and the role, if any, played by the defendant, resort to *res ipsa* is unnecessary since the relevant evidence would simply no longer be circumstantial. Short of such proof, however, most courts hold that the introduction of some evidence of negligence does not bar *res ipsa*. *See* Sammons v. Smith, 353 N.W.2d 380 (Iowa 1984). *But see* Marrero v. Goldsmith, 448 So.2d 543 (Fla. App.1984) (*res ipsa* not applicable when one of plaintiff's experts testified that the cause of her post-operative arm injury was incorrect positioning or failure to change position during surgery).

f. Procedural Effect

As previously noted, *res ipsa loquitur* has basically two dimensions: first, whether the doctrine is *applicable* ; and second, if the doctrine does apply, what is its *procedural effect*? In some cases it will be so clear that the elements have or have not been satisfied that the doctrine will be held to be applicable or inapplicable as a matter of law. If, however, the court decides that reasonable minds can differ on whether all the elements have been established, under the preferred approach, the jury decides whether those elements have in fact been satisfied so as to render *res ipsa* "applicable." *See* II, D, 3, d, i. Just because *res ipsa* is held to be applicable does not necessarily mean that the plaintiff will prevail. To be sure, application of *res ipsa* usually operates to avoid a nonsuit or directed verdict by allowing plaintiff to get to the jury. But in most instances it does not automatically guarantee ultimate success. Rather, the outcome will depend on the application of the procedural effect given to the doctrine.

Assuming the doctrine is found to be applicable—meaning the required elements have been proven—it must be decided what procedural effect the doctrine should have. The courts have followed three approaches. The first and prevailing view holds that the doctrine merely creates a per-

missible inference of negligence. *See* Wiles v. Myerly, 210 N.W.2d 619 (Iowa 1973); Young v. Caspers, 311 Minn. 391, 249 N.W.2d 713 (1977). If the
doctrine is found to be applicable, plaintiff usually
avoids a nonsuit, but might not win even if defendant rests without introducing any contrary evidence. The jury is, in other words, free to accept
or reject the inference. The burden of proof remains on the plaintiff. The effect of the doctrine
depends entirely upon the persuasive strength of
the inference of negligence.

A second approach essentially shifts the burden
of going forward with the evidence to the defendant or creates a rebuttable presumption of negligence. *See* Tenn.Code Ann. § 29–26–115(c) (1980);
Mudd v. Dorr, 40 Colo.App. 74, 574 P.2d 97 (1977).
Not only does plaintiff usually avoid a nonsuit, but
if there is no countervailing evidence explaining
the accident or rebutting the inference of negligence, plaintiff will be entitled to a verdict as a
matter of law.

A third rule shifts the burden of persuasion to
the defendant. Thus, in order to avoid an adverse
result on the question of fault, defendant must
prove by a preponderance of the evidence that he
was not in fact negligent or did not cause the
injury.*

---

* Some courts have taken this last view even further. In
Anderson v. Somberg, 67 N.J. 291, 338 A.2d 1 (1975), a rongeur
broke off while being manipulated in plaintiff's spinal column.
In an action against physicians, hospital, supplier, and manufacturer, the court held that when an unconscious or helpless

The inference of negligence or the defendant's countervailing evidence may, in rare circumstances, be so overwhelming that reasonable minds could not differ, warranting a decision for the plaintiff or defendant as a matter of law. In most cases, however, the ultimate decision whether to apply the procedural effect in question rests with the jury. Generally, the effect of this evidence along with all the other evidence should be for the jury to determine in light of its overall probativeness, assuming that reasonable minds could differ on both the question of whether the elements of the doctrine have been satisfied as well as the ultimate question of negligence. An especially troublesome issue is how to handle the situation in which the defendant simply testifies and offers evidence that everything he did conformed to the applicable professional standards, but does not otherwise establish a cause of the harm for which he would not be responsible. The most sensible approach would be to hold that such evidence should not automatically nullify *res ipsa,* but should be factored into the jury's overall calculus. The jury should be allowed, in such circumstances, to decide

plaintiff suffers a mishap unrelated to the scope of the surgery and *res ipsa* applies, the burden of proof shifts to all those who owed the patient a duty of care or a duty not to furnish a defective instrument. More significantly, since all parties had been joined who could reasonably have been responsible for the negligence or defect, and if no explanation for the accident other than the negligence of defendants or the defectiveness of the rongeur was forthcoming, the court held that a verdict against at least one of the defendants was compelled.

whether the defendant's evidence is believable or worthy of acceptance in light of the suggestion of negligence created by the circumstantial evidence.

The permissible inference rule is probably the approach most consistent with the basic theory of *res ipsa*. The doctrine should be only as outcome-determinative as the persuasiveness of the inference of negligence warrants. Under this view, however, the jury must sometimes wrestle twice with inferences to be drawn from the occurrence— once in deciding whether the elements of *res ipsa* have been satisfied (*see* II, D, 3, d), and if so, then in deciding whether the inference is persuasive enough considering all of the evidence to establish negligence.

Ultimately the most sensible course may lie in completely abandoning *res ipsa*, with all of its convoluted and redundant perturbations. A rule might be adopted in its place in which a plaintiff would simply be entitled to prove his case with circumstantial or direct evidence, or both. The judge would decide whether, under all the evidence including circumstantial evidence, reasonable minds could differ on the issue of negligence. If so, the jury would be instructed that the weight of the circumstantial evidence should depend upon its persuasiveness in light of all of the facts. It would also be instructed that both circumstantial and direct evidence might be considered in determining whether the plaintiff satisfied his burden of proof.

CHAPTER III

THE PATIENT'S RIGHT TO SELF-DETERMINATION AND INFORMATION

A. NATURE OF PATIENT'S RIGHT TO SELF-DETERMINATION AND INFORMATION

An individual's right to self-determination with respect to his physical integrity is vigorously guarded by the courts. Justice Cardozo long ago declared that "[e]very human being of adult years and sound mind has a right to determine what shall be done with his own body." Schloendorff v. Society of N.Y. Hosp., 211 N.Y. 125, 129, 105 N.E. 92, 93 (1914).

Analytically, the subject of the patient's right of self-determination can be divided into several dimensions. First, there is the threshold question of when a person will be deemed to have *consented* to a medical procedure. *See* III, B. Second, there is the question whether the patient's choice of a medical course of action was sufficiently *informed*. *See* III, C. Third, the effects of misrepresentation and nondisclosure of information on the patient's rights to informed decision-making must be considered. *See* III, D.

Treatment performed in the absence of valid consent may constitute a battery and be actionable without expert testimony on the standard of care. Moreover, since recovery may be based on the invasion of one's dignitary interests, one may recover for battery even in the absence of physical harm. When there has been consent to the medical procedure, but that consent was not sufficiently informed, the physician may be liable, usually under a negligence theory, for harm that would have probably been avoided had the required disclosures been made.

B. REQUIREMENT OF CONSENT

1. Forms of Consent

a. *Consent by the Patient*

Effective consent may be based upon either of two conditions. First, the patient* may have in fact been willing to undergo the medical procedure in question. Second, irrespective of his actual willingness or unwillingness, the patient may through his conduct have sufficiently manifested consent that the law will find a valid consent. *See* Restatement § 892 & Comment b.

When the patient was in fact willing that the contact occur, this alone may satisfy the consent requirement. *See Id.* § 892 & Comment b & Illus-

* The term "patient" as used here should be read to include the patient's surrogate when the patient's age, incompetency, or incapacity necessitates substituted consent. *See* III, B, 1, d.

tration 1. Thus, if it were established, perhaps through admissions of the patient, that he was in fact willing that his adenoids be removed if medically indicated during the course of a tonsillectomy, such actual willingness should satisfy the consent requirement under the Restatement view. Similarly, the fact that a parent was willing for a minor child to visit a doctor's office for a specified treatment of an infection might, depending on all of the facts, be sufficient evidence of actual parental willingness to satisfy the consent requirement. Generally, however, a finding of consent will seldom be based on proof of actual willingness alone. Patients who were in fact willing to undergo the procedure seldom would sue for a lack of consent. And in any event, proving actual willingness to undergo a specific procedure of a patient claiming a lack of consent would in most cases be difficult.

Consent may also be based on conduct that manifests a willingness to undergo the procedure, irrespective of the actual state of mind or even unexpressed unwillingness of the patient. *See Id.* § 892 & Comment c. The conduct must, however, be reasonably understood by the defendant as intended to signify consent. *Id.* Moreover, the defendant must also have acted in good faith in believing that the manifestation of consent accurately reflected the patient's true willingness to undergo the procedure. A patient can signify his consent to treatment in a number of ways. A written acquiescence is the most unequivocal manifestation of consent. However, unless there is a specific statutory requirement for written consent for certain types of procedures, unwritten consent may also be valid. Thus, a patient's consent may be manifested orally or even by his act of submission to a specified procedure. Grannum v. Berard, 70 Wash. 2d 304, 422 P.2d 812 (1967); *see* O'Brien v. Cunard S.S. Co., 154 Mass. 272, 28 N.E. 266 (1891) (lining up and submitting to a vaccination constituted valid consent). When, however, a patient on a prior occasion has expressly withheld his consent to a particular procedure, a clearer manifestation of consent may thereafter be required than might otherwise be necessary. Obviously, written consent is preferred from an evidentiary standpoint.

Plaintiff's consent should be addressed to the specific medical procedure contemplated, to the extent it is known in advance. This does not mean that the patient must specifically consent to each constituent step of a single, unified medical procedure. But consent must at least signify a realization by the patient of the basic type and nature of the procedure proposed.

One's consent may be invalid when it is procured by duress or misrepresentation concerning the nature of the invasion or extent of the harm, when the patient is acting under a serious misapprehension of which defendant is aware concerning such matters, or when the patient is a minor, is incompetent, or is in a non-lucid state. *See generally* Restatement §§ 892A(2)(a), 892B. Consent to conduct that constitutes a crime—such as illegal abortion—may also be deemed invalid, although the authorities are divided on the question. *See* Prosser at 122.

The traditional rule, at least with respect to unemancipated minors, is that, absent an emergency requiring immediate treatment to save the patient's life or to prevent serious bodily harm, the consent of the minor's parent or guardian should be obtained prior to treatment. *See* Zoski v. Gaines, 271 Mich. 1, 260 N.W. 99 (1935) (addressing immature minors). This rule appears to have been relaxed by some courts when the minor was mature enough to understand the nature and consequences of the treatment and to knowingly consent. This has been especially true when the patient's parents were not readily available, the procedure was performed primarily for the benefit of the patient, and the procedure was a relatively simple one. *See, e.g.,* Younts v. St. Francis Hosp. and School of Nursing, Inc., 205 Kan. 292, 469 P.2d 330 (1970) (seventeen-year-old undergoing minor surgical repair and skin graft on a lacerated finger); Restatement § 892A, Comment b; *cf.* Kan. Stat.Ann. 38–123b (1973).

Some statutes and cases provide that the consent of an "emancipated" or married minor may also be valid. The definition and legal effect of emancipation varies from state to state, but often requires that the minor be married or have a separate residence from his parents and be responsible for his own financial situation. Relinquishment of parental control or conduct inconsistent with continuing parental rights and responsibilities may also be required. Emancipation often occurs irrespective of parental acquiescence, however, when the minor marries or enters military service.

A number of states have enacted special legislation rendering a minor's consent valid for certain purposes. Examples include treatment of sexually transmitted disease, of the minor's own children, in connection with pregnancy, for drug and alcoholic dependency, blood donations, examination following rape, and prescription of birth control pills. One statute, in addition to recognizing the validity of a minor's consent for some specific types of treatment, allows minors 14 years of age or older and certain others to consent to any legitimate treatment. *See* Ala.Code §§ 22–8–4 to 22–8–7 (1984). A Louisiana statute has gone even farther, allowing valid consent by a minor without an express age limitation who is or believes himself afflicted with an illness or disease. La.Rev.Stat. Ann. § 40:1095 (West 1977).

The United States Supreme Court has declared that the provisions of a statute imposing a blanket requirement of parental consent before a minor female could obtain an abortion (when otherwise entitled to one) were unconstitutional. *See* Planned Parenthood of Central Mo. v. Danforth, 428 U.S. 52 (1976). A later case, however, suggested that parental consent for an abortion could be required if the state provides an alternative procedure whereby the patient could dispense with such consent if she could show either that she is sufficiently mature to make the decision or that the abortion would be in her best interest. *See* Bellotti v. Baird, 443 U.S. 622 (1979) (plurality decision). *See also* H.L. v. Matheson, 450 U.S. 398 (1981) (upholding requirement of parental notice for immature minor seeking abortion, at least if the minor is afforded opportunity to avoid notice by proof of maturity or proof that abortion without notice would be in her best interest).

When a patient has been adjudged legally incompetent, consent to treatment must be secured from the patient's legal guardian. When no judicial determination of incompetency has been made, the consent of the spouse or parent should be obtained when incompetency is reasonably apparent. A patient who is normally a competent adult may be held to lack the requisite capacity to consent under special circumstances. Thus, in Demers v. Gerety, 85 N.M. 641, 515 P.2d 645 (Ct.App.1973), *rev'd on other grounds,* 86 N.M. 141, 520 P.2d 869 (1974), plaintiff, whose native language was French and who possessed a sixth grade education, signed a consent form after being awakened following sedation. Plaintiff had previously expressly withheld consent to performance by the defendant of the surgical procedure in question. The court held that the evidence supported a verdict for the plaintiff based on a lack of consent.

b. Implied Consent

In some cases consent will be "implied" by law even though there has been neither proof of actual willingness nor sufficient manifestation of consent by the patient. The most common occasions for implying consent involve emergencies in which the patient is a minor, unconscious, incompetent, or otherwise incapable of consenting. Such emergencies must generally endanger the life or health of the patient and require such prompt medical intervention that obtaining substituted consent (*see* III, B, 1, d) does not reasonably appear feasible. *See* Jackovach v. Yocom, 212 Iowa 914, 237 N.W. 444 (1931); Moss v. Rishworth, 222 S.W. 225 (Tex.Civ. App.1920). Further, the defendant must have no reason to believe that the patient (or someone authorized to consent for him) would decline treatment if he had the opportunity to consent. *See* Restatement § 892 D.

c. Scope of Consent

Even if the patient has consented to medical intervention, an issue may be presented regarding the scope of that consent. This question really has two possible dimensions. First, there is a question of whether the medical procedure actually performed was within the scope of the patient's consent. And second, there may be a question whether the patient's consent included performance by the physician in question.

On the first question, the traditional rule has been that a physician has no more right to extend the scope of an operation or other medical procedure without the patient's consent than he does to perform it in the first instance without authorization. *See* Mohr v. Williams, 95 Minn. 261, 104 N.W. 12 (1905). Under certain circumstances, however, consent to an extension of a procedure not specifically authorized has sometimes been found or implied. Various theories have been relied upon to accomplish that result. First, when an unanticipated condition arises during an authorized procedure requiring immediate action for the preservation of the life or health of the patient, courts have held that the physician may extend the scope of the treatment if it is impracticable to first obtain consent of the patient or a surrogate. Preston v. Hubbell, 87 Cal.App.2d 53, 196 P.2d 113 (1948).

Second, some courts have held that when the patient has given a general authorization permitting the physician to exercise his reasonable judgment to remedy any unforeseen condition injurious to health that he encounters during surgery, an extension of the operation may be justified. However, most of these cases have also involved a condition posing a serious threat to the patient's life or health, thus tending to cloud the question of the legal effect of the patient's general authorization. *See* Danielson v. Roche, 109 Cal.App.2d 832, 241 P.2d 1028 (1952); Rothe v. Hull, 352 Mo. 926,

180 S.W.2d 7 (1944). In the absence of an emergency situation, the courts are divided on the validity of a general consent form. Some courts have relied on a general consent form authorizing, for example, "therapeutically necessary" procedures in addition to those specifically contemplated. Such language was held to justify removal of what turned out to be a benign ovarian tumor and a hysterectomy to control the bleeding of a patient who had expressly authorized a caesarean section and tubal ligation. *See* Davidson v. Shirley, 616 F.2d 224 (5th Cir.1980) (Georgia law). Other courts, however, have been less willing to tolerate extensions in the absence of an emergency even when there was a general consent form. *See* Rogers v. Lumbermens Mutual Cas. Co., 119 So.2d 649 (La.App.1960).

In one recent case, the patient had specifically consented to a laparotomy. She had also signed a general consent form authorizing additional procedures that the physicians "may consider necessary or advisable in the course of the operation." During surgery the surgeon encountered such extensive endometrial adhesions that he concluded that the patient was already sterile and that later surgery would be necessary unless he performed a total hysterectomy and bilateral palpingo-oophrectomy, which he did. The patient sued, arguing that she had not consented to the latter procedures. Moreover, the surgeon was aware of the patient's desire to have children. Finding the evidence clear that no emergency existed that threatened the patient's life or health, the court held for the plaintiff as a matter of law. It stated: "Regardless of the reasonableness of the surgery or its eventual necessity, a physician may not act beyond his patient's authorization, except when a situation seriously threatens the health or life of the patient." Karl J. Pizzalotto, M.D., Ltd. v. Wilson, 437 So.2d 859, 861 (La.1983). The court rejected the blanket authorization form as ambiguous and of no weight since it failed to designate the nature of the operation authorized. There were vigorous dissents in *Pizzalotto*. One justice noted: "[T]his writer wonders which way the sword would have swung had the doctor subjected the plaintiff to another operation which may either have caused her serious pain and suffering or possibly loss of life." *Id.* at 868 (Blance, J., dissenting).

A compromise might be to uphold such general open-ended authorizations even in the absence of emergencies when a condition was encountered that was not reasonably anticipated and reasonably required treatment, and the treatment neither involved removal of an organ or member nor alteration of sexual function, and ordinarily did not entail serious additional risks. Perhaps a general consent should also be valid when there was specific consent to contemplated surgery that was to be exploratory in response to specific symptoms or was to achieve a specific objective, it was understood that reasonable additional steps might be taken to treat the condition, those steps were reasonably described in general to the patient, and the benefits of the additional steps taken clearly outweighed the risks.

Finally, without relying on either an emergency or a general authorization, some cases have recognized a privilege under certain circumstances to extend an operation. One case involved the unauthorized puncturing of an ovarian cyst during an appendectomy. In implying consent as a matter of law, the court relied upon the following factors: (1) the condition encountered could not reasonably have been diagnosed prior to surgery; (2) there was no indication of patient unwillingness to undergo the extended procedure; (3) the extension was in the area of the original incision; (4) sound medical practice dictated such an extension; and, (5) neither the patient nor a surrogate was immediately available to give consent. Kennedy v. Parrott, 243 N.C. 355, 90 S.E.2d 754 (1956).

Given the complexities of modern surgery and other medical procedures, it is seldom feasible to suspend an operation each time an unexpected condition is encountered. Moreover, the inherent risks of general anesthesia and surgery militate against repeated surgical invasions when a single operation would suffice. Under these circumstances, the *Kennedy* approach probably represents the most acceptable accommodation of the patient's physical well-being with his right of self-determination. Having the patient execute a general authorization for treatment of unexpected conditions would, when combined with the *Kennedy* criteria, increase the likelihood of a finding of implied consent to an extension of the surgery.

The fact that a patient consents to surgery or other procedure by one physician does not ordinarily constitute consent to performance by a substitute physician. The original physician may be subject to liability. *See* Perna v. Pirozzi, 92 N.J. 446, 457 A.2d 431 (1983). And, the substitute physician might be liable for battery in the absence of valid consent or an emergency. *See* Guebard v. Jabaay, 117 Ill.App.3d 1, 72 Ill.Dec. 498, 452 N.E. 2d 751 (1983) (dicta); *Perna, supra.* When, however, a situation arises that was not reasonably anticipated, that makes performance by the original physician impossible, and that does not permit time to afford the patient a reasonable opportunity to select a substitute physician, the substitution should be excused.

If a team of physicians is to be involved in the performance of a medical procedure, this should be explained to the patient and appropriate consent obtained. Such general authorization, however, may not ordinarily without more permit a substitution for the primary physician. Thus, a consent form naming several doctors "and such assistants as are assigned to this case," did not authorize a first-year resident to act as the "primary performer" of the surgery even though under direction and supervision of named surgeon. *See* Guebard, *supra* (dicta).

When the patient's condition or the nature of the physician's practice makes it infeasible for the physician to schedule the patient's treatment, the physician should obtain the patient's consent to a specified substitute physician or physicians. For example, the availability of a specific obstetrician may not coincide with the onset of labor. This type of arrangement should, however, be explained to the patient in advance. Similarly, when time permits, a patient to be hospitalized should be informed of and consent to arrangements for coverage by other physician during anticipated absences of the admitting physician.

d. Substituted Consent and the Right to Refuse Treatment

When the patient is not competent to consent because of age or mental incapacity, substituted consent by a surrogate is usually required if the patient's condition allows sufficient time to obtain such consent. Statutes or cases often provide that such substituted consent may be given by certain specified persons, typically a guardian, spouse, parent, person *in loco parentis,* or perhaps some other person. Under some circumstances, court approval may be required. Many states also have statutes governing the required authorization for treatment of institutionalized incompetent patients.

Courts are increasingly called upon to decide difficult questions about the limits of authority for consenting for another. One question arises when a surrogate seeks to consent to or judicial approval for a medical procedure that is not designed primarily for the benefit of the patient, such as the donation of an organ for transplant to another. *Compare* Little v. Little, 576 S.W.2d 493 (Tex.1979) (upholding Probate Court's authorization of guardian of mentally retarded minor to consent to donation of kidney to brother), *with* Lausier v. Pescinski, 67 Wis.2d 4, 226 N.W.2d 180 (1975) (refusing to authorize transplant).

A serious dilemma may arise when parental consent is required but has been expressly withheld. A physician who treats a patient under such circumstances runs the risk of committing a battery. On the other hand, if treatment is withheld, serious injury to the patient may result, and perhaps the attending physician might even conceivably be charged with abandonment of the patient or negligence in some cases. To avoid this dilemma, physicians and hospitals have increasingly sought judicial intervention. Courts have sometimes relied upon "child neglect" statutes for authority to appoint a guardian to consent for the child or to give the court authority to approve treatment. Even when the parents object to treatment on religious grounds, the courts have ordered treatment in appropriate cases. *See* State v. Perricone, 37 N.J. 463, 181 A.2d 751 (1962). Most cases have involved treatment necessary to avert death or serious injury. The courts are divided on the extent to which parents should be allowed to decide whether treatment should be withheld for less critical conditions. *Compare* Matter of Sampson, 29 N.Y.2d 900, 326 N.Y.S.2d 398, 278 N.E.2d 918 (1972) (upholding family court's authorization, over the religious objections of the patient's mother, for surgery to repair serious facial deformity in order to improve the minor's appearance), *with* In re Green, 448 Pa. 338, 292 A.2d 387 (1972), *appeal after remand* 452 Pa. 373, 307 A.2d 279 (1973) (refusing to allow the state to override parental refusal to permit spinal fusion surgery, at least in the absence of a conflict between the desires of the parents and those of the minor).

Sometimes parents will not withhold consent to all treatment, but rather refuse to consent to conventional medical therapies. One example encountered in recent years has involved parental opposition to conventional cancer therapies (surgery, radiation, or chemotherapy) in favor of treatment with unproven and potentially dangerous substances such as laetrile. Most courts have recognized that the best interest of the child should guide the court in deciding whether to appoint a guardian to assure proper medical care. *See* Custody of a Minor, 378 Mass. 732, 393 N.E.2d 836 (Mass.1979) (upholding order requiring conventional chemotherapy for child with acute lymphocytic leukemia and forbidding laetrile). Occasionally, however, a court will unfortunately retreat from the preceding straightforward analysis.*

Generally, a competent adult has a constitutionally protected right to refuse treatment, absent a compelling state interest. The question of the right to refuse treatment sometimes arises when the patient is terminally ill. Certainly, a terminally ill patient with advanced cancer should not be forced to submit to "heroic" treatments against his will when the prospects for cure or significant remission are remote. Some courts have held that a terminally ill competent adult may even order the discontinuation of life-supporting respirator. *See* Satz v. Perlmutter, 379 So.2d 359 (Fla.1980). Courts have occasionally been asked to order treatment or appoint a guardian when a competent adult patient withholds consent to potentially life-saving treatment. The outcomes have varied. In Lane v. Candura, 6 Mass.App. 377, 376 N.E.2d 1232 (1978), the court upheld a competent patient's right to refuse a life-saving amputation. But, compulsory vaccinations have been required for the protec-

* In Matter of Hofbauer, 47 N.Y.2d 648, 419 N.Y.S.2d 936, 393 N.E.2d 1009 (1979), the court took a dangerously narrow view of the scope of judicial oversight of the parent's decision, stating: "[T]he court's inquiry should be whether the parents, once having sought accredited medical assistance and having been made aware of the seriousness of their child's affliction and the possibility of cure if a certain mode of treatment is undertaken, have provided for their child a treatment which is recommended by their physician and which has *not been totally rejected* by all responsible medical authority." 393 N.E.2d at 1014, (emphasis added).

tion of both society and the patient. The cases are divided on whether a patient has a right to refuse a life-saving blood transfusion. Some patients have relied on religious objections. Factors sometimes relied upon to varying degrees to support orders to save the patient's life have included the necessity of preserving the *status quo* ; the temporary mental incapacity of the patient; the prevention of the orphaning of children; the necessity of giving guidance and protection to medical personnel; and, the prevention of suicide. Opposing arguments have sometimes included freedom of religion; the right of privacy and self-determination; the fact that refusal of consent was unequivocal and released the medical personnel from liability; and, the fact that the patient had no minor children.

A further nuance arises when a patient who is sustained by artificial means is comatose or incompetent, and the family or guardian withholds consent for continuation of such life-support measures. A comatose or incompetent patient is generally held to have the same constitutional right to refuse treatment that is accorded a competent adult patient. The problem is how to effectuate that right. This type of situation really presents two questions. First, what criteria must be satisfied before the artificial life supports may be withdrawn or withheld? And second, who applies those criteria?

A number of courts have approved cessation of artificial life support when the patient was comatose with virtually no chance of ever regaining a cognitive, sapient state. Thus, in the Matter of Quinlan, 70 N.J. 10, 355 A.2d 647 (1976), the court held that the respirator could be withdrawn when the attending physicians concluded that there was no reasonable possibility of the patient ever emerging from her present comatose condition to a cognitive, sapient state; the hospital ethics committee concurred in the foregoing conclusion; the attending physicians were of the opinion that the life-support apparatus should be discontinued; and the guardian and family of the patient concurred in the decision.

Other cases have involved incompetent but non-comatose patients who suffered from a terminal condition that would probably result in death irrespective of treatment. *See* Supt. of Belchertown State School v. Saikewicz, 373 Mass. 728, 370 N.E.2d 417 (1977) (upholding lower court order withholding chemotherapy from incompetent, profoundly retarded leukemia patient).* When a terminally ill incompetent patient is non-comatose, however, some courts appear reluctant to approve the withholding of the less "heroic" therapies or

---

* A few cases have considered the rights of permanently incompetent elderly patients not suffering from a specific terminal disease. *See* Matter of Hier, 18 Mass.App.Ct. 200, 464 N.E.2d 959 (1984) (withholding surgery from 92 year old incompetent nursing home patient under the circumstances); Matter of Conroy, 98 N.J. 321, 486 A.2d 1209 (1985) (examining prerequisites for withholding or withdrawing life-sustaining treatment from incompetent nursing home resident with life expectancy of less than a year).

life support measures. *See* Matter of Storar, 52 N.Y.2d 363, 438 N.Y.S.2d 266, 420 N.E.2d 64 (1981) (denying the right to discontinue life-supporting blood transfusions for a terminally ill mentally retarded patient).

Another question on which there has thus far been little case law, relates to the type of medical life-support treatment or intervention that can be withheld or withdrawn. Most cases have dealt with major life support systems such as respirators or extensive treatment modalities such as surgery or cancer chemotherapy. A few cases, however, have addressed the withholding or withdrawal of less complex measures. *See* Barber v. Superior Court, 147 Cal.App.3d 1006, 195 Cal.Rptr. 484 (1983) (comatose patient).

In addition to satisfying medical criteria relating to the patient's irreversible condition and the nature of the life-prolonging procedure, the courts have also usually required an exercise of substituted judgment with respect to whether to withdraw or withhold treatment of a comatose or incompetent patient. The decision makers are usually "to determine with as much accuracy as possible the wants and needs of the individual involved." Superintendent v. Saikewicz, 373 Mass. 728, 370 N.E.2d 417 (1977).

The criteria for deciding, and the identity and nature of involvement of the individuals—such as physicians, family, guardian, and hospital committee—deciding to withhold or withdraw artificial life support for a comatose or incompetent patient varies from court to court. *Compare Quinlan, with* John F. Kennedy Mem. Hosp., Inc. v. Bludworth, 452 So.2d 921 (Fla.1984). Assuming the conditions precedent to withholding or withdrawal of therapy. have been identified and satisfied, the question then becomes whether judicial intervention is required. Courts have taken basically two approaches. Most courts have held that court-approval should not be routinely required. It has been emphasized, however, that the courts should remain open to hear these matters when the parties desire judicial intervention. See Bludworth, *supra.* Other cases suggest that invocation of the court's jurisdiction should be regarded as optional. *See* Matter of Storar, 52 N.Y.2d 363, 438 N.Y.S.2d 266, 420 N.E.2d 64 (1981). Of course, when the designated decision-makers cannot agree, judicial intervention would be necessary.

A few courts have held that judicial approval may be required, at least in certain circumstances. These include, for example, situations in which an appropriate family member is not available to consult with attending physicians or in which the court's jurisdiction has already been invoked. *See* Custody of a Minor, 385 Mass. 697, 434 N.E.2d 601 (1982) (court approval required for "no code" order for abandoned child with incurable terminal illness). *See also* In the Matter of Spring, 380 Mass. 629, 405 N.E.2d 115 (1980) (identifying other relevant factors affecting the question of when judicial approval is required). Furthermore, judicial intervention is sometimes required by statute for certain types of medical procedures.

In recent years, many states have enacted so-called "Natural Death" or "Living Wills" statutes. Although the statutes vary markedly, the California statute offers a good example. It provides, *inter alia*, a procedure whereby a terminally-ill adult person may execute a directive for withholding or withdrawal of life-sustaining procedures in the event he has a terminal condition, he is unable to personally give such directions, and death becomes imminent whether or not the life-sustaining procedures are utilized. *See* Calif.Health & Safety Code §§ 7185 *et seq.* (Supp.1985). The act also provides that its provisions are cumulative in the sense that they do not impair any other rights independent of the act with respect to the withholding or withdrawal of life-sustaining procedures. *Id.* § 7193.

A growing number of states have also enacted statutory definitions of death based on brain-death criteria. These statutes have eliminated some of the questions in this area.

To place these matters into perspective, the likelihood of a plaintiff succeeding in a torts action in cases in which life-sustaining treatment has been withheld or withdrawn is remote. First, the plaintiff would have to prove that the patient's consent or substituted consent was invalid and that the patient was not already legally dead (under increasingly broad definitions of death) at the time of the alleged withdrawal or withholding of life support. Second, those claiming damages for the death of the patient might, under some statutes governing death actions in some states, be subject to defenses based on their consent to the conduct in question. *See generally* Prosser at 958–59. Furthermore, the likelihood of such decedents' lives, given their usual profound permanent disability, being worth much in damages is unlikely.*

2. Standard for Consent

The validity of consent may be affected by questions with respect to the outward manifestations of willingness to undergo the procedure, the patient's age (or other status), mental competency, and relationship to another giving substituted consent, and the existence of an emergency situation. One question the courts have seldom adequately addressed concerns the standard by which the conduct of the person securing the consent will be judged with respect to the foregoing variables. There are at least three possible approaches. First, the person rendering care could be held to act at his peril. Despite reasonable appearances to the contrary, if the patient were in fact unwilling to proceed, if he were in fact incompetent or under age, or if a bona fide emergency did not exist, the health care provider could be liable. Second, an

---

* If, however, the withholding of treatment caused additional harm to the patient and the patient survived at least for a time, the potential damages could be significant if liability were established.

objective standard could be used under which the defendant would be held to a reasonable person standard. If he reached a reasonable conclusion as to these variables consent would be valid. Finally, a good faith standard might be adopted, requiring simply that the physician make a subjective good faith effort to reach the correct conclusion with respect to the foregoing variables.

With respect to the manifestations of willingness, most authorities agree that an objective test should apply. If a reasonable person in the position of the physician would have concluded that the patient's actions manifested a willingness to undergo the contemplated medical procedure, that should be sufficient to constitute consent. *See* Restatement § 892, Comment c; J. Waltz and F. Inbau, *Medical Jurisprudence* 165–66 (1971).

The state of the law is less clear with respect to the standards for the other variables—age or emancipation (or maturity in jurisdictions recognizing a "mature minor" rule), existence of emergency, or authority of another to render substituted consent. Few if any states that have explicitly addressed the question require that the physician act at his peril. Some states have adopted a reasonable person standard with respect to some aspects of the consent problem, such as whether there exists an emergency. *See* Nev.Rev.Stat. 41 A. 120 (1983); *see also* Restatement § 892D. Others have gone further, adopting a good faith standard with respect to some matters. A Pennsylvania statute provides that the consent of a minor claiming to be old enough to give valid consent shall be effective if the physician relies in good faith upon the representations of the minor. Pa.Stat.Ann. tit. 35 § 10105 (Purdon 1977). *See also* Ga.Code Ann. § 31–9–6(c) (1985) ("Any person acting in good faith shall be justified in relying on the representations of any person purporting to give such a consent, including, but not limited to, his identity, his age, his marital status, his emancipation and his relationship to any other person for whom the consent is purportedly given."). A more general Idaho provision states that if the consenting person appears to the physician or dentist securing the consent to possess intelligence and awareness sufficient to comprehend the need for, nature of, and inherent risks of the procedure, the care may be administered. Idaho Code § 39–4302 (1977).

Unfortunately, in many respects the law remains unclear regarding the standards for testing a physician's judgment in connection with the foregoing variables. Explicit adoption of an objective standard that would protect reasonable judgments by physicians on all of the foregoing matters would add much needed certainty to this area of the law.

C. INFORMED CONSENT AND DECISION MAKING

1. In General

Not only must the patient have effectively consented to the contemplated medical procedure, but that consent must also have been informed. Before a patient undergoes a medical procedure, he must first receive certain information about it, especially concerning its inherent risks. Liability for a failure to obtain the patient's informed consent does not require negligence in the choice of treatment or in the manner in which it was administered. Rather, liability is based upon the materialization of certain inherent risks of a medical procedure about which the patient received insufficient information.

While the informed consent doctrine serves a number of functions, foremost among them is protection of the patient's right of self-determination. Indeed, a central premise of the doctrine is that the patient's freedom to decide what shall be done with his body may be an even more paramount interest than preservation of the patient's health. Some have perceived the rise of the doctrine of informed consent as simply another expression of an overly litigious society in crisis. Others, however, view it as a symbol of frustration by patients with some physicians who for reasons of inadvertence, time, paternalism, self-interest, or insensitivity, have been unwilling to involve their patients in the medical decision making process in a meaningful way.

2. Battery or Negligence?

Although there is some authority to the contrary, the prevailing view is that otherwise authorized treatment administered in the absence of informed consent is actionable under a negligence rather than a battery theory. *See* Tex.Rev.Civ.Stat. art. 4590i § 6.02 (Vernon's Supp.1985); Cobbs v. Grant, 8 Cal.3d 229, 104 Cal.Rptr. 505, 502 P.2d 1 (1972). Under this view, only when there was no consent, or the consent was to a medical procedure substantially different than the one actually performed, or the physician knew that the patient did not understand the nature of the procedure, or consent was otherwise invalid (*see* III, B, 1, a), might a battery theory apply. *See* Logan v. Greenwich Hosp. Assn., 191 Conn. 282, 465 A.2d 294 (1983). *See generally* III, B; IV, B.

3. Standard of Disclosure

a. *Various Approaches*

A central question in informed consent relates to the standard of disclosure by which the adequacy of the physician's disclosure is tested. Under the majority rule, the standard of disclosure is much the same as the standard of care in cases involving negligent diagnosis or treatment. The extent of a physician's duty to disclose is determined by professional standards. *See, e.g.* Idaho Code § 39–4304 (1977); N.Y.Pub.Health Law § 2805–d(1) (McKinney 1977); Tenn.Code Ann. § 29–26–118 (1980); Hook v. Rothstein, 281 S.C. 541, 316 S.E.2d 690 (1984). Some courts have adopted a modification of the professional standard wherein once the plaintiff proves that the defendant failed to inform him of inherent risks of the procedure, the burden shifts to the doctor to prove that his failure to disclose conformed to the applicable professional standards. *See* Blades v. DaFoe, 666 P.2d 1126 (Colo.App.1983), rev'd on other grounds, 704 P.2d 317 (1985).

Generally, courts adhering to a professional standard of disclosure reason that, given the complexities of medical science, the determination of what risks warrant disclosure is better left to the judgment of members of the medical profession. Without a professional standard, physicians would be left with no real premonition of what disclosures would be legally sufficient and might be held liable even though their conduct completely conformed to the expectations of their profession. Establishing the facts of non-disclosure often depends on conflicting recollections of plaintiff and defendant of their conversation. As a result, the issue of informed consent is peculiarly susceptible to selective recollection or even fabrication. Finally, one might argue that the time medical practitioners devote to satisfying the requirements of informed consent represents a misallocation of limited medical resources.

In 1972, the landmark decision of Canterbury v. Spence, 464 F.2d 772, 783 (D.C.Cir.1972), rejected the view that a "physician's obligation to disclose is either germinated or limited by medical practice." Instead, the court required disclosure of all material risks. Risks were deemed material when a reasonable person in the patient's apparent position would likely attach significance to the risks in question in deciding whether or not to proceed with the proposed therapy. Thus, while the court adopted an objective standard of disclosure, it rejected the conclusiveness of professional standards. The standard of disclosure was to be based on a reasonable lay person rather than a reasonable physician frame of reference. The court reasoned that there might not even be a discernible professional custom with respect to the standard of disclosure. More significantly, the court feared that arrogating to the medical profession the decision concerning what information should be disclosed might be in derogation of the patient's right of self-determination.* The court noted that what risks are material represents a non-medical judgment. Finally, the court seemed to question the view that the prevailing medical practice should conclusively establish the standard of care generally.

The *Canterbury* decision has attracted significant support from the courts and a few legislatures. *See* Logan v. Greenwich Hosp. Assn., 191 Conn. 282, 465 A.2d 294 (1983); Harnish v. Children's Hosp., 387 Mass. 152, 439 N.E.2d 240 (1982); Pa. Stat.Ann. tit. 40 § 1301.103 (Purdons Supp.1985); Rev.Code Wash. § 7.70.050(2) (Supp.1985). To a considerable extent, however, a trend favoring a

* A reasonable person standard would also allay fears of professional bias favoring under-disclosure motivated by non-therapeutic considerations such as economic advantage. *See* Schneyer, *Informed Consent and the Danger of Bias in the Formation of Medical Disclosure Practices,* 1976 Wis.L.Rev. 124.

lay standard of disclosure has been checked by a proliferation of malpractice statutes, most of which have adopted a professional standard of disclosure.

It should be noted that even under the *Canterbury* standard of disclosure, expert testimony will usually still be necessary for some purposes. It would not be required to prove *which* risks and other information were material. It would, however, usually still be needed to establish whether the nondisclosed matters *were in fact* risks of, alternatives to, or other inherrent aspects of the particular procedure in question as well as the prognosis if the patient went untreated, and whether a reasonable practitioner should have been aware of such information. Expert testimony would also ordinarily be required to establish that the patient's injury was caused by a materialization of risks of a procedure about which there was inadequate disclosure.

In addition to the two main lines of authority, there have been a number of other approaches to the standard of disclosure. Some of these are simply variations on the two major themes. Other approaches, however, may represent a different direction. A number of state statutes have created a presumption that informed consent was given when a written consent form, *inter alia*, sets forth in general terms the nature and purposes of the procedure together with the known risks of "death, brain damage, quadriplegia, paraplegia, the loss or loss of function of any organ or limb, or disfiguring scars . . ., with the probability of each such risk if reasonably determinable." Iowa Code Ann. § 147.137 (Supp.1985). A Texas statute provides for an even more specific list of information.*

Perhaps the most restrictive position has been the judicial interpretation given to a Georgia statute that creates a conclusive presumption of validity (absent fraudulent misrepresentation) for a written consent when the "general terms" of treatment are disclosed. Ga.Code Ann. § 31–9–6(d) (1985). The Georgia Court of Appeals has concluded, relying in part on the statute, that the physician's duty of disclosure did not include an obligation to reveal the risks of treatment. Simpson v. Dickson, 167 Ga.App. 344, 306 S.E.2d 404 (1983). *See also* Holbrook v. Schatten, 165 Ga.App. 217, 299 S.E.2d 128 (1983) (implying that the statute would be satisfied by information given *orally*).

---

* It creates a Medical Disclosure Panel that is charged with responsibility for identifying those medical procedures that do and do not require disclosure of risks, the disclosure required, and the form in which it is to be made, as well as for periodically updating such guidelines. *See* Tex.Rev.Civ.Stat.Ann. art. 4590i, § 6.04 (Vernon's Supp.1985). Written and signed acknowledgement of disclosure of the information prescribed by the panel, or the fact that the procedure was identified as one not requiring disclosure, is admissible and creates a rebuttable presumption that the statutorily created duties of informed consent have been satisfied. Conversely, a failure to disclose information prescribed by the Panel creates, subject to exceptions, a rebuttable presumption of negligent failure to obtain informed consent. *Id.* § 6.07(a). If a medical procedure has not yet been addressed by the panel one way or the other, the standard of disclosure is not affected by the statutory procedure. *Id.* § 6.07(b).

In addition to the standard of disclosure, the duty of disclosure has also been addressed from a more topical perspective, focusing on the types of information that must be revealed. Some courts not only require disclosure of the material risks, but also a description of *alternative courses* of action and the prognosis if the patient went untreated. *See* Canterbury, *supra* at 787–88. Others have added, *inter alia,* the duty to disclose the diagnosis, the general nature of the procedure,* and the probability of success. *See* Hook v. Rothstein, 281 S.C. 541, 316 S.E.2d 690 (App.1984). Some courts have also held that if the patient specifically inquires about a risk, he has a right to know even if disclosure would not otherwise be required. *See* Harbeson v. Parke Davis, Inc., 746 F.2d 517 (9th Cir.1984).

Regardless of the standard of disclosure, a health care provider can only be expected to know of risks and other information that a similarly situated reasonable practitioner would be expected to know. Before disclosure of a risk or other information can even be *potentially* required, it must first appear that a reasonable practitioner should have been aware of it. Thus, the duty to disclose is generally held to be *no broader* than those matters that the physician knew or reasonably should have known (but may be narrower depending on which of those

* A failure to disclose the general nature of the procedure might also support a claim for battery if there was so little general information given that it could be held that the patient's "consent" was meaningless and invalid. *See* II, B.

matters are required to be disclosed under the standard of disclosure). *See* Holton v. Pfingst, 534 S.W.2d 786 (Ky.1975). Thus, even courts following a lay standard of disclosure have added that expert testimony may be required to establish "that it is accepted medical practice to know" of the risks. *See* Reinhardt v. Colton, 337 N.W.2d 88, 96 (Minn. 1983). One court has suggested that the physician may be required to conduct a reasonable literature search to determine the risks and that the duty may sometimes encompass potential risks even if not yet conclusively established or accepted as definite risks by the medical profession, especially if the patient specifically inquires about such risks. *See* Harbeson, *supra.*

A number of general rules have evolved in some cases and statutes that help temper the informed consent doctrine. It has been held unnecessary to discuss the risks that might materialize from improper performance of the medical procedure. *See* Mallett v. Pirkey, 171 Colo. 271, 466 P.2d 466 (1970). Some jurisdictions recognize a defense when the patient assured the health care provider that he would undergo the treatment regardless of the risks or that he did not want the information to which he was entitled. *See* Del.Code Ann. tit. 18, § 6852(b)(2) (Supp.1984). Some courts have held that the duty to disclose does not include "information the physician reasonably believes the patient already has . . . ." Harnish v. Children's Hosp., 387 Mass. 152, 439 N.E.2d 240, 243

(1982). Some statutes have stated that there is no liability for failure to disclose commonly known risks. *See* Alaska Stat. § 09.55.556(b)(1) (1983); N.Y.Pub.Health Law § 2805–d(4)(a) (McKinney 1977).

b. *Suggested Solution*

Perhaps the ultimate solution to the standard of disclosure question lies in the creation and continuing revision of specific risk and information profiles containing the required information for the more frequently performed medical procedures. Most other situations not covered by specific profiles could be handled by standard disclosure guidelines such as those adopted in the Iowa statute. When written forms are used, added safeguards might be provided by requiring that the physician orally discuss the contents of the forms with the patient and invite questions from him. For information not encompassed under the preceding formulation, such as material facts relating to alternative procedures and the patient's prognosis under his various options, one of the general standards of disclosure could be employed. Since the particularized information will afford the patient significant protection, these remaining matters could perhaps be handled under a professional standard of disclosure without seriously undermining the patient's autonomy.

4. Causation

Mere proof of a violation of a duty to disclose does not entitle one to recover unless plaintiff also proves causation, which has several dimensions in informed consent. First, the fact that the required information was not disclosed must have been outcome-determinative to the patient's decision to proceed with the medical procedure in question. Three different tests have been employed in connection with this aspect of causation. Under the so-called "objective" test representing the majority view, the plaintiff must prove that a reasonable person in the patient's position would have declined the proposed treatment had he been adequately informed. *See* N.Y.Pub.Health Law § 2805–d(3) (McKinney 1977); Hartke v. McKelway, 707 F.2d 1544 (D.C.Cir.1983) (applying D.C. law); Hook v. Rothstein, 281 S.C. 541, 316 S.E.2d 690 (1984). Under the "subjective" test, plaintiff has to establish that he personally would have withheld consent had the required information been disclosed. *See* Alaska Stat. § 09.55.556(a) (1983). Finally, some courts require that both objective and subjective tests be satisfied. *See* Harnish v. Children's Hosp., 387 Mass. 152, 439 N.E.2d 240 (1982).

The objective test prevents retrospective second-guessing by the patient. The subjective test, on the other hand, may more accurately reflect true causation. Perhaps the best approach would be to require that the plaintiff satisfy an objective test.

Even if he did, however, the defendant should still be allowed to avoid liability if he can establish that the subjective test was not satisfied. *See* Truman v. Thomas, 27 Cal.3d 285, 165 Cal.Rptr. 308, 611 P.2d 902 (1980). The outcome determinative component of causation, when based on an objective test, should significantly reduce a physician's potential liability under informed consent. With respect to relatively safe procedures necessary to preserve life or health, such as appendectomies, there should be little doubt in most instances that a reasonable patient would have consented to the treatment even if all the required risks and information had been revealed. This aspect of the causation requirement would, however, be more readily satisfied in cases involving elective surgery, innovative or relatively untested procedures, and situations in which cost-benefit advantages of a procedure were less self-evident.

As a second dimension of causation, some courts have also required that the harm complained of must have been a materialization of the undisclosed risks that should have been disclosed. *See* Canterbury v. Spence, 464 F.2d 772 (D.C.Cir.1972). It is unclear, however, how far the *Canterbury* court really intended its broad statement to go. A number of situations may arise that were not contemplated by the court. What if, for example, a patient were injured by the materialization of a *disclosed* risk or one *for which disclosure was not required,* but the physician had also failed to disclose other significant risks (which did not materialize), or alternatives, or other information requiring disclosure? Imposing liability in such cases would not, strictly speaking, even have to be based on a battery theory (which has been overwhelmingly rejected for informed consent cases). Although a negligence theory would not redress dignitary interests alone (as would a battery theory) it would at least cover physical harm. Thus, the question is not whether to classify informed consent cases as batteries, but rather should be whether materialization of the risks in question should be deemed a proximate result of the negligent nondisclosure.

Assume, for example, that a patient suffered a severe reaction to the injected contrast media used during an X-ray procedure and that the patient was fully informed of this risk. Assume, further, that considering the nature of the patient's condition, an ultrasound procedure was a viable diagnostic alternative, but was not disclosed to the patient. Or, consider a case involving cosmetic surgery that entailed risks of paralysis and hearing loss, the disclosure of both of which was required. What if the risk of paralysis was disclosed, hearing loss was not, and paralysis or some unforeseeable and nondisclosable risk ensued? In both situations, the defendant negligently failed to reveal a risk or information requiring disclosure yet some other risk materialized. If applied literally, the *Canterbury* causation requirement in the preceding paragraph could nullify much of the duty of disclosure.

Perhaps liability for such harm should be recognized even under the prevailing negligence theory of informed consent in the first situation—when the defendant failed to disclose viable alternative procedures when their disclosure was required. Although this approach concededly would extend the scope of liability in informed consent cases, it would in doing so afford the patient an additional measure of protection. Moreover, plaintiff would still have to prove that in failing to disclose this information defendant violated the standard of disclosure and that the lack of such information was outcome-determinative to his decision to undergo the procedure in question.

A third dimension of causation is the requirement that the harm complained of have been caused by the medical procedure. *See generally* V, A. Thus, although a cardiac arrest may be a risk of a specific surgical procedure, the patient could not recover under informed consent even though he was not informed of that risk and did suffer a cardiac arrest if it were not established that his surgery caused this complication.

At least one case has recognized a fourth requirement—that plaintiff demonstrate that the injury suffered was measurably greater than the patient's condition would have been if he had foregone the therapy. *See* Haven v. Randolph, 342 F.Supp. 538 (D.D.C.1972), *aff'd,* 494 F.2d 1069 (D.C.Cir.1974);

Restatement § 920;* *cf.*, Waltz & Scheuneman, *Informed Consent to Therapy,* 64 N.W.U.L.Rev. 628, 649 (1970).

5. Privileges to Withhold Information

When because of an emergency it is not feasible to obtain the informed consent of the patient or a surrogate, the physician may be justified in not disclosing otherwise required information. Thus, there was no requirement for the doctor to discuss possible consequences and methods of treatment with a snake-bit victim "while the venom was being pumped through the patient's body." Crouch v. Most, 78 N.M. 406, 432 P.2d 250, 254 (1967). Similarly, if because of incapacity, incompetency, or minority, the patient cannot give valid consent, and the patient's condition does not permit substituted consent, the physician would also be privileged in not obtaining informed consent. When substituted informed consent is feasible, it should be obtained from a surrogate after the required disclosures.

The physician's failure to make an otherwise required disclosure may also be excused when it reasonably appears that the information might so upset the patient that it would unreasonably affect

---

* The Restatement provides that "[w]hen the defendant's tortious conduct has caused harm to the plaintiff . . . and in so doing has conferred a special benefit to . . . the plaintiff that was harmed, the value of the benefit conferred may be considered in mitigation of damages, to the extent that this is equitable."

his health. *See* Alaska Statutes § 09.55.556(b)(4) (1983); N.Y.Pub.Health Laws § 2805–d 4(d) (McKinney 1977). Reasonably limiting the extent of disclosure might, under some views, also be justified when further disclosure could be expected to adversely affect the outcome of the treatment. *See* Del.Code Ann. tit. 18: § 6852(b)(3) (Supp. 1984).*

In Nishi v. Hartwell, 52 Hawaii 188, 473 P.2d 116 (1970), the court, while upholding the privilege to withhold information to protect the patient, also held that there was no need to obtain the substituted consent of the patient's spouse because she could not halt the operation since the patient was competent. Other courts, however, have suggested that informed consent should be obtained from a surrogate in such circumstances. *See* Canterbury v. Spence, 464 F.2d 772 (D.C.Cir.1972).

Most courts would probably place the burden of proof on the privilege question on the defendant who seeks to rely on that privilege.

---

* Occasionally, it has also been suggested that nondisclosure may be justified when it appears likely to so disturb the patient that a rational decision is foreclosed. *See Canterbury, supra.* The court, however, also cautioned that the physician may not remain silent simply because the patient might otherwise forego the contemplated procedure. One court, however, in a questionable decision, recently excused an alleged failure to disclose risks of tardive dyskinesia from psychotropic drugs because it would probably have caused the psychiatric patient to refuse the treatment. *See* Barclay v. Campbell, 683 S.W.2d 498 (Tex.Civ.App.1984).

6. Who Must Disclose?

A question may arise not only with respect to *what* information must be disclosed, but *who* must disclose it. Most courts hold that the duty of disclosure rests with the physician performing the medical procedure in question. *See* Nevauex v. Park Place Hosp., 656 S.W.2d 923 (Tex.Ct.App. 1983) (duty was on radiologist directing cobalt therapy rather than on the technician or the hospital).

The question of responsibility is complicated when a number of physicians are involved in a patient's care. In Halley v. Birbiglia, 390 Mass. 540, 458 N.E.2d 710 (1983), a child undergoing an arteriogram suffered severe complications from thromboses that ultimately required amputation of his right foot. A neurologist serving as a consultant had recommended the arteriogram and his notes contained a direction to proceed with it. Another unidentified doctor actually appeared to have ordered it. The neurologist was neither the admitting nor the attending physician. Further, he did not speak to the parents about the test. A radiologist actually performed the procedure. The court held that the neurologist owed no duty to obtain the informed consent, but that the radiologist did owe a duty. The status of other physicians not named as defendants is unclear from the opinion. Other cases have held that a referring physician who requests a consultation is not responsible for securing the patient's informed consent with respect to procedures performed by the consulting

physician. *See* Johnson v. Whitehurst, 652 S.W.2d
441 (Tex.Civ.App.1983) (surgeon, but not referring
internist, owed duty of disclosure in connection
with partial stomach resection and vagotomy).

Matters are further complicated when multiple
physicians actually participate in the medical procedure. In one case, the patient's hypoglossal
nerve was severed during neck surgery, resulting
in almost total loss of tongue function. The surgeon in charge of the operation, who was also the
admitting physician, was assisted in the operation
by two other physicians. The court held that a
proper case for the jury was made against the
surgeon in charge and one assistant who had actually discussed the risks of surgery with the patient.
See Harnish v. Children's Hosp. Med. Ctr., 387
Mass. 152, 439 N.E.2d 240 (1982). The court upheld dismissal as to the other assistant, holding
that his participation was not sufficient to support
a duty of disclosure. Thus, a duty may arise not
only with respect to the surgeon in charge, but also
as to others who actually undertake to assure a
sufficient disclosure to the patient. But in Logan
v. Greenwich Hosp. Assn., 191 Conn. 282, 465
A.2d 294 (1983), the court held that there was no
duty to inform his patient owed by an internist
when he did not participate in the kidney biopsy
performed by a urologist. The court noted that
although the internist did provide some information to the patient, he also told her that a more

detailed explanation would be made by the urologist.

When another physician such as an anesthesiologist acts not merely as assistant, but is charged with responsibility for a discrete aspect of the surgery, both he and surgeon may have a duty to disclose. *See* Cornfeldt v. Tongen, 262 N.W.2d 684 (Minn.1977). *But see* Bell v. Umstattd, 401 S.W.2d 306 (Tex.Civ.App.1966) (duty owed by surgeon, but ordinarily not by anesthesiologist absent inquiry by the patient). Some courts hold that whether the person administering anesthesia has a duty to communicate the required information about the anesthesia for informed consent depends on what the applicable professional standards require. *See* Forney v. Mem. Hosp., 543 S.W.2d 705 (Tex.Civ. App.1976).

The following is a suggested approach. The surgeon or other practitioner in charge of performing the procedure should be primarily responsible for assuring adequate disclosure to the patient with respect to all aspects of the procedure, except to the extent that it is understood and agreed that someone else participating or assisting him who is competent to do so will communicate the required information. Another participant such as an anesthesiologist (or a qualified assistant) performing discrete services should perhaps *also* be responsible for reasonably assuring that the appropriate information is disclosed with respect to those services unless it is agreed that the surgeon will do so.

Thus, with respect to anesthesia, for example, both the surgeon and anesthesiologist would be expected to take reasonable steps to assure that at least one of them (or their qualified assistants) communicates the necessary information to the patient with respect to the anesthesia. Perhaps even a referring physician who also continues to actively attend the patient but does not participate in the procedure should be required to assist in disclosure to the extent that information, such as non-surgical alternatives to the contemplated procedure, is required and within the ambit of his expertise and responsibilities. A duty should not otherwise be imposed on a non-participating physician unless they have agreed to provide information or have actually undertaken to do without the kind of expressed reservations stated by the physician in the *Logan* case, *supra*.

7. Informed Refusal

Traditionally the primary emphasis has been upon assuring adequate disclosure of the risks and alternatives of a contemplated medical procedure. A few decisions have significantly expanded the physician's potential liability by expressly recognizing a duty to disclose the *risks of refusing* a recommended medical procedure. In a leading California case, a family practitioner recommended to his patient that she have a pap smear. He never specifically informed her of the risks of not having the test. The patient declined the test and later died of cervical cancer. There was also evidence that the patient declined the test because she did not want to spend the money. The test itself was virtually risk free. The California Supreme Court held that a physician owed a duty to inform his patient of the material risks not only of accepting, but also of rejecting a recommended procedure. Significantly, the court defined "material" information as that "which the physician knows or should know would be regarded as significant by a reasonable person in the patient's position when deciding to accept or reject the recommended medical procedure." Truman v. Thomas, 27 Cal.3d 285, 165 Cal.Rptr. 308, 611 P.2d 902, 905 (1980). The court added that the duty applied to information that is not commonly known by patients. And, of course, causation must be established. *See* III, C, 4.

Cases like *Truman* have potentially serious implications. How does a practitioner know what risks of refusal of a recommended procedure a reasonable patient would want to know? Ultimately, the jury may have to decide. What if a patient undergoing a routine physical examination refuses to submit to a complete blood count that analyzes a whole host of blood characteristics? The number of conditions such a test could reveal is staggering. Perhaps when a harmless diagnostic screening procedure is not designed to rule out a single disease, a brief explanation of the general screening nature of the test should be held sufficient. Moreover, adoption of a professional standard to determine what information should be disclosed to the reluctant patient would seem more sensible than the lay standard of *Truman.*

D. OTHER INFORMATIONAL NEEDS OF THE PATIENT

1. Subsequently-Discovered Dangers

A number of cases have recognized a duty to disclose dangers of a medical procedure that were discovered *after* its performance. Thus, in Tresemer v. Barke, 86 Cal.App.3d 656, 150 Cal. Rptr. 384 (1979), the court held that a gynecologist owed a duty to warn the patient of the dangers of an intrauterine device when, subsequent to its insertion, the physician obtained newly discovered knowledge of the dangers.

2. Misrepresentation, Concealment, and Nondisclosure

To the extent that accurate information should reasonably be imparted to the patient to protect his health, the matter of misrepresentation, concealment, and nondisclosure will fall within basic negligence principles. *See* II. Thus, for example, if a physician made a fraudulent or negligent misrepresentation to the patient that adversely affected his health, he would be subject to liability for the harm caused by the patient's justifiable reliance on the misinformation. *See* Restatement §§ 310–311.

An action might also lie when the physician fraudulently or negligently misrepresents risks or other information about a medical procedure to which the patient consents in justifiable reliance on the untrue information.   Thus, for example, even if a physician satisfied the applicable standards of disclosure for informed consent purposes, he still might be subject to liability for negligently misrepresenting facts extrinsic to his duty to warn but which nevertheless influenced the patient's decision.   *See* Bloskas v. Murray, 646 P.2d 907 (Colo.App.1982) (alleged misrepresentation about prior experience with ankle replacement surgery and about a risk perhaps not requiring disclosure).

There may also be situations in which actionable misrepresentation (or concealment or nondisclosure) by the physician causes harm unrelated to personal injury.   An action for fraudulent misrepresentation would require knowing or reckless falsehood and justifiable reliance by the plaintiff. *See* Restatement § 525.   Negligent misrepresentation requires a negligently false representation, a duty to exercise care, and justifiable reliance by the plaintiff.   *See id.* § 552.   Generally, a duty would exist when the representation was made in the course of the defendant's profession.   Examples of potential liability for misrepresentation for harm unrelated to personal injury might include a situation in which a physician fraudulently or negligently misrepresented that a prior injury was not caused by himself or another treating physician and the plaintiff's legal rights are adversely affected by the lack of such information. Or, a physician hired by prospective adoptive parents to examine a child being considered for adoption might negligently misrepresent the health or condition of the child.

The most difficult cases arise in situations in which a physician or other health care provider does not make an express misrepresentation, but rather conceals or fails to disclose certain information from the patient, such as the existence and source of an injury caused by prior medical treatment. When a treating physician discovers the presence of a condition, irrespective of who caused it, that poses a danger to the patient's health, he clearly must disclose such information or risk being held liable for negligence. *See* LeBlang & King, *Tort Liability for Nondisclosure: The Physician's Legal Obligations to Disclose Patient Illness and Injury,* 89 Dick.L.Rev. 1 (1984). A less clear situation is presented if the patient's health could not be affected by the disclosure, perhaps because death intervened. Or, what if the surgeon or a subsequent physician disclosed a dangerous condition, but failed to disclose that the surgeon caused it? If a physician took affirmative steps, such as destroying or altering records, to conceal the source of the patient's injury, liability even for non-physical injury should be imposed, equating the conduct to express misrepresentation. *See* Restatement § 550. Even absent such affirmative acts of concealment, all those who participated in the procedure in which the prior injury occurred should have a duty to disclose not only the nature of the condition but also its cause. Furthermore, a compelling argument can be made that given the fiduciary nature of the physician-patient relationship, any subsequent attending physician should also have a duty to disclose a condition and its cause which he discovered even if it did not currently threaten the health of the patient. There is, however, little law on point. *See generally* Vogel and Delgado, *To Tell The Truth: Physician's Duty to Disclose Medical Mistakes,* 28 U.C.L.A.L. Rev. 52 (1980). A patient who can prove a violation of the duty to disclose should be entitled to recover all proximately caused damages from the nondisclosure.*

Nondisclosure of information could also suspend the running of the statute of limitations in some jurisdictions. *See* VIII, A, 3, b and 4.

---

* Any detriment to the patient's health from a delay in discovery that could have been avoided by disclosure by the defendant should of course be recoverable. Even in the absence of such harm, however, damages should also be recoverable for any other losses attributable to the nondisclosure to the extent that a duty to disclose is recognized for such losses. They might include, for example, pecuniary losses due to a failure to bring a timely lawsuit due to ignorance of the existence of cause of the injury.

CHAPTER IV

INTENTIONAL AND MISCELLANEOUS TORTS

A. INTENTIONAL TORTS IN MALPRACTICE

Liability for medical malpractice is for the most part a matter of negligence law. Nevertheless, intentional and other torts may sometimes play a role. One potential advantage of an intentional tort as opposed to a negligence theory is that under the former approach expert evidence may not be necessary to establish the standard of care. Also, for many intentional torts such as battery, unlike negligence, an action will lie for purely "dignitary" harm without any physical harm. Liability for some intentional torts may sometimes not be covered by one's liability insurance—depending on the insurance contract and the public policy of the state.

The element of "intent" required for intentional torts may be satisfied in several ways. One may act for the purpose of achieving a result that invades another's interests. Or, he may realize that such a result is substantially certain to follow from his actions.

Some of the torts discussed in this chapter are exclusively intentional torts. Others may be based on either intentional or negligent conduct and are included here because they involve special problems.

B. BATTERY AND ASSAULT

One may be liable for a battery when he intentionally causes a nonconsensual, unprivileged, and impermissible contact with another that is harmful or offensive. An assault is similar to a battery except that the offending result is the apprehension of a harmful or offensive contact.

A physician will often be required to perform procedures that are painful or unpleasant to the patient. Generally, however, this will not constitute a battery because of the patient's consent. Most assault and battery cases in malpractice are intentional torts only because the patient's consent to an otherwise legitimate medical procedure was lacking or invalid. *See* III, B. Situations involving other kinds of assault and battery are uncommon in the medical setting. Physicians who have disciplined a misbehaving minor patient have occasionally been sued for battery. Psychiatrists have also been charged with malpractice for allegedly beating a patient, even when such conduct was purportedly for a therapeutic purpose. *See* Hammer v. Rosen, 7 N.Y.2d 376, 165 N.E.2d 756, 198 N.Y.S.2d 730 (1960). Sexual misconduct has sometimes been alleged as a form of battery against physicians, especially psychiatrists. There are several arguments that to varying degrees may nullify

ostensible consent in the context of sexual relations with a patient. First, some courts may hold
that consent is ineffective when the conduct constitutes a crime. Second, there is at least an argument that the consent should be invalid because it
was coerced or involuntary.

Alleged sexual contact with patients sometimes
gives rise to an action by a patient's spouse for
criminal conversation or alienation of affections.
See Mazza v. Huffaker, 61 N.C.App. 170, 300 S.E.2d
833 (1983). Sexual relations with a patient may
also be challenged as negligent malpractice.

C. FALSE IMPRISONMENT AND WRONGFUL COMMITMENT

False imprisonment requires the intentional, unprivileged, and nonconsensual confinement of an
individual. There have been cases in which patients have been detained in a hospital for failure
to pay their bills. Such detention would, of course,
constitute false imprisonment. When one's mere
carelessness results in the confinement of another,
an action might lie for negligence if a duty were
owed.

There are a number of potential tort theories
that may operate when a physician's allegedly
tortious conduct contributes to the detention or
commitment of a person for purported psychologi-
cal conditions. In Marcus v. Liebman, 59 Ill.App.
3d 337, 16 Ill.Dec. 613, 375 N.E.2d 486 (1978),
plaintiff was voluntarily admitted to a hospital

where she was placed in psychiatric floor. She
alleged that a psychiatrist coerced her into staying
against her will by threatening to have her committed to a state hospital. The court held that
plaintiff was entitled to present her case to the
jury for false imprisonment.

Liability for wrongful commitment might also be
based on wrongful use of civil proceedings when a
physician who lacks probable cause takes an active
part in the initiation or continuation of commitment proceedings primarily for some improper purpose, and the proceedings terminate in favor of the
person committed (a requirement at least when he
was represented by counsel). *See* Restatement
§ 674. Other potential theories for wrongful detention or commitment include, depending on the
circumstances, assault, battery, abuse of process,
defamation, infliction of mental distress, and possibly negligent evaluation of an individual's condition (assuming a physician-patient relationship existed or that a duty of care was otherwise owed to
the examinee). In addition, even assuming that
the physician has not been guilty of tortious conduct in connection with the detention or commitment, there may be limits on the permissible scope
of medical services that may be administered to a
patient while detained or committed to an institution. These may depend on the nature of the
detention or commitment, the mental condition of
the patient, and the nature of the medical service
or procedure in question.

There may be substantial obstacles to recovery against a physician for wrongful commitment. The foregoing theories of liability are often difficult to establish. Certain occasions may be privileged, such as those involving testimony in judicial proceedings. Some statutes purport to confer a degree of immunity on the physician or limit his liability in connection with certain detention or commitment procedures. Some states condition such immunity on the exercise of good faith and reasonable care by the physician. A physician may in some jurisdictions be immune from liability while serving in an official or a quasi-official capacity, such as a member of an official or court-appointed commitment committee.

D.   UNAUTHORIZED COMMUNICATIONS AND DISCLOSURE

1.   Defamation

One may be subject to liability for defamation for communicating orally (slander) or in writing (libel) to a third person an untrue statement about another that tends to significantly damage his reputation. There are manifold occasions in which defamation might occur in the medical setting. For example, the false imputation of certain diseases or psychiatric impairments to another is a common form of defamation.

Recent decisions suggest that plaintiff may have to prove that defendant (courts disagree, *inter alia*, on whether the rule applies to non-media defendants) was at least negligent in believing the truth of the information he communicated in the case of most private plaintiffs, or that defendant had knowledge of the statement's falsity or a reckless disregard for whether it was true or false in the case of public officials or public figures. The requirements of fault may be Constitutionally required, at least for statements involving matters of public concern. *See generally* Dun & Bradstreet, Inc. v. Greenmoss Builders, Inc., 105 S.Ct. 2939 (1985) (focusing on damages question); Gertz v. Robt. Welch, Inc., 418 U.S. 323 (1974); Prosser, at 771–848.

A combination of the "fault" test for defamation along with a liberal application of traditional privileges (*see* IV, D, 4) should afford sufficient protection for physicians.

2. Invasion of Privacy

The tort of invasion of privacy has been divided into four categories: (1) intrusion upon seclusion; (2) appropriation of plaintiff's name or likeness; (3) publicity of plaintiff's private life; and, (4) publicity placing plaintiff in a false light. Restatement § 652A. The practice of medicine, inherently involving as it does intimate and extensive intrusions into private spheres of a patient's life, affords numerous occasions for invasions of privacy.

Invasions of privacy based on unauthorized communications (categories 2–4 above) are discussed in this subsection. Liability for intrusion on seclusion is discussed in IV, E.

One may be subject to liability for appropriating for one's own benefit the name or likeness of another. *See id.* at § 652C. This type of liability might arise when a physician wrote a book on fitness and included a photo of a well known personality on the cover without his authorization.

Liability may result from publicity of even truthful information concerning one's private life if highly offensive to a reasonable person and not of legitimate concern to the public. *See id.* § 652D. This theory may overlap with liability for divulgence of confidential information. *See* IV, D, 3. Such an invasion might occur, for example, when motion pictures or photographs of the patient, or information about his medical condition, are publicized without consent.

Publicity placing another in a false light may be actionable if the disclosure would be highly offensive to a reasonable person and the defendant had knowledge of the matter's falsity or showed a reckless (or perhaps even negligent) disregard for its truth or falsity. *Id.* at § 652E.

What might otherwise constitute liability-producing invasions of privacy are often not actionable because of the express or implied consent of the patient or some other applicable privilege. *See generally* VI, D, 4.

3. Divulgence of Confidential Information

A physician may be liable for the unauthorized disclosure of confidential information about the patient acquired in the course of the physician-patient relationship. *See* Humphrers v. First Interstate Bank, 68 Or.App. 573, 684 P.2d 581 (1984) (recognizing potential liability of physician for breach of confidential relationship for allegedly providing means whereby adopted daughter could discover identity of natural mother, the plaintiff). Unlike defamation, liability for disclosure of confidential matters may be based on an entirely true statement. This theory of liability may also differ from invasion of privacy. A right of privacy is accorded all citizens. The right to prevent disclosure of confidential information, on the other hand, is based on a duty rooted in certain special relationships, including the physician-patient relationship.*

There are multiple grounds upon which the duty not to reveal information obtained in the course of medical care might be based. *See generally* Horne v. Patton, 291 Ala. 701, 287 So.2d 824 (1973). In some cases the duty is based on the doctor-patient relationship. The policy against disclosures is set forth in the A.M.A. Principles of Medical Ethics, and in some legislation. The rationale for the duty

---

* Another possible difference is that less extensive publication may be necessary to render a disclosure of confidential information actionable than is required by some courts for an invasion of privacy. Moreover, perhaps a less offensive disclosure of confidential information might be actionable than might otherwise be required under an invasion of privacy theory. Finally, liability based on breach of a confidential information may be less vulnerable to constitutional challenge than invasion of privacy arguably is.

is that patients seeking medical attention should be free to reveal private matters to their physicians without fear of unwarranted disclosures.

Licensing and "testimonial privilege" statutes have also been relied on, with varying degrees of success, to sustain a cause of action for disclosure of confidential matters.* Some privilege statutes prohibit both judicial and extra-judicial disclosures of confidential information, while many others are limited to judicial (testimonial) disclosures. Most licensing and testimonial privilege statutes do not expressly provide a civil remedy for their violation. Therefore, courts relying on such statutes in civil cases when applicable have held that such statutes helped to support the duty upon which common law liability could be based or, occasionally, that such statutes impliedly created a cause of action. Even in the absence of a relevant statutory prohibition, a duty not to make extra-judicial disclosures of confidential information has been recognized by a number of courts. When a physician is required

---

* The law in this area has been confused by the use of the term "privilege" in two entirely different senses. The "privilege statute" terminology has an entirely different meaning from the phrase, a "privilege to disclose." A "privilege statute" provides that a physician (subject to certain important exceptions) cannot, without the consent of the patient, testify in certain legal proceedings or, under some statutes, make extrajudicial statements, with respect to confidential information about the patient. *See generally* McCormick §§ 98–105. A "privilege to disclose" on the other hand refers to an otherwise actionable statement or disclosure made by a defendant that the law has chosen for some reason to shield from civil liability. *See* IV, D, 4.

to testify in legal proceedings, he should not be liable for divulging confidential information except possibly when he violated a testimonial privilege statute prohibiting such testimony.

Patients have also claimed that the physician breached an implied contract to preserve private information.

Generally, the duty of confidentiality should be qualified if the patient is seen by a physician for some purpose other than for medical care. Thus, a physician conducting pre-employment or insurance examinations should be permitted to make disclosures to those who retained him as long as the patient was aware of the purpose of the examination. To reduce the possibility of misunderstanding the physician should at the outset obtain the patient's consent for the anticipated disclosure of information to others.

4. Privileges to Disclose

The rights of the patient to his good reputation, privacy, and confidentiality, must be accommodated with the interests of society in the disclosure of information that furthers a significant social interest. This accommodation occurs not only through the elements of a particular cause of action, but also through a catalogue of occasions when certain disclosures will be deemed not actionable based on a "privilege to disclose." A privilege may be either absolute or conditional.

A patient may expressly or impliedly consent to an otherwise actionable disclosure. Applications and claims forms for insurance, for example, commonly contain authorizations by patients for the release of medical information. *See* Millsaps v. Bankers Life Co., 35 Ill.App.3d 735, 342 N.E.2d 329 (1976). By placing his medical condition in issue in legal proceedings, a patient is often held to have impliedly waived his right under a testimonial privilege statute to prevent the physician from testifying. *See* Sagmiller v. Carlsen, 219 N.W.2d 885 (N.D.1974). Reasonable consultations and appropriate exchanges of information among physicians in connection with a patient's care should usually be protected by the patient's implied consent or a privilege, at least to the extent that the patient authorized the consultation. Generally, the extent of a privilege based on consent is determined by the terms of the consent. *See* Restatement § 583, comment d.

Physicians may be conditionally privileged to disclose certain matters to appropriate persons when a sufficiently important interest of the defendant, the recipient, a third person, the patient, or a shared interest among them, warrants or reasonably appears to warrant such disclosures. *See* §§ 594–597. When the interest is that of the recipient or of a third person, circumstances must justify a correct or reasonable belief that the interest is a sufficiently important one and that the communication is based on a legal duty or is otherwise within generally accepted standards of decent conduct. *See id.* at § 595.

A number of statutes require or permit certain disclosures to designated officials and expressly or impliedly insulate physicians to varying degrees from liability for such disclosures. These statutory provisions have included reports of drug abuse, gunshot wounds, contagious diseases, child abuse, and various other matters. Some statutory provisions also confer a privilege on physicians to provide pertinent information to those involved in quality and cost control activities. In addition to statutory authorizations, a privilege may also exist when there is a duty to communicate information about a patient to a non-patient third party in order to protect a person's safety. *See generally* II, B, 6. A privilege to make disclosures to a minor patient's parent or (according to one view on which the courts are divided) a patient's spouse is sometimes recognized by statute or case law even when such disclosures are not necessary for the protection of someone. This privilege, when recognized, is based on the community of interest in the patient's health shared by other members of the family. A privilege would also normally exist when substituted consent to treatment by one other than the patient was required. *See generally* III, B, 1, d.

A fairly liberal application of the privilege concept is found in Berry v. Moench, 8 Utah 2d 191, 331 P.2d 814 (1958). Defendant, a former physician of the plaintiff, supplied information to another physician who requested it for the stated purpose of passing it on to the parents of a girl who was then associating with plaintiff. The defendant had administered psychiatric treatment to the plaintiff seven years earlier. The defendant's letter, critical of the plaintiff, was relayed by the other physician to the parents. The court held that the letter was conditionally privileged, and remanded the case to determine whether the privilege had been abused. The court noted that whether a conditional privilege based on the protection of the interests of third persons exists depends, *inter alia,* upon generally accepted standards of decent conduct.

Courts have held that a conditional privilege may be lost or "abused" under certain circumstances. Defendant's state of knowledge may defeat a conditional privilege if he knows that his statement is false or he acts with reckless disregard as to its truth or falsity. *See* Restatement § 600. Some courts hold that a conditional privilege may be lost even when defendant is merely negligent in not realizing the falsity of his statement. However, given the trend to require at least negligence in defamation, permitting negligence to defeat the privilege would render the privilege largely redundant. A conditional privilege may also be abused when the publication is not made for the purpose of protecting the interest for which it is conferred. *See id.* at § 603. Conditional privileges may also be abused in other ways, such as by excessive publication. *See generally id.* at §§ 604–605A.

There are also a few situations in which courts have recognized an absolute privilege that may not be lost by most traditional grounds for abuse. These situations may include, for example, statements by parties or witnesses made during judicial proceedings so long as they are pertinent to the proceedings. *Id.* at §§ 587, 588. This privilege may, however, be subject to the patient's right, under "testimonial privilege" statute, to demand that a treating physician refrain from making disclosures of confidential information at trial. When not subject to a testimonial privilege statute, or when falling within an exception to it, a physician will generally not be civilly liable for testifying as a witness in legal proceedings as long as his statement has some relation to those proceedings. *See id.* § 588. A witness testifying falsely under oath, of course, remains subject to criminal penalties. Communications between husband and wife are also usually considered absolutely privileged. *See id.* at § 592. When one is required by law to communicate otherwise actionable matters, his statement may, depending on the statutory language, be absolutely privileged. On other absolute privileges, see generally *id.* at §§ 583–592A.

Special statutorily-created privileges may be either absolute or conditional.

E. INTRUSIVE INVASION OF PRIVACY

An invasion of privacy may occur when one intentionally and without consent intrudes upon the seclusion of another or into his private concerns in a way that would be highly offensive to a reasonable person. *Id.* at § 652B. In one case, a jury question was presented whether defendant surgeon violated a dying patient's privacy by intruding on his seclusion by taking his photograph. *See* Estate of Berthiaume v. Pratt, 365 A.2d 792 (Me.1976) (recognizing potential liability absent consent or therapeutic necessity). Or, a treating physician may be liable if, without first securing the patient's consent, he allows a third party who has no professional connection with the patient to observe a medical procedure. It would be advisable to obtain the patient's express consent for such situations. Consent should also be obtained before significant exposure or contact is permitted between the patient and others such as medical students and even interns, residents, and other medical personnel unless they are involved in the care of the patient and covered by his prior consent. The same goes for consultations as well as the procedures for coverage of the patient during anticipated absences of the primary attending physician.

F. INFLICTION OF MENTAL DISTRESS

In most situations involving claims for mental distress, there have been initial physical injuries that produced the distress—such as surgical carelessness causing physical injury that causes mental suffering—or some other accompanying tortious conduct such as defamation. Liability in such cases is often based on traditional negligence or intentional tort theories. The element of mental distress in such cases is usually compensable simply as part of the damages recoverable for the underlying tort.* There are, however, other situations in which the initial injury may be purely emotional in nature and not covered by another tort theory. These situations are discussed below.

Liability for the tort of infliction of mental distress has traditionally been divided into two categories. First, there has been more serious conduct, often denominated "outrageous conduct," by which the defendant intentionally or recklessly inflicts severe emotional distress on the victim. *See* Restatement § 46. Second, there are other situations involving negligently or intentionally inflicted emotional distress that fall short of outrageousness. The most significant difference between the two is that most courts do not require that the mental distress have produced physical conse-

* *See* J. Stein, Damages and Recovery §§ 33–47 (1972). Even when mental distress was the result of a direct physical injury, and thus normally compensable, there appear to be limits to the willingness of some courts to redress a few types of mental distress. There has, for example, been a split of authority over whether cancerophobia caused by an alleged negligently-inflicted injury should be compensable independently of possible recovery for the future materialization of the cancer itself. *Compare* Howard v. Mt. Sinai Hosp., 63 Wis.2d 515, 219 N.W.2d 576 (1974) with Ferrara v. Galluchio, 5 N.Y.2d 16, 176 N.Y.S.2d 996, 152 N.E.2d 249 (1958).

quences—such as a heart attack or miscarriage—
when the conduct is outrageous, but most do for
other less egregious forms of infliction in order to
be actionable.

The case of Johnson v. Woman's Hosp., 527
S.W.2d 133 (Tenn.App.1975), is a graphic illustration of this tort in the medical setting. Six weeks
following the loss at birth of her premature infant,
the mother, wishing clarification of a notation on
her chart, sought information from her physician
regarding the disposition of the child's body. Ultimately she was directed to a hospital employee
who thereupon allegedly presented the plaintiff
with a jar of formaldehyde containing the body of
the infant. The court had little difficulty in holding that a jury could find such conduct would
constitute actionable outrageous conduct.

Not every disturbance will support an action for
outrageous conduct. The most difficult cases have
involved alleged verbally inflicted emotional distress. In Anderson v. Prease, 445 A.2d 612 (D.C.
App.1982), recovery was permitted when the physician allegedly cursed at his patient and screamed
at her to leave his office. The court noted that the
physician apparently had knowledge of the patient's susceptible nervous disposition. On the other hand, in Ferlito v. Cecola, 419 So.2d 102 (La.
App.1982), recovery for outrageous conduct was
denied where plaintiff alleged that defendant re-
sponded to her complaints by saying that she
needed a psychiatrist and on another occasion ut-

tered profanity concerning the plaintiff when unaware of her presence.

An action for infliction of mental distress not rising to the level of outrageous conduct might be actionable under a negligence theory when mental distress was intended which unreasonably subjected a plaintiff to a risk of resulting bodily harm; when defendant failed to act reasonably in the face of a foreseeable risk of unnecessarily causing mental distress and resulting illness or bodily harm; or when defendant created an unreasonable risk of initial bodily harm that produced emotional disturbance. *See* Restatement §§ 306, 312, 313, 436, 436A.

Although there is a split of authority, most cases involving non-outrageous conduct probably require that the mental distress have produced physical consequences. *Compare* Di Giovanni v. Latimer, 390 Mass. 265, 454 N.E.2d 483 (1983) (requiring physical consequences) *with* Molien v. Kaiser Fdn. Hosp., 27 Cal.3d 916, 167 Cal.Rptr. 831, 616 P.2d 813 (1980) (not requiring such consequences).

In some situations, a non-patient plaintiff suffers mental distress because of concern about the condition of a patient. A majority of courts have held that such plaintiffs may not recover under such circumstances unless they were personally in the zone of danger of some physical impact or physical harm independent of any fear for the safety of the patient.* *See* Vaillancourt v. Medical Center

* There is a division of authority following this view on whether the plaintiff must also have actually feared direct personal harm.

Hosp. of Vt., Inc., 139 Vt. 138, 425 A.2d 92 (1980); Whetham v. Bismark Hosp., 197 N.W.2d 678 (N.D.1972) (mother observing newborn infant allegedly being dropped). A few courts have rejected the zone of danger requirement and allow recovery so long as the non-patient was closely related to the patient, suffered physical consequences from the mental distress, was present, and actually observed the injury to the patient. Some courts rejecting the zone of danger requirement and allowing recovery in principle have added the requirement that the plaintiff not have been a voluntary witness to the occurrence. *See* Justus v. Atchison, 19 Cal.3d 564, 139 Cal.Rptr. 97, 565 P.2d 122 (1977) (denying recovery because, *inter alia,* the father-plaintiff was voluntarily present in the delivery room when the complications allegedly occurred resulting in the death of the fetus). Another California case has expanded liability at least for one type of situation. It held that if as a result of negligence (if proven), the husband of a patient was erroneously informed that she suffered from syphilis, he could recover for his emotional distress without satisfying all of the preceding requirements. *See* Molien v. Kaiser Fdn. Hosp., 27 Cal.3d 916, 167 Cal.Rptr. 831, 616 P.2d 813 (1980). The court also abandoned the requirement that the mental distress produce physical consequences not only for the instant case, but for cases involving negligent infliction of mental distress generally.

CHAPTER V

CAUSATION, DAMAGES, AND
SCOPE OF DUTY

A. IN GENERAL

Proof of negligence, intentional misconduct, or other liability producing conduct is never alone sufficient to support recovery. Plaintiff must also establish that the injury was caused in fact and proximately caused by the defendant's actionable conduct. Thus, in Fall v. White, 449 N.E.2d 628 (Ind.App.1983), plaintiff alleged that one defendant was negligent in prescribing a decongestant for flu-like symptoms for a patient with coronary artery disease. The court held that plaintiff could not recover for the heart attack death of the patient absent sufficient proof that the medication was a contributing cause. *See also* Fountain v. Cobb Gen. Hosp., 167 Ga.App. 36, 306 S.E.2d 37 (1983) (allegedly negligent delay in removing an epidural catheter not shown to have caused the defect in spinal column that necessitated back surgery); Paige v. Manuzak, 57 Md.App. 621, 471 A.2d 758 (1984) (hospital not liable for negligently administering penicillin to patient allergic to drug for subsequent post-operative complications absent proof of causal connection).

Cause in fact or "causation" refers to the cause and effect relationship that must be established between the tortious conduct and the loss before liability for the loss may be imposed. The term "proximate cause" is sometimes used as a connotation for causation. For present purposes, however, proximate cause will refer to the body of rules to determine the extent to which liability should not be imposed despite the fact that a loss was caused in fact by tortious conduct.

B. CAUSATION AND VALUATION

1. Test of Causation

The time-honored test of causation is the "but for" or "*sine qua non*" test. Causation exists when the loss would not have occurred "but for" the defendant's tortious conduct. Both negligent acts and omissions may constitute causes of an injury. Thus, a physician may be deemed a cause of a patient's death by negligently prescribing the wrong drug or by negligently failing to diagnose and treat shock. An alternative test advocated by some requires that the defendant's tortious conduct have been a "substantial factor" in bringing about the injurious result. *See* Restatement § 431. The difference between the two tests is, however, largely semantic. The substantial factor test retains "but for" causation as an essential feature except when two or more actively operating forces, for only one of which the defendant was responsible, combine to bring about the harm, and each one alone would have been sufficient to produce the harm.

2. Proof of Causation

Causation must be established by a preponderance of the evidence standard of proof. This usually requires that the plaintiff prove that it was "more likely than not" that the defendant's tortious conduct caused the harm. *See* Miles v. Edward O. Tabor, M.D., Inc., 387 Mass. 783, 443 N.E.2d 1302 (1982); Harvey v. Fridley Med. Center, 315 N.W.2d 225 (Minn.1982).

Unless a causal connection is so obvious that it falls within the common knowledge of laymen, expert testimony (or possibly a substitute such as an admission by the defendant) is required to establish causation. *See* First Nat'l Bank of Chicago v. Porter, 141 Ill.App.3d 1, 69 Ill.Dec. 796, 448 N.E.2d 256 (1983); Harvey, *supra.* A question that has generated more confusion than it should concerns the required form of the expert testimony. Traditionally, many courts stated that an expert should state his opinion on causation "with reasonable medical certainty." Unfortunately, there has been little concensus on either the meaning of this phrase or how strictly such semantic preferences should be enforced. Under one interpretation, "reasonable medical certainty" simply requires that the expert have been provided enough facts and possess enough understanding of the subject to form an opinion with reasonable medical certainty. A second interpretation equates reasonable medical certainty with the traditional standard of proof—in effect equating reasonable medical certainty with "more likely than not." The most sensible approach would be to construe the "reasonable medical certainty" language in the former sense—as referring to the ability of the expert to formulate a sufficiently definite opinion. The standard of proof would then be addressed by the "more likely than not" phrase or similar language. Thus, an expert's testimony would be sufficient to support a finding of causation if he stated that he had formed an opinion *with reasonable medical certainty* that the allegedly tortious conduct *more likely than not* was a cause of the harm.* The courts should, however, allow other formulations that communicate essentially the same meaning.

---

* Matters are sometimes further confused by a failure to explain whether the court is addressing the *admissibility* of the testimony or its *sufficiency* to allow the plaintiff to reach the jury. The preferred approach would be to *admit* expert testimony expressed in terms of a "possibility" of causation, and to reserve final decision on the *sufficiency* of plaintiff's proof until all of his evidence has been presented. This is especially important since, as a number of courts have held, an expert's testimony should be evaluated as a whole rather than piecemeal. *See* Largent v. Acuff, 69 N.C. 439, 317 S.E.2d 111 (1984); Vassos v. Roussalis, 658 P.2d 1284 (Wyo.1983). However, a directed verdict would be appropriate unless the expert's testimony ultimately supported the conclusion that the alleged tortious conduct more likely than not ("probably") rather than "possibly" was a cause of the harm in question. Thus, language indicating a mere possibility of a causal connection would not be enough unless there was other expert testimony that causation "probably" existed.

Occasionally, it has been suggested that the expert must testify with actual certainty as to causation. This not only reflects specious reasoning, but also may pose a semantic trap for the unwary. In the first place, it is often unclear whether certainty refers to the quality of the opinion or the standard of proof. Second, and in either event, actual certainty is simply never possible and to insist that the expert state his opinion in those terms means that he either must fail or must overstate his opinion.

Causation may be based on direct or circumstantial evidence, or both. *See* Van Zee v. Sioux Valley Hosp., 315 N.W.2d 489 (S.D.1982). Whether based on direct or circumstantial evidence or both, proof of causation will require expert testimony unless the issue is within the common knowledge of laymen.

3. Multiple Causes

Occasionally a court will speak in terms of proof that the defendant's conduct was "the" cause of the harm. Technically, this is incorrect since there is never a single cause of anything. In order to satisfy the causation requirement, it is only necessary that defendant's conduct be *a* cause, not the only one. *See* Restatement § 430, Comment d. Thus, the fact that there may have been other causes of the harm (even other tortious causes) will not preclude liability so long as the defendant's conduct was also a cause, unless such other conduct is deemed a superseding cause for the purpose

of *proximate* cause.   *See* Davison v. Mobile Infirmary, 456 So.2d 14 (Ala.1984); V, C, 1. One can
imagine numerous instances of multiple tortious
causes in the malpractice setting.   A physician
may negligently prescribe medication in an obviously excessive dosage.   A nurse may administer
the drug without seeking some confirmation.   Or,
two physicians may both make negligent misdiag-
noses, resulting in unnecessary surgery.

When the negligence of two or more tortfeasors
causes the same harm, most jurisdictions hold each
tortfeasor jointly and severally liable to the plaintiff for the entire harm.   Although plaintiff could
obtain a *judgment* against each joint tortfeasor,
each judgment could be *satisfied* only up to the
point at which plaintiff had been fully compensated for his injuries; he could not receive double
recovery.   Such jointly and severally liable tortfeasors might have a right to seek contribution from
each other as appropriate.   In a few states such
tortfeasors are not subject to joint and several
liability for the entire liability, but their liability to
the plaintiff is apportioned, often according to
their relative fault.

4. Preexisting Conditions and Loss of a Chance

Many courts have failed to distinguish causation
from the *value* of the interest adversely affected.*

---

* The analysis of this subject is to some extent derived from:
King, *Causation, Valuation, and Chance in Personal Injury*

There will always be forces and conditions other than the defendant's conduct that must be considered in deciding questions of causation and valuation. Some of these forces will constitute other contributing causes of the injury. Some forces will constitute preexisting conditions. A "preexisting condition" is defined here as a disease, condition, or force that has become sufficiently associated with the victim to be factored into the value of the interest destroyed, and that has become so before the defendant's conduct has reached a similar stage. A force would qualify if its effect on the value of the interest in question could not be avoided even if the victim were aware of it, and had reached that stage before defendant's conduct had reached a similar stage. Thus, in assessing damages because a patient was killed by a negligently prescribed drug, the fact that the patient suffered from a preexisting cancer should obviously affect damages.

A condition or force may constitute a contributing cause of an injury in one respect and a preexisting condition in another. A physician may fail to diagnose a preexisting cancer, allowing it to progressively worsen with harmful effects. The disease was a cause of the harmful effects, but the physician's negligence may also have been a contributing cause of the harm that would have been avoided by due care. The disease was also a preex-

Torts Involving Preexisting Conditions and Future Consequences, 90 Yale L.J. 1353 (1981).

isting condition whose irreversible effects should be taken into account in assessing damages.

A defendant should be subject to liability only to the extent that he tortiously contributed to the harm by allowing a preexisting condition to worsen or by aggravating its harmful effects, or to the extent he caused other harm to the patient. The courts have disagreed on how preexisting conditions should be taken into account. A physician may, for example, fail to make a timely diagnosis of a heart attack or cancer, thereby losing an opportunity to prevent or reduce the adverse effects from the condition. Most courts have failed to identify that destroyed opportunity itself as the compensable loss. Instead, they have regarded the chance of avoiding the loss as if it were either a certainty or impossibility depending on the degree of likelihood that the harm could have been avoided. This confusion of valuation with causation has resulted in an all-or-nothing approach to the loss of a chance.

Most courts following this all-or-nothing approach deny recovery unless the patient was deprived of at least a better-than-even chance of surviving or of some other favorable outcome with proper care. Thus, in one case, recovery was denied for the death of a child whose skull fracture was allegedly misdiagnosed. At trial, the strongest evidence plaintiff produced on causation was expert testimony that there was about a 50% chance that the victim would have survived had surgery been timely performed. The supreme court held that the plaintiff had failed as a matter of law to establish the requisite causal connection between the allegedly negligent misdiagnosis and the patient's death. The court held that the plaintiff must establish that the defendant's negligence *probably* caused the death, which the court interpreted as requiring that the decedent have had a *better than* 50% probability of survival with proper care. *See* Cooper v. Sisters of Charity of Cinn., Inc., 27 Ohio St.2d 242, 272 N.E.2d 97, 56 Ohio Op. 2d 146 (1971); *accord* Gooding v. University Hosp. Bldg. Inc., 445 So.2d 1015 (Fla.1984).

Some courts, struck by the apparent harshness of the traditional approach have adopted various rules to ameliorate it. A few have held that once there is evidence that defendant's tortious conduct increased the risk of harm or reduced or destroyed a chance (even a not-better-than-even chance) of a better outcome, and the harm was sustained or the better outcome not realized, the plaintiff is entitled to reach the jury on the question of causation. *See* Herskovits v. Group Health Co-op of Puget Sound, 99 Wn.2d 609, 664 P.2d 474 (1983). In *Herskovits,* expert testimony indicated that the six month delay in diagnosing this patient's lung cancer reduced the chance of long term survival by 14% by reducing a 39% chance of survival to a 25% chance.* The approach of *Herskovits* and similar

---

* In *Herskovits,* the decedent was not shown to have had a better-than-even chance of survival with prompt diagnosis. Moreover, since the patient did die of cancer, he apparently was

decisions fails to explain how the jury is to harmonize the relaxed rule with respect to the form of expert testimony with the all-or-nothing approach under the traditional standard of proof. Nor does the court explain whether damages are to be reduced to reflect the fact that the decedent was deprived of a slim chance of long term survival. A few other cases have suggested that plaintiff should recover if it appeared that the patient was negligently deprived of a "substantial possibility" of recovery. *See* Hicks v. United States, 368 F.2d 626 (4th Cir.1966) (dictum).

All of the preceding all-or-nothing approaches miss the mark. They confuse the question of causation with the question of the nature of the loss and how it should be valued. Some all-or-nothing approaches tend to regard destruction of not-better-than-even chances as worthless, as in *Cooper.* Or, they treat them as a certainty, as in *Hicks.* Or they let the jury treat them either way as in *Herskovits.* In so doing they deny recovery to some worthy plaintiffs despite a real loss and overcompensate others.

not even within the 25% who would survive after the six month delay. Thus, loss of a 14% chance *probably* would not have made a difference even knowing that the decedent was not within the 25% who would survive even after the delayed diagnosis (since decedent's chances would then have been reduced by a fraction of 14/75). Nevertheless, the court held that the evidence was sufficient to allow the jury to decide whether the alleged negligence caused the death. *See also* Roberson v. Counselmann, 235 Kan. 1006, 686 P.2d 149 (1984).

A more sensible approach would hold that once it is established that a defendant's tortious conduct more likely than not deprived the patient of or reduced any chance (including a not-better-than-even chance) of a more favorable result, the focus should shift to a determination of how much that chance was worth or reduced. A number of cases have advocated recognition of chance itself as a compensable loss. *See* Thompson v. Sun City Community Hosp., 141 Ariz. 597, 688 P.2d 605 (Ariz. 1984); Herskovits, *supra* (Pearson, J., concurring) (urging recognition of the loss of a not better than even chance as an actionable injury).

There are persuasive reasons for recognizing the loss of a chance as a compensable interest in its own right. First, the all-or-nothing approach is arbitrary. Second, it subverts the deterrence and loss allocative objectives of tort law. Third, it creates irresistible pressures to manipulate and distort traditional causation and damages rules to avoid injustice. Fourth, the all-or-nothing rule sometimes gives defendants the benefit of an uncertainty that was caused by their own negligence. And finally, loss of a chance is worthy of redress. *See id.* ; King, *supra*, 90 Yale L.J. at 1376–78.

Although a few cases have advocated recognizing loss of a chance as a compensable interest in its own right, they seldom have explored the complex matter of how damages for such lost chances should be computed. A suggested approach would be to value a tortiously destroyed chance by the percentage probability by which the defendant's tortious conduct diminished the prospects for achieving some more favorable outcome.*

5. Burden of Proof

The burden of proof on causation, valuation, and damages questions has traditionally been placed on the plaintiff. In a number of situations, however, some courts have shifted the burden of proof to the defendant. When the patient with a preexisting condition establishes that the defendant was a cause of at least some harm, there is a definite split of authority on the question of who must prove the effect of the preexisting condition on damages. A number of decisions shift the burden of proof to the defendant on how a loss should be apportioned between that portion not reasonably avoidable due to the preexisting condition and the portion that was. In Fosgate v. Corona, 66 N.J. 268, 330 A.2d 355 (1974), the patient sued the defendant-doctor for failing to diagnose the patient's longstanding tuberculosis. The New Jersey Supreme Court, noting the difficulty of separating the harm that had been reasonably avoidable with timely diagnosis from that which was not, held that the defendant had the burden of segregating damages for which he was responsible from those that could not have been avoided.

* For a more detailed discussion of the chance-valuation process, see King, *supra,* 90 Yale L.J. at 1381–87.

When two or more individuals are alleged to have committed wrongful conduct, but it is asserted that they all could not have caused the injury, some courts (under the better-reasoned approach) have shifted the burden to the defendant to prove that his actions were not the cause. *See* Restatement § 433B(3). In Incollingo v. Ewing, 444 Pa. 263, 282 A.2d 206 (1971), the patient's death was caused by aplastic anemia induced by Chloromycetin. One defendant argued that no causal connection had been established between the doses he allegedly prescribed and the patient's death, contending that the damage had already been done by the Chloromycetin prescribed by another physician. The court held that, under such circumstances, the burden was on the defendant to prove which doses caused the fatal condition.

Assuming the plaintiff proves that the defendant caused some harm and proves the total loss suffered by the victim, and the only question is how that total loss should be allocated between the preexisting condition and the tortious conduct, the following approach is suggested. If the plaintiff can show that because of the passage of time or other circumstances, he had no reasonable opportunity to evaluate the status of his condition at the time of the alleged negligence so as to reasonably allocate the loss between the unavoidable harm due to the preexisting condition and that due to the tortious conduct, the burden should be shifted to the defendant to do so.

C. PROXIMATE CAUSE AND SCOPE OF LIABILITY

1. Nature of Proximate Cause and Scope of Duty Limitations

The requirement that defendant's conduct have *proximately* caused the plaintiff's injury is a separate matter from the cause-in-fact ("causation") question. The concept of proximate cause as used herein, whether articulated in terms of "proximate cause," "legal cause," the "foreseeability" of the injury, or the scope of one's duty, is based on the premise that at some point one's liability even for injuries in fact caused by the defendant, should extend no further. Proximate cause has served as essentially a catchall phrase for the host of considerations that have prompted courts to limit liability for injuries that were caused by otherwise actionable conduct. It is based more on considerations of public policy than on the conceptualism that characterizes the causation question.

Most proximate cause questions in the malpractice setting are addressed under the "duty" analysis and relate to whether or not there existed a doctor-patient relationship or some other basis that would give rise to a corresponding duty of care. *See* II, B. Once the requisite professional relationship has been established, issues of proximate cause have for the most part been subject to the general tort rules regarding proximate cause. Generally, the victim must be within the ambit of risk the creation or disregard of which rendered the defendant's conduct tortious. This rule is often articulated in terms of a requirement that the victim must have been reasonably foreseeable. There is less agreement on whether the result, as opposed to the victim himself, must have been within the ambit of foreseeable risk. Most courts hold that the fact that the victim suffers greater harm from an accident or omission than a normal person would have ordinarily suffered does not relieve defendant from liability.* It is also generally held that the extent of the harm to an otherwise foreseeable victim need not itself be foreseeable. Nor must the manner of the harm be foreseeable if the result is otherwise foreseeable. Moreover, if a defendant's negligent diagnosis or treatment is a cause of the need for further medical intervention, the defendant is subject to liability for the foreseeable complications of such subsequent therapy even if caused by the negligence of

---

* It is important here to distinguish three ideas. The fact that a victim would not, for example, have died at all from negligently severed blood vessels had he been healthy rather than suffering from a bleeding tendency related to preexisting leukemia does not relieve the defendant from liability. This is a rule of *proximate cause*. Nor does the fact that the victim, who died from the incision in July, would have died from the leukemia in December prevent the defendant from being the cause of the harm in July. This is a rule of *causation*. The fact, however, that the victim had preexisting leukemia that would be fatal should quite clearly affect the value of the victim's life as it existed at the time of his death in July. This is a rule of *valuation and damages*.

Ch. 5   *SCOPE OF LIABILITY*   213

others.* Apart from the foregoing rules, the state of the law is less clear on whether other aspects of the "result" must have been foreseeable. When there has also been an intervening cause of the injury, most courts would probably hold that either the intervening cause or the result usually must be foreseeable.

2. Special Problems on Scope of Liability

a. Assisting in Non-Therapeutic Matters

A physician may sometimes be hired for a non-therapeutic purpose. Prospective adoptive parents might, for example, retain a physician to examine a child they are considering for adoption. Or, a professional football team may have its team physician examine an athlete before he is signed. The non-therapeutic duty to the contracting parties** would be based on the contractual understanding.

A physician who has undertaken to actually render care to a patient may also owe the patient a duty to cooperate with certain non-therapeutic interests of his patient. Thus, a physician had a duty to exercise reasonable care to provide correct information to the Social Security Administration for the purposes of a disability determination. *See*

* *See* Prosser, at 309–10. When the subsequent treatment clearly goes beyond ordinary negligence and involves highly extraordinary misconduct, such as intentionally inflicted harm, it may constitute a superseding cause of the ensuing harm for which the original tortfeasor would not be liable.

** A potential duty to the examinees in such non therapeutic examinations is addressed in II, B, 5.

Albert v. Ertan, 457 So.2d 241 (La.App.1984). And, a plaintiff alleged a valid cause of action when he charged that as a result of the physician's allegedly negligent misrepresentation of the extent of his injury following an automobile collision, he had improvidently settled a personal injury claim against a third party for too small a sum. *See* Rosenthal v. Blum, 529 S.W.2d 102 (Tex.Civ.App. 1975).

A physician similarly must act with reasonable dispatch and accuracy in completing insurance forms for the patient. And, if necessary, a physician may be required to testify at a trial (or at least by deposition in some jurisdictions) or hearing in connection with a patient's claim for Workers' Compensation, for insurance benefits, or for personal injury damages.

When a treating physician is called as a witness at a trial, an issue sometimes arises concerning the scope of the physician's duty to testify, especially in malpractice cases. An attending physician can, of course, be compelled to testify with respect to pertinent *facts* of which he has knowledge. Furthermore, a treating physician, or any competent physician for that matter, may willingly agree to serve as an expert witness for the plaintiff. However, the extent to which a treating physician can be *compelled* to give an *expert opinion,* absent an express statutory requirement that he do so, remains unclear.*   Although there is a division of authority, the trend appears to require the treating physician to give an expert opinion when questioned during his testimony, especially when provisions are made for his compensation at a level commensurate with the value of his time as an expert. The societal interest in obtaining a fair trial, the difficulty patients encounter in obtaining medical experts, the treating physician's familiarity with the case, and the inherent difficulty in separating matters of fact from opinion all militate in favor of requiring expert testimony from the treating physician.

As a practical matter, the foregoing issue arises infrequently in malpractice cases. In some cases the attending physician will be willing to offer his expert opinion. When he is not, most litigants will be reluctant to force the issue, being cognizant of the imponderables of calling as an expert an unwilling witness.

A related question is whether a treating physician may offer expert opinion testimony for the *defendant* in connection with a claim by the patient. Some decisions appear to allow it, assuming that such testimony is within an exception to any applicable testimonial privilege statute. *See* Trujillo v. Puro, 101 N.M. 408, 683 P.2d 963 (App. 1984). Other cases disagree. In Piller v. Kovarsky, 194 N.J.Super., 392, 476 A.2d 1279 (1984),

* For a discussion of this question as applied to the defendant-physician, see II, D, 2, c.

the court held that under an exception to the testimonial privilege statute, a treating physician was not prevented from testifying as a *fact* witness, but that the fiduciary relationship between the physician and patient precluded him from testifying against his patient as an *expert,* at least in a malpractice action involving the same condition for which this physician treated the patient.

b. *Peer Review and Related Matters*

Physician members of a hospital staff are often charged with responsibility for screening and evaluating other physicians seeking or holding staff privileges, and sometimes even for supervising the quality of care administered. An action might lie against members of the hospital medical staff when an injury to a patient results from an exercise of hospital privileges by or conduct of a physician that would have been averted by reasonable care by the responsible professional staff in carrying out the preceding responsibilities. *Cf.* Corleto v. Shore Mem. Hosp., 138 N.J.Super. 302, 350 A.2d 534 (1975). *See generally* IX, C, 2, d and e.

Although few cases have addressed the matter, a physician probably should be held to a duty not to refer a patient to another physician who is not competent to perform the contemplated medical procedures when he knows or has reason to know of the other's incompetence. The referring physician does not, however, ordinarily guarantee the competency of another physician. Nor would he be vicariously liable for the acts of another physician when he merely referred a patient, absent some other relationship between the physicians. *See* VI, C.

c. Disposition of Dead Bodies and Human Tissue

The obligations of a physician and hospital may not end at the conclusion of a medical procedure or upon the death of the patient if decedent's body or significant human tissue remain to be disposed of. If such disposition occurs in an improper manner, liability may result regardless of the quality of the prior treatment.

The law generally recognizes that the next of kin have a legally-protected interest in a dead body for the purposes of burial, autopsy, and other legitimate postmortem procedures such as organ transplantation, at least assuming that the decedent in his lifetime had not made different arrangements.

The failure to secure appropriate consent from the next of kin or persons with the burial rights may result in liability when a body is disposed of in an unauthorized manner. A number of legal theories have at various times been employed to support such actions. Some cases, especially the older ones, considered the interests invaded as basically property rights. Other cases have relied upon a theory of infliction of mental distress. Liability for negligent infliction of mental distress has sometimes been facilitated in cases involving the mishandling of dead bodies by abandonment of the usual requirement of resulting physical consequences from the distress. *See* Prosser, at 362; Restatement § 868 & Comment a. *But cf.* Brooks v. South Broward Hosp., 325 So.2d 479 (Fla.App. 1976) (physical impact required in order to recover for emotional distress when hospital negligently misplaced body of deceased infant and never again located it). *See generally* IV, F. Mental distress cases may involve some form of unauthorized mutilation of the corpse, an unauthorized burial, or even failure to dispose of the body. *Cf.* Johnson v. Women's Hosp., 527 S.W.2d 133 (Tenn.App.1975).

There may be situations in which, depending on the applicable statutory, regulatory, and case law, the physician or hospital can legally dispose of the corpse or at least take actions affecting it in the absence of the express consent of the next of kin. These may include situations when next of kin or a responsible party cannot be identified or are unwilling to claim the body; when precautions are required to prevent the spread of infectious diseases; when an autopsy is authorized by statute; or when the patient had prior to his death expressed a preference with respect to the disposition of his remains under the Uniform Anatomical Gift Act or similar statute.

Although there are few cases on point, there is a possibility that consent will be required prior to disposition of some human organs or tissue removed incident to treatment. One decision found that the patient, by his silence, had impliedly consented to the hospital's usual procedures for disposing of amputated organs. *See* Browning v. Norton-Children's Hosp., 504 S.W.2d 713 (Ky.App.1974). Rather than relying on an implied consent theory, hospitals would be well advised to obtain the express consent of the patient in advance.

d. Birth as an Injury

i. Nature of the Problem. The practice of medicine is not always committed exclusively to the propagation of life. With increasing frequency, physicians are being called upon to assist, through sterilization, birth control measures, and abortions, in the prevention and termination of unplanned or unwanted pregnancies. Physicians are also often required to make an accurate diagnosis of pregnancy, fetus-threatening diseases such as rubella, or genetic defects, and to perform abortions in appropriate cases. Modern technologies such as amniocentesis now facilitate advance detection of genetic abnormalities in time to allow the option of terminating the pregnancy.

Physicians have sometimes been charged with negligence in performing these activities, or in rare cases with breaching a guarantee of a specific result.* This has presented the difficult questions of the scope of liability and damages for the birth

* Although most of these cases are based on negligence, plaintiffs sometimes rely on a breach of a promise of a specific result. *See generally* VII, A, 2. One's theory of recovery could conceivably affect the measure of damages. *See* VII, A. It has not, however, apparently had much practical effect thus far on these types of cases.

of a child whose life the plaintiff alleges was tortiously allowed to come into existence.

ii. Birth of Normal Child. There was once serious doubt whether any action would lie as a result of a pregnancy culminating in the birth of a normal child. The early decisions tended to regard such occurrences as blessed events, concluding that an award of damages would contravene public policy. Recent years have witnessed significant changes in the social and legal framework on which these early decisions rested. The right to practice contraception and a woman's right to seek an abortion have, subject to some limitations, been invested with constitutional protection under the right of privacy. *See* Roe v. Wade, 410 U.S. 113 (1973) (rights to abortion prior to viability and, if necessary to preserve life or health of the mother, thereafter); Griswold v. Connecticut, 381 U.S. 479 (1965) (contraception). Reflecting these developments, the decided trend of authority holds that a negligent sterilization or abortion and subsequent childbirth may give rise to actionable injury. There has, however, been much less agreement as to precisely what damages are recoverable.

Once all the elements of liability are established, most courts would probably allow recovery for damages attending an unwanted pregnancy and delivery (or abortion), including the pain and suffering of the mother due to the birth (or abortion), medical expenses (including the cost of the unsuccessful operation as well as those medical expenses for the birth of unplanned child or termination of the pregnancy), and lost income because of the pregnancy and childbirth (or abortion). *See* Beardsley v. Wierdsma, 650 P.2d 288 (Wyo.1982). Some courts also recognize loss of consortium of the husband. *See* Coleman v. Garrison, 327 A.2d 757 (Del.Super.1974), *aff'd*, 349 A.2d 8 (Del.1975). Presumably, if there were damages associated with complications of the birth (or abortion), those too would be fully compensated.

The majority of courts have drawn the line here and have refused to allow damages to either the child or the parents for the costs of supporting a healthy child. *See* Nanke v. Napier, 346 N.W.2d 520 (Iowa 1984). The following are the arguments most commonly relied on to deny such relief, along with some counter arguments.

First, it has been suggested that such damages would be too speculative, that the cost of supporting a life and the value of life are incommensurables, difficult to compare. *See* Coleman, 349 A.2d at 12. There has also been concern about the possibility of fraudulent claims. *See* Beardsley, *supra.* Conversely, other courts respond that such costs are quantifiable under settled rules and readily available data. *See* Jones v. Malinowski, 299 Md. 257, 473 A.2d 429 (1984).

Second, some argue that to compel compensation for the costs of rearing the infant would impose liability wholly out of proportion to the defendant's culpability. Rieck v. Medical Protective Co. of Fort

Wayne, Ind., 64 Wis.2d 514, 219 N.W.2d 242 (1974). To this some might respond that, as between an innocent patient and a negligent physician, who should better bear the loss?

Third, some courts have argued that the benefits of a normal healthy child outweigh any burden as a matter of law. *See* Nanke, *supra.* Contrariwise, other courts contend that allowing child-rearing expenses is not to disparage the value of life, but to protect the parents' freedom of choice not to have children. *See* Jones, *supra.* It has also been recognized that in many situations, an unplanned child will cause serious emotional or economic problems that will outweigh the benefits. *See* Univ. of Ariz. v. Sup. Ct., 136 Ariz. 579, 667 P.2d 1294 (1983).

Fourth, occasionally it is argued that the parents have a duty to mitigate damages by seeking an abortion or placing the child for adoption. Although this argument is seldom taken seriously even by courts following the majority rule, a corollary argument, that the failure to choose abortion or adoption establishes that the benefit of the child outweighs the burden, seems somewhat more persuasive. *See* Coleman, *supra.* On the "duty to mitigate" argument, other courts reply that the best interests of the child and the natural instincts of the parents make it unreasonable to require parents to abort the child or place it for adoption. *See* Jones, *supra. See also* Cal.Civil Code § 43.6 (West 1982).

Finally, some courts have expressed concern about the effect on the child of discovering not only that he was not wanted, but that he was reared by funds supplied by a stranger. *See* Boone v. Mullendore, 416 So.2d 718 (Ala.1982). Conversely, other courts observe that the parents seek damages not because they do not love the child, but because the physician's fault has forced on them burdens which they sought to and had a right to avoid. *See* Jones, *supra.* Moreover, a child might even encounter less resentment if, as a result of an award of damages, he consumed less of a family's scarce resources.

Few courts have allowed damages for the full cost of raising the child. A significant minority of courts, however, have adopted an intermediate position. Under this approach, recovery for the costs of rearing the child up to majority is allowed only to the extent that such costs exceed the benefit parents derive from the parent-child relationship. *See* Jones, *supra*; Restatement § 920.

A number of courts following the burden-minus-benefits approach have allowed recovery for both pecuniary and non-pecuniary (emotional) costs of rearing and education of the child up to majority offset by both pecuniary and non-pecuniary benefits. *See* Univ. of Ariz., *supra.* The right to recover has, however, sometimes been qualified by the rule that in calculating the burden of the child, the parents' reasons for not wanting a child (*e.g.,* economic, maternal health, genetic) should be considered. *See* Jones, *supra.* Thus, for example, where a parent sought sterilization to avoid a genetic defect, the jury could easily find that the uneventful birth of a healthy child was a blessing. *See* Univ. of Ariz., *supra.*

Thus far few courts have been receptive to actions by the unplanned healthy infant himself. Such an action would have to be premised on the untenable assumption that life had a negative value. Damages would be impossible to quantify. Nor have the courts looked kindly on actions by siblings for loss attributable to the arrival of a new child.

iii. Birth of Deformed or Disabled Child. Sometimes as a result of a physician's failure to diagnose or ascertain potential fetal-threatening conditions or birth defects or to prevent or terminate a pregnancy as requested, a child is born with a deformity or disability. In the situation addressed in this section, the negligence of the physician did not cause the birth defect itself,* but was a cause of the progression to life of a child who would

---

* If the physician's tortious conduct causes the condition itself (as opposed to merely failing to prevent the birth), the physician would generally be subject to liability under traditional torts damages principles. Thus, for example, if he negligently fails to protect the mother or deal with a preventible condition potentially transmissible to a fetus, the physician may be liable for the ensuing birth defects. Similarly, if the physician carelessly causes hypoxia during delivery, resulting in brain damage to the infant, he would be liable for the disability. These cases are distinguishable from the ones discussed in the instant section.

suffer from conditions that originated totally independent of the physician.

The central issue is whether there may be recovery for at least some of the costs of supporting a child born with birth defects where a child is born whose conception or birth would have been prevented had the physician not committed malpractice.

While the courts are divided, the decided trend of recent cases has been to allow recovery for the extraordinary (over and above those ordinarily required for any child) medical, educational, and other expenses necessitated by the birth defect. *See* Schroeder v. Perkel, 87 N.J. 53, 432 A.2d 834 (1981). Thus, in Harbeson v. Parke-Davis, Inc., 98 Wash.2d 460, 656 P.2d 483 (1983), a mother suffering from epilepsy who took anticonvulsive medication during pregnancy gave birth to two children who suffered from fetal hydantoin syndrome, producing a spectrum of developmental deficiencies and deformities. The parents alleged that certain physicians negligently failed to discover and disclose the risks of birth defects associated with the medication. The only injury addressed was the failure to prevent the births; potential liability for causing the deformities was not considered. In approving a remedy, the court observed:

> . . . [Health care providers owe a duty] to impart to their patient material information as to the likelihood of future children being born defective, to enable the potential parents to de-

cide whether to avoid the conception or birth of such children. If medical procedures are undertaken to avoid the conception or birth of defective children, the duty also requires that these procedures be performed with due care.

656 P.2d at 491. The court held that damages should include, *inter alia,* those medical, educational, and other expenses in excess of the costs of birth and rearing of normal children.

Although many courts have allowed the parents to recover for extraordinary expenses, most have refused to recognize a cause of action in favor of the defective child himself. Recent decisions, however, have gone both ways on the question. *Compare* Nelson v. Krusen, 678 S.W.2d 918 (Tex.1984) (denying cause of action for child for "wrongful life"), *with* Procanik v. Cillo, 97 N.J. 339, 478 A.2d 755 (1984) (approving a cause of action for the child for wrongful life to recover extraordinary medical expenses attributable to the birth defect). When a cause of action is recognized on behalf of the child, damages would have to be reduced to the extent that there had been overlapping damages awarded to the parents for the same expenses. *See* Harbeson, *supra.*

Another question is whether the extraordinary expenses may also be recovered for those expenses incurred after the child reaches majority. Some courts have granted recovery only until the child reaches majority. *See* Ramey v. Fassoulas, 414 So. 2d 198 (Fla.App.1982). Other courts have allowed recovery for expenses incurred after majority, often when they have recognized a separate cause of action on behalf of the child. *See* Procanik, *supra.*

Other damages have also sometimes been awarded in such cases. Some courts, for example, have awarded damages for the emotional suffering of the parents attributable to the birth of the impaired child. *See* Harbeson, *supra.* The court in *Harbeson* stated that such damages should be reduced by any countervailing emotional benefit attributable to the birth of the child. Some courts would also allow recovery for medical expenses of the mother attributable to the delivery. Perhaps damages for any pain and suffering and disability resulting from the pregnancy and delivery might also be recoverable. Most of the courts recognizing a child's cause of action for the "wrongful life", however, have refused to allow recovery for the impaired child's emotional distress at being born. *See* Procanik, *supra;* Harbeson, *supra.*

e. *Self-Inflicted Injury*

Sometimes a patient will intentionally kill or injure himself, and a physician or hospital will be sued for contributing to his injury. In addition to establishing that the health care provider was at fault and a contributing cause of the suicide, plaintiff must also overcome the argument that the patient's conduct constituted a superseding intervening cause under proximate cause concepts, thereby relieving the defendant of liability.*

A physician (or other health care provider) can contribute to a patient's self-destructive acts in two ways. First, a physician may tortiously cause an injury or condition that in turn causes a patient's self-destructive acts. A physician might, for example, negligently sever a nerve or blood vessel, leaving the patient with chronic pain. Or, negligently administered anesthesia may produce brain damage which in turn causes the patient to kill himself. A key question is whether the physician is liable not only for the initial injury, but also for the effects of the self-destructive acts. The prevailing rule has been that when insanity or mental incapacity prevents one from realizing the nature of his act or from controlling his self-destructive impulses, suicide (or presumably other self-inflicted injuries) are not superseding causes and do not relieve the defendant from liability for the effects of the plaintiff's acts. *See* Prosser, at 310–11; Restatement § 455.

Second, a defendant may be sued for a patient's suicide or other self-inflicted injury when the defendant negligently *fails to prevent* such acts when he was under a duty to do so. The most hotly contested issues in such cases are whether the defendant was in fact negligent in not preventing

* Defendant might also argue that the patient was contributorily negligent, a defense that is discussed elsewhere. *See* VIII, B.

the harm and whether that negligence in fact caused the self-destructive events. Relatively little attention has been paid to the question whether the patient's self-destructive acts constituted a superseding cause that would defeat liability. Indeed, a number of cases seem to confuse the proximate cause question with the reasonable-care and cause-in-fact questions. The following is a suggested approach. If a negligent failure to protect the patient is shown to have been a cause of the self-inflicted injury, a flexible approach is recommended. Rather than treat self-inflicted injury as superseding unless it is the product of mental incapacity that prevents understanding or self-control (under the rule applied in the first type of situation), a more general inquiry should focus on whether the self-inflicted injury was reasonably foreseeable* or was a part of the risk that made the defendant's failure to prevent it negligent.

D. DAMAGES

Traditional rules governing the measure of damages for personal injury tort actions usually apply with equal force to medical malpractice claims. Thus, in addition to recovering for pecuniary losses

---

* In one case the court held that proximate cause could be found unless the intervening events were highly extraordinary. It refused to find it extraordinary that a delusional psychotic patient might wedge herself between a mattress and side rail in attempting either to hurt herself or extricate herself from confinement. *See* Pisel v. Stamford Hosp., 180 Conn. 314, 430 A.2d 1 (1980).

such as past and future medical expenses and loss of earning capacity, an aggrieved patient may also recover for pain and suffering and mental distress. Punitive damages may also be awarded when the conduct was sufficiently eggregious because of the defendant's evil motive or his reckless indifference to the rights of others. Restatement § 908(2).

When a claim against a health care provider is based on breach of a contract guaranteeing a specific result or upon some other uniquely contractual theory, the measure of damages may vary from the traditional torts approach. *See* VII, A–C.

In response to what many perceive as recurring crises in medical malpractice claims in the last decade, some state legislatures have enacted a number of reforms addressing the matter of damages. *See* X, C.

CHAPTER VI

VICARIOUS LIABILITY

A. IN GENERAL

Normally one's liability for injuries suffered by a patient is predicated on a finding that the defendant himself failed to exercise the requisite level of care. Under the doctrine of vicarious liability, however, one party ("A"), who may be innocent of any personal fault, may under certain circumstances, be held liable for the liability-producing acts of another ("B"). For example, a nurse employed by a physician may injure a patient by the negligent manner in which a blood sample is drawn from the patient, rendering the physician vicariously liable. Vicarious liability is a hybrid concept of loss allocation, one that does not fit exclusively into either fault or strict liability categories. It is not a purely fault-based theory of liability since A may be liable even when he has personally exercised proper care. Nor is it exclusively a form of strict liability, since some substandard conduct by B is usually required in order to trigger the liability of A.

In some situations, A may also have been directly negligent himself and his negligence may have contributed to the patient's injury even though it occurred at the hands of B. A might, for example, have negligently hired an incompetent assistant, have been derelict in supervising him, or have assigned tasks to him beyond the latter's ability or level of training. A might be *directly* liable in such a case for the injury to the patient that was a reasonably foreseeable result of his negligence. In addition, when the requisite elements are satisfied, the liability of A might also be grounded on a theory of *vicarious* liability.

There are two preconditions for the imposition of vicarious liability. First, the required *relationship* must exist between A and B. This usually, though not always, involves what has been termed a "master-servant relationship," most commonly that of employer and employee. *See* VI, B. Vicarious liability may also be based on other relationships such as "borrowed servants" and partnerships. *See* VI, D, E.

The second precondition requires that B must have been acting within the contemplated *scope of the relationship when he committed the tort.* In an employer-employee relationship, for example, it is commonly said that B must have been acting within the "scope of his employment." One's conduct is usually within the scope of his relationship when "it is not a serious departure from authorized conduct in manner or space, is actuated in part by a motive to serve the master, and, as to the intentional use of force, not unexpectable." W. Seavey, Law of Agency 148 (1964). Some courts in recent years have focused on the foreseeability of B's actions in determining the scope of relationship question. *See* Prosser, at 504.

Imposition of vicarious liability on A does not exculpate B. Thus, a plaintiff will often sue both A and B for his injury. Moreover, A may have, depending on the nature of his own and B's conduct, a right to seek indemnity or contribution from B, or under some circumstances, a duty to indemnify or pay contribution to B. *See* Restatement §§ 886A, 886B.

A number of reasons have been advanced to justify vicarious liability. First, the doctrine helps to assure that an injured plaintiff will have a solvent defendant, or a "deep pocket," to look to for redress. Second, vicarious liability helps to assure that the loss will be borne by the party who is in a position to redistribute it or "spread the loss" through higher charges for goods or services. Third, such losses can be reflected in the costs of goods and services thereby informing consumers of the "true costs" of competing goods and services. Finally, the threat of vicarious liability may serve as an incentive to encourage A to exercise greater care in the management of his servants.

B. LIABILITY OF PHYSICIANS FOR THEIR EMPLOYEES' TORTS

In most cases, a physician will be held vicariously liable for the torts of his employees occurring within the course of their employment. The mere status as an employee is usually enough to establish the required master-servant relationship. The requirement that an employee's conduct have been within the scope of his employment rarely presents a serious problem in connection with medical services performed by a physician's employees. Since most medical care is dispensed in a physician's office or other treatment facility, it is usually manifest that the employee was acting within the scope of his employment.

C. LIABILITY FOR TORTS OF OTHER PHYSICIANS

One physician may occasionally be held vicariously liable for the malpractice of another physician. Situations in which vicarious liability is a possibility include when one physician is actually an employee of another physician (*see* VI, B); when two or more physicians are partners or satisfy the specific requirements to be deemed members of a "joint enterprise" (*see* VI, D); or, when one physician is held to be a "borrowed servant" of another physician (*see* VI, E, 4).

If one physician is actually employed by another, the latter will usually be liable under a *respondeat superior* theory for the torts of the former committed in the course of his employment. The fact that some economic relationship exists between two physicians may not automatically create a master-servant relationship. Because of the judgment and freedom of action that inheres in the practice of medicine, it is possible that a physician will be classified as an "independent contractor" rather than a servant, thereby destroying the requisite master-servant relationship. Generally, however, when there is a formal relationship involving payment of wages and a right to control the manner of performance, a master-servant relationship is more likely to be found.

Apart from the foregoing situations, a physician will not ordinarily be vicariously liable for the conduct of another physician merely because they have both been involved in the care of the same patient. Thus, the mere fact that a physician refers a patient to another physician or recommends one does not support vicarious liability. *See* Mincey v. Blando, 655 S.W.2d 609 (Mo.App.1983) (referral); Dahlberg v. Ogle, 268 Ind. 30, 373 N.E. 2d 159 (1978) (recommendation). Nor is a physician who arranges for another physician to cover his patients vicariously liable for the conduct of the other physician in the absence of some other relationship between them. *See* Settoon v. St. Paul Fire & Marine Ins. Co., 331 So.2d 73 (La.App.1976). When, however, the relationship between the defendant and the covering physician rises to the level of a master-servant relationship, there may be vicarious liability. *See* Impastato v. DeGirolamo, 117 Misc.2d 786, 459 N.Y.S.2d 512 (Sup. 1983).*

---

* Here there was evidence that the covering physician was serving the defendant's patients exclusively; used his office, staff and files; and turned over a portion of certain fees collect-

Even if in a particular situation a physician is not vicariously liable for another, he may still be held *directly* liable if he were personally negligent. Thus, if a physician refers a patient to a physician whom he knows or has reason to know is incompetent, he might be directly liable. The same may be true if he fails to leave adequate instructions for a covering physician. *See* Reams v. Stutler, 642 S.W.2d 586 (Ky.1982). One of two physicians actively participating in a patient's care may also have a duty to confront or warn the other physician when he is following a course inconsistent with sound medical practice. *See* McMillin v. L.D. L.R., 645 S.W.2d 836 (Tex.App.1982) (duty of assistant surgeon to warn lead surgeon that he was removing too much skin without grafting new skin); Vassos v. Roussalies, 658 P.2d 1284 (Wyo. 1983) (duty of family physician attending patient to express concern to surgeon about failure to treat intra-abdominal abscess with surgical drainage and continued antibiotics).

D. PARTNERSHIPS AND PROFESSIONAL CORPORATIONS

One physician may be held vicariously liable for the torts of another physician who is a member of the same partnership for conduct committed in the

ed during defendant's absence (which defendant characterized as rent and administrative services).

scope of partnership activities.* Moreover, partners may also be held vicariously liable for the torts of the employees of the partnership. *See* J. Crane & A. Bromberg, *Law of Partnership* § 64 (1968). The partnership entity itself may also be vicariously liable for the torts of its partners and employees in many states.

Most states have enacted statutes authorizing the formation of professional corporations. The fact that a physician is a shareholder or employee of a professional corporation does not relieve him of *direct* liability for his personal tortious conduct. There remains, however, the question to what extent a physician-shareholder might be held vicariously liable for the acts of other physician-shareholders as well as for the acts of other employees of the corporation performing medical services on behalf of the corporation. Some statutes explicitly address at least some aspects of this question.

---

* Vicarious liability may also theoretically be imposed when "A" and "B" have engaged to treat the patient as part of a joint enterprise or venture. Mutual control and cooperation is necessary for such arrangements. The principles here are similar to those involved in partnerships, except that in joint undertakings, the relationship is usually less formal and less permanent. Commonly, in addition to an agreement to manage a patient's care as a joint enterprise, the participants must share a common purpose, an equal right of control, and a pecuniary interest. *See* Restatement § 491, comment c. Given the characteristic independence of medical practitioners, vicarious liability of physicians has, except for true partnerships, seldom been successfully based on the joint enterprise or venture type of relationship.

Other statutes are silent, leaving the matter to be resolved by the courts.

Although generalization is difficult, professional corporation statutes fall roughly into the following categories regarding the vicarious liability of physician-shareholders for others performing medical services on behalf of the corporation.* First, a few statutes appear to retain vicarious liability for physician-shareholders of a professional corporation for the torts of certain persons, such as other physician-shareholders, acting on behalf of the corporation, thus essentially treating them as partners. Second, some statutes appear to impose vicarious liability on the physician-shareholders for the acts of the corporation's employees (including presumably its physician-shareholder employees) unless the physicians and other employees of the corporation or the corporation maintain specified liability insurance coverage. Third, some statutes subject a physician-shareholder to vicarious liability only for the acts of persons under his direct supervision or control. Fourth, some statutes state that a physician-shareholder shall not be subject to vicarious liability by reason of his being a shareholder of a professional corporation. Finally, some statutes are silent on the effect of incorporation on the vicarious liability of physician-shareholders.

On balance, the most sensible approach would be to relieve physicians-shareholders of all vicarious

* See Black, *Professional Corporations and Medical Malpractice* (May 3, 1985) (unpublished manuscript).

liability for the acts of persons employed by or shareholders in their professional corporation, so long as the corporation itself is well insured and remains vicariously liable for the conduct of its employees. But the physicians should remain subject to *direct* liability for their own torts.*

E. NON–EMPLOYEES AND THE "BORROWED SERVANT" RULE

1. Theory of the Borrowed Servant

The Restatement (Second) of Agency § 227 (1958), states: "A servant directed or permitted by his master to perform services for another may become the servant of such other in performing the services" rule. The foregoing principle is known as the "borrowed servant." When a patient is treated in a hospital, the treating physician is usually supported by other physicians (including residents and interns), nurses, medical technicians, and a host of others. Many of these individuals will be self-employed or employed by the hospital, but few if any will be formal employees of the treating physician. The central question then becomes when does a master-servant relationship between a physician and someone assisting him exist despite the lack of a traditional employment relationship between them. One's status as a borrowed servant largely depends upon a finding that

---

* Whether individual physician-shareholders would remain subject to vicarious liability for employees of the corporation or hospital employees under the borrowed servant rule should also be clarified. *See generally* VI, E.

the master possessed the required degree of control over the assistant. Courts have tended to scrutinize the control question more closely in the borrowed servant cases than in situations in which the purported servant was a regular employee of the physician. In the latter cases, the requisite level of control has generally been inferred from the existence of the formal employment relationship.

There are a number of explanations for the use of the borrowed servant doctrine in malpractice. First, charitable and governmental immunity, especially in the past, often insulated hospitals from tort liability, including that based on the actions of hospital employees. *See* IX, D. By applying the borrowed servant rule against physicians courts hoped to assure that injured plaintiffs would have at least one potentially solvent defendant against whom to proceed. Second, the threat of vicarious liability helped assure that ultimate responsibility for the patient would lie in the hands of a single individual, such as a surgeon, during procedures requiring a team effort.

To impose vicarious liability under the borrowed servant rule, plaintiff must prove, *inter alia,* that the person assisting the physician was at least negligent, that the physician possessed the required degree of control, and that the assistant was acting within the scope of his role as assistant. Plaintiff need not prove any direct negligence on the part of the physician.* Thus, by relying on the borrowed servant theory of vicarious liability, plaintiff may be able to obtain a judgment against the physician while proving the negligence of only the assistant. Moreover, even though proof of negligence on the part of a nurse or other assistant would often require expert testimony, the difficulties of proof would seldom match the complexities and expense of proving direct negligence by a physician himself.

2. Absent Physicians

When a physician is absent during the allegedly negligent acts of a hospital employee ·or other person not employed by him, most courts have refused to apply the borrowed servant rule. Thus, in Elizondo v. Tavarez, 596 S.W.2d 667 (Tex.Civ. App.1980), a post-operative patient eviscerated following attempted insertion by a hospital nurse of a levin tube down his throat to relieve abdominal distension. The physician had ordered the insertion of the tube, but it was not done in his presence. The court held that as a matter of law the

* Occasionally a physician's conduct and relationship to someone assisting him will support liability based on both *direct* and *vicarious* liability principles. Thus, the physician may have been personally negligent in supervising someone assisting in a medical procedure and in so doing contributed to the patient's injury, rendering the physician *directly* liable. And, if the degree of control over his assistant satisfies the applicable prerequisites for the borrowed servant rule, the physician may also be *vicariously liable.* Direct and vicarious liability of a physician are not mutually exclusive.

borrowed servant rule was not applicable. *See also* Variety Children's Hosp., Inc. v. Perkins, 382 So.2d 331 (Fla.App.1980). In cases involving pre-operative or post-operative care administered in the absence of the physician, courts generally reason that application of the borrowed servant rule would be improper since the physician lacked even an opportunity to control the other individual and the latter was presumably qualified to perform the tasks assigned. A few cases have, however, recognized the potential vicarious liability of an absent physician for the acts of non-employees. *See* McCullough v. Bethany Med. Ctr., 235 Kan. 732, 683 P.2d 1258 (1984) (surgeon-obstetrician could be vicariously liable for the acts of a nurse anesthetist performed in his absence if it were determined that he had a right to control the work). A few cases following the so-called "Captain of the Ship" doctrine (*see* VI, E, 3, b) have sometimes extended its scope to apply to a physician not present when the negligence occurred.

A few other cases in which an absent physician has been held vicariously liable for the acts of a non-employee are probably *sui generis*. Thus, in Naccash v. Burger, 223 Va. 406, 290 S.E.2d 825 (1982), a physician allegedly agreed to oversee and supervise a cytogenetics laboratory and the technicians who performed its day-to-day activities. Although the technician was paid by the hospital, the physician was held to be vicariously liable for the alleged negligence of the technician that occurred in his absence. This case may, however, be distinguishable from the usual borrowed servant situation in that in *Naccash* the supervisory relationship was a long-term one rather than for a specified event.

An absent physician may, of course, be held directly liable for his personal negligence when for example, he reasonably should have been present to supervise or was negligent in the instructions he left. *See* Winchester v. Meads, 372 Mich. 593, 127 N.W.2d 337 (1964) (as a result of physician's allegedly incomplete and unsigned written medication order, patient received an improper intravenous solution from the nurse).

3.　Physicians Present During Patient Care

a.　In General

Most cases addressing the borrowed servant question have involved a tortious injury that occurred while the physician was physically present. The early decisions tended to impose vicarious liability almost automatically on a physician who was present and had a right to control the actions of another, especially in a surgical setting. More recently, however, a number of courts have rejected a right to control test. They have held instead that the borrowed servant rule depends not on whether a physician had a right to control, but on whether he in fact exercised or assumed control over the other individual. *Cf.* 49 Notre Dame L. 933 (1974). These two approaches to the borrowed servant cases are discussed in the following sections.

b. The Right to Control Standard

Under the traditional borrowed servant formulation, a physician might be held vicariously liable for an individual assisting in the patient care but employed by someone else when the physician had a right to control that individual. Thus, in Baird v. Sickler, 69 Ohio St.2d 652, 433 N.E.2d 593, 595 (1982), the court observed in dicta that "it is unnecessary that such right of control be exercised; it is sufficient that the right merely exist." *See also* Sparger v. Worley, 547 S.W.2d 582 (Tex.1977).

Some courts following a "right to control" test have invoked a "captain of the ship" analogy, particularly with respect to surgeons. Some courts seem to equate that terminology with the ordinary right to control formulation. *See* McCullough v. Bethany Med. Center, 235 Kan. 732, 683 P.2d 1258 (1984). Others have interpreted the captain of the ship concept as dispensing with the need to establish even a right of control, or at least as creating a presumption of a right of control merely from a person's status, such as lead surgeon. *See* Kitto v. Gilbert, 39 Colo.App. 374, 570 P.2d 544 (1977) (a confusing decision not expressly mentioning captain of ship terminology). The captain of the ship variation has not been followed by most courts, even those adhering to a right to control test generally. Thus, in the *Baird* case, the court noted that it made "no attempt to impose upon an operating physician the duty of overseeing all that occurs in the highly technical milieu in which he works," but limited the borrowed servant rule to those matters over which the physician realistically possessed the right to control. 433 N.E.2d at 595. *See also* Sparger, *supra.*

A few courts apply a variation of the right to control test based on a distinction between an assistant's duties involving professional skills and those that are simply ministerial, under which a physician might be vicariously liable for the former, but not the latter. *See* Beaches Hosp. v. Lee, 384 So.2d 234 (Fla.App.1980).

c. *Assumption or Exercise of Control*

Some cases seem to require that the physician have actually assumed or exercised control over the conduct of another individual before the borrowed servant rule can apply. In May v. Broun, 261 Or. 28, 492 P.2d 776 (1972), a patient was burned by an electric cauterizing machine during surgery. The evidence justified an inference that the circulating nurse had either hooked up the machine incorrectly or operated it improperly. Although the purported negligence of the nurse occurred during surgery and in the presence of the surgeon, the court held that the surgeon was not vicariously liable for her acts. The court observed:

> [W]here the nurse is in the general employ of the hospital and is performing services for the hospital as well as for the surgeon, courts do not

usually hold that she changes from a general employee of the hospital to a special employee of the surgeon until she is under the surgeon's direct supervision and control.

.   .   .

[W]hen technical equipment and the personnel to operate it are furnished by the hospital to the surgeon and injury is caused by malfunctioning equipment or negligent operators, and it is not shown that the surgeon was personally negligent or that the circumstances were such that it was practical for him to exercise direct supervision or control over the machine or its operation, *respondeat superior* liability does not attach to the surgeon.

492 P.2d at 780–82.

The *May* court reasoned that the burden of insuring the proper selection and training of hospital employees and maintenance of hospital equipment in such cases more properly rests with the hospital than with the surgeon. For this reason, the court concluded that it was the hospital that would have the best opportunity to prevent such occurrences in the future.

Similar reasoning and results have sometimes been reached even in cases involving relatively simple procedures when the individual assisting in the patient care was a member of a highly-trained field, such as a nurse-anesthetist. *See* Starnes v. Charlotte-Mecklenberg Hosp. Auth., 28 N.C.App. 418, 221 S.E.2d 733 (1976) (surgeon not vicariously liable for alleged negligence of a nurse-anesthetist in burning infant with hot-water bottle during surgery). In Sesselman v. Muhlenberg Hosp., 124 N.J.Super. 285, 306 A.2d 474 (1973), a patient suffered injury to her teeth during childbirth. A nurse anesthetist had administered anesthesia through an airway and catheter she had inserted into patient's mouth. Although the exact cause of the injury was unexplained, there were inferences from which the jury might have found that it was attributable to the negligence of the nurse-anesthetist. The court refused to hold the obstetrician vicariously liable merely because the nurse had received instructions from him as to what work was to be performed. The court noted that there was no evidence that the physician undertook to exercise control over the nurse. Other courts have emphasized that some tasks are so routine that they may not fall within the ambit of the physician's special supervisory responsibility, and thus are not subject to the borrowed servant rule. *See* Nichter v. Edmiston, 81 Nev. 606, 407 P.2d 721 (1965).

A few cases have tended to underscore the inevitability in modern surgery of at least a rough separation of responsibility among the surgeon and other personnel assisting in the operation. In Grant v. Touro Infirmary, 254 La. 204, 221–22, 223 So.2d 148, 154 (1969), the court recognized in dictum that "operations performed under modern techniques require team performance, and the nurses and other personnel assisting in the operating room are not at all times under the immediate supervision and control of the operating surgeon so as to bring the case strictly within the 'borrowed servant' doctrine."

4. Responsibility for Other Physicians

Multiple physicians may be involved in a medical procedure. For example, an anesthesiologist may be present to administer the anesthetic and to monitor the patient's vital signs during surgery, and a cardiologist might be present when difficulties with the heart are anticipated. Interns and residents are also frequently involved in patient care. While theoretically, other physicians might be deemed the borrowed servants of a physician in charge of a procedure, in practice the courts often seem more reluctant to characterize other participating physicians, particularly specialists, as borrowed servants.

A California case is illustrative of the general trend. The patient suffered severe brain damage caused by hypoxia induced by an adverse reaction to an anesthetic administered by an anesthesiologist. In affirming a verdict for the surgeon, the court held that he could not be held vicariously liable for the actions of the anesthesiologist over whose performance he had (in the absence of evidence to the contrary) no control or right to control. *See* Marvulli v. Elshire, 27 Cal.App.3d 180, 103 Cal.Rptr. 461 (1972). *Accord* Thompson v. Presbyterian Hosp., Inc., 652 P.2d 260 (Okla.1982).

Other courts, however, have sometimes applied borrowed servant status to other physicians assisting in the surgery under certain circumstances. *See* Kitto v. Gilbert, 39 Colo.App. 374, 570 P.2d 544 (1977) (anesthesiologist); Schneider v. Albert Einstein Med. Center, 257 Pa.Super. 348, 390 A.2d 1271 (1978) (anesthesiologist).

Given the increasing complexity and specialization in surgery and other medical procedures, the notion that the lead surgeon or physician in charge will have a reasonable opportunity for realistic control over facets of a procedure peculiarly within the expertise of another specialist is questionable. While a single physician should retain ultimate control over the course of surgery or procedure, that he would or even reasonably could actively supervise the many specialized details of a medical procedure that are the immediate responsibility of another specialist makes even a theoretical right to control largely illusory with respect to many of the specialized details of such procedures. Moreover, most established physicians are insured. Thus, borrowed servant status appears particularly inappropriate in the case of other physicians, especially other specialists. While application of borrowed servant status to residents and interns may be less objectionable than in the case of established physicians, it is still subject to the criticisms of the doctrine generally. *See* VI, E, 6. If borrowed servant status is applied to residents and interns at all, the assumption-of-control test should be used. *See* VI, E, 3, c.

5. Effect on Hospital Liability

If the borrowed servant rule renders a physician vicariously liable for the torts of a hospital employee, the question arises whether the hospital may also be subject to vicarious liability for its employee. The courts are divided on the question. The better reasoned view holds that the hospital may be vicariously liable along with the physician. *See* City of Somerset v. Hart, 549 S.W.2d 814 (Ky.1977); Piehl v. Dalles Gen. Hosp., 280 Ore. 613, 571 P.2d 149 (1977); Restatement (Second) of Agency § 226 (1958). A number of courts have, however, relieved the hospital of vicarious liability for the acts of hospital employees for whom the physician is liable. *See* Kitto v. Gilbert, 39 Colo.App. 374, 570 P.2d 544 (1977).

Given the hospital's continuing responsibilities for training and evaluating its employees as well as for anticipating liability and insuring against it, a persuasive case can be made for preserving the vicarious liability of the hospital even when the borrowed servant rule is applied.

6. The Borrowed Servant: A Reappraisal

The continuing validity of the purported justifications for the borrowed servant rule is open to question. The argument that the borrowed servant rule fosters greater care by the physician is questionable. The threat of liability for personal

negligence should be a sufficient deterrent to ensure physician accountability. To encourage (by
the threat of vicarious liability) a physician's active
exercise of control over a qualified hospital employee or even over another self-employed physician
when sound medical practice does not require it,
might actually endanger the patient under some
circumstances.

While a physician not actually exercising direct
control over the work of another is often in no
position to minimize risks of injury at the hands of
the other, the hospital-employer is. It has the
primary responsibility for the hiring and ongoing
training, discipline, and evaluation of hospital employees. Not only is the hospital in a better position than the physician to respond to the incen-
tives and disincentives created by vicarious
liability for the actions of hospital employees, but
it is also better able to anticipate and redistribute
losses caused by its employees. Certainly, in those
jurisdictions where the hospital may itself remain
vicariously liable for the negligence of its employees even when they are assisting physicians not
employed by the hospital, there seems little justification to also hold the physician vicariously liable.

Even in situations when the physician actually
exercises control over the details of another's work,
a good argument can be made that it is only the
regular employer (usually a hospital) that should
normally be vicariously liable. The fact that an
assistant was not within the immediate control of

hospital personnel should not affect hospital liability. The element of control where the servant is an employee is largely implied by the employment relationship in any event. Moreover, the hospital employees do not cease furthering the interests of their regular employer merely because they temporarily become subject to the control of another. And if the physician were personally negligent in his control of the other, he would, of course, then be *directly* liable independent of the borrowed servant doctrine.

Even the "deep pocket" argument is questionable. The gradual erosion of governmental and charitable immunity has meant that the physician usually no longer stands alone as the only "deep pocket." The growing prevalence of liability insurance among nurses and others also helps to ensure the existence of a financially responsible defendant.

Another question about the borrowed servant rule that has yet to be adequately resolved is what effect the fact that a physician has incorporated should have on his potential vicarious liability under the borrowed servant rule. This complication is another reason for abrogating the rule.

CHAPTER VII

CONTRACT AND STRICT LIABILITY THEORIES OF RECOVERY

A. CONTRACT ACTIONS

1. In General

Although the physician-patient relationship is essentially a consensual one and is usually based on an implied contract, most malpractice cases are governed by tort principles. *See* I, C. In some situations both tort and contract theories *conceptually* support recovery and are coterminous. This would be true, for example, when plaintiff alleges that the physician failed to exercise the requisite degree of care, thereby breaching his implied contract to do so as well as the duty of due care imposed by tort law. The decided trend has been to deal with such cases exclusively under tort principles. A significant exception to the predominance of tort principles, however, occurs when a physician not only undertakes to perform in accordance with the applicable standard of care, but also promises to do something more, such as produce a specific therapeutic result, employ a specific technique, or perform specific services for the patient. The freedom of parties to contract has generally been held to include the right of the physician and the patient to enter into such arrangements. In such cases, the physician has promised to do more than the law otherwise requires, and to that extent contract principles may apply not only with repect to liability, but in other respects as well unless otherwise provided by special malpractice legislation. Thus, when a contract promising a specific therapeutic result is established, the time-honored tort axiom that the liability of a physician cannot ordinarily be based solely on the fact that treatment was unsuccessful may not prevent liability based on the contractual guarantee. A different measure of damages might also be applicable to uniquely contract actions than is employed by personal injury tort actions. Three alternative measures of damage for breach of contract were explored in Sullivan v. O'Connor, 363 Mass. 579, 296 N.E.2d 183 (1973) (identifying the "expectancy," "restitution," and "reliance" measures, and endorsing the latter one). Generally, there has been some disagreement among the courts as to the appropriate theory of damages as well as the compensability of pain and suffering under uniquely contract causes of action.

2. Contracts Promising Specific Results

a.   The Dilemma

Liability based on a contract to produce a specific therapeutic result beyond that required by due care has evoked an ambivalent response from the courts. Considering the uncertainties which attend the practice of medicine, and the inherent variations in human anatomy and psychology, doctors seldom can realistically (and never should) guarantee specific therapeutic results. Moreover, unrestricted allowance of such claims might threaten the physician with liability for what were essentially therapeutic reassurances to his patient. A physician found to have breached such a contract becomes an insurer to the extent provided by the contract. This means that even the fact that the physician exercised due care will not exculpate him. There are sometimes temptations for a plaintiff with a devastating illness or a predisposition to litigate to attempt to convert an unsuccessful or otherwise untoward result of therapy into a sizeable judgment despite the innocence of the physician. This may invite patient fraud or at least a good deal of selective recollection of what was said by the physician. The possibility of taking advantage of a longer statute of limitations period that may exist in some jurisdiction for contract actions than for tort actions may further enhance the attraction of the contractual guarantee theory. *See* VIII, A, 2. Moreover, traditional tort doctrines afford most patients ample protection. When the physician's assurances distort the risks of the proposed medical procedure, an action might lie under the informed consent doctrine or for misrepresentation. Furthermore, depending on the terms of the insurance policy, a claim based on a breach of a contract promising a specific result might not be covered by some physicians' malpractice liability insurance policies.

On the other hand, without such a cause of action, there is concern that patients who were enticed by unrealistic guarantees to accept treatment might be left remediless when the promised results fail to materialize.* The threat of liability may serve to check overselling or even misrepresentation by physicians to further their own economic or professional interests. Such actions, by helping to insure a more accurate flow of information to the patient, also serve to vindicate the patient's right of self-determination.

b. Possible Approaches to the Problem

Judicial and, more recently, legislative attitudes toward the problem of alleged contracts guaranteeing a specific therapeutic result have varied. The most patient-oriented approach is typified by the case of Guilmet v. Campbell, 385 Mich. 57, 188 N.W.2d 601 (1971).** The patient underwent a

---

* The contract action may be easier for the patient to utilize than other legal theories. For example, no proof that the defendant violated a professional standard of disclosure would be required for such contract actions, but would under an informed consent theory in many jurisdictions. See III, C, 3. Moreover, a physician could conceivably make all of the required disclosures for informed consent purposes, yet still guarantee a specific therapeutic result.

** The effect of the Guilmet case in Michigan has been largely dissipated by enactment of a statute of frauds provision requiring that such contractual guarantees be in writing and signed. See Mich.Comp.Laws Ann. § 566.132(g) (West Supp. 1985).

vagotomy (severance of the vagus nerve to retard the flow of stomach acid) for a peptic ulcer. Surgery was followed by a host of complications that required three subsequent operations (with blood transfusions that may have caused hepatitis), and posed an ongoing threat of recurrent infections. Plaintiff testified that his surgeon had told him, among other things, that the proposed surgery would take care of all of his troubles; that there was nothing to the operation at all; that he would be out of work for four weeks at most; and, that he could throw his pill box away. The jury returned a verdict of "no negligence" but awarded $50,000 damages for breach of contract to produce a specific result, which was affirmed by the supreme court. The court held that questions concerning what was said by the parties and whether there was such an oral contract (and if so, what it was) were all matters for the jury to decide in the instant case. The alleged contract in *Guilmet* was based entirely on plaintiff's recollection of the alleged words of his physician. No express words of guarantee or warranty were alleged, and no additional consideration was paid for the alleged promise.

Other courts have taken a more restrictive approach. For some, this has taken the form of closely scrutinizing the alleged promise to see if it rose to the level of a guarantee. Thus, in Ferlito v. Cecola, 419 So.2d 102 (La.App.1982), allegations that defendant dentist stated that the proposed crowns would "please" plaintiff and make her teeth "pretty" did not constitute a guarantee. *See generally* La.Rev.Stat.Ann. § 40:1299.41, C (1977). Other courts emphasize that to support a warranty of a specific result, an express warranty must be established by clear and convincing evidence. *See* Burns v. Wannamaker, 281 S.C. 352, 315 S.E.2d 179 (App.1984). In Rogala v. Silva, 16 Ill.App.3d 63, 305 N.E.2d 571 (1973), the court posited a three-part requirement: (1) the making of an express warranty; (2) plaintiff's reliance thereon; and (3) separate consideration. The *Rogala* standard imposes significant limitations on liability for breach of a contract promising a specific result. Even when the language expressly creating a warranty is alleged, a finder of fact would often find allegations that a physician would offer such an express guarantee doubtful and unworthy of belief. The "reliance" requirement might oblige plaintiff to show that except for the alleged promise he would not have proceeded with the treatment, or at least that the promise was a substantial factor in his decision. Finally, the separate consideration requirement, if strictly enforced, would be difficult to prove and would probably defeat recovery in most cases.

It has also been suggested as a possible solution that prior to treatment patients should be asked to sign a form disclaiming any promises of specific results. *See* Tierney, *Contractual Aspects of Malpractice,* 19 Wayne L.Rev. 1457, 1478 (1973). Others have suggested a rule requiring corroborative evidence to establish a contractual guarantee. *See* 41 Tenn.L.Rev. 964, 974 (1974). Under this approach, some proof apart from the bare assertions of the plaintiff would be required, such as testimony of third party witnesses, written evidence, or additional charges paid by or billed to the patient. A number of states have enacted statutes of frauds requiring that contracts guaranteeing specific therapeutic results be memorialized in writing and signed to be enforceable. *See* Ind.Code Ann. § 16–9.5–1–4 (Burns 1983) (for providers qualified under statute). Since most physicians would be unlikely to memorialize such alleged promises in writing, these statutes would often wipe out the cause of action for breach of such contracts.

3. Other Uniquely Contractual Actions

Although breach of a contract to produce a specific result represents the most common contractual theory of malpractice that may not involve tortious conduct, there remain several other potentially uniquely contractual bases of liability. If a physician expressly agrees to employ a specific medical technique and then uses some other method, he may be liable for breach of contract. For example, in Stewart v. Rudner, 349 Mich. 459, 84 N.W.2d 816 (1957), a physician who had agreed to arrange delivery by a cesarean section was held liable for breach of contract when the child was delivered by normal methods.

Occasionally a patient will sue a physician for breach of contract when the physician allegedly agreed to care for the patient and thereafter refused to do so. Liability under such a theory will depend on the precise nature of the contractual arrangements between the parties. Of course, when the physician has agreed or undertaken to care for the patient and thereafter terminates the relationship in an unreasonable manner, a tort action might also lie for intentional abandonment or negligence. *See* II, B, 3.

B. STRICT LIABILITY

1. Physicians

Strict liability* is a theory under which a defendant may be held liable for injuries he caused even though he acted with reasonable care. In personal injury actions generally, the most common instances of strict liability have occurred in the field of products liability and in connection with abnormally dangerous activities. However, absent a promise by the defendant guaranteeing a specific therapeutic result, a physician or other individual medical practitioner has generally not been subject to strict liability for injuries arising out of professional medical services. *See* Magner v. Beth Israel Hosp., 120 N.J.Super. 529, 295 A.2d 363 (1972); Barbee v. Rogers, 425 S.W.2d 342 (Tex.1968). This rule has been frequently applied to professional services. *See* Finn v. G.D. Searle & Co., 35 Cal.3d

---

* Unless otherwise stated, the term "strict liability" will be used in its broad sense to mean strict liability based on either strict tort or breach of implied warranty theories.

691, 200 Cal.Rptr. 870, 677 P.2d 1147 (1984) (diagnosis); Hoven v. Kelble, 79 Wis.2d 444, 256 N.W.2d 379 (1977), (cardiac arrest during lung biopsy). Courts have similarly rejected strict liability based on an implied warranty theory for professional services. *See* Batiste v. American Home Products Corp., 32 N.C.App. 1, 231 S.E.2d 269 (1977) (prescribing oral contraceptive); Dennis v. Allison, 678 S.W.2d 511 (Tex.Civ.App.1984) (psychiatric services).

Even when an allegedly defective product causes harm while it is being used or administered by the physician, strict liability (under either a tort or implied warranty theory) has generally not been imposed on physicians. *See* Magrine v. Krasnica, 94 N.J.Super. 228, 227 A.2d 539 (1967), *aff'd sub nom,* Magrine v. Spector, 100 N.J.Super. 223, 241 A.2d 637 (1968), *aff'd per curiam* 53 N.J. 259, 250 A.2d 129 (1969) (defective hypodermic needle used by dentist). In such cases courts have emphasized one or more of the following considerations: (1) the essential nature of the association between practitioner and patient involves a professional service rather than a sale; (2) the practitioner is in no position to discover or to take measures to prevent latent defects; (3) the product manufacturers and suppliers rather than the practitioners are in the best position to anticipate and distribute losses by higher prices and charges; (4) the fear of liability might distort medical priorities by discouraging physicians from using some devices or from employing some techniques.

Application of strict products liability to physicians and other individual practitioners would ordinarily not appear justified when the injury occurred in the course of medical care. It is conceivable, however, that under some circumstances a physician might legitimately be regarded as a provider of goods for the purposes of strict products liability. Thus, for example, an ophthalmologist might offer for sale without any professional consultation non-prescription contact lens cleaning materials. It is possible that a court might consider that such transactions so far departed from the rendition of professional services that essentially a sale of goods was involved that should be subject to strict liability.

2. Hospitals

Most courts have refused to apply strict liability to hospitals when the injury was allegedly caused by professional services. *See* Hoven v. Kelble, 79 Wis.2d 444, 256 N.W.2d 379 (1977). A similar rule has been applied when the professional services employed a non-defective mechanical device. Thus, in Greenberg v. Michael Reese Hosp., 83 Ill. 2d 282, 47 Ill.Dec. 385, 415 N.E.2d 390 (1980), plaintiff alleged that radiation therapy of the tonsils and adenoids ultimately caused cancer or nodular growths. The court refused to apply strict liability for such injuries. The court noted that plaintiffs did not allege that the radiation equipment was defective, but rather challenged the appropriateness of radiation treatment for plaintiffs' condition. *See also* Nevauex v. Park Place Hosp., Inc., 656 S.W.2d 923 (Tex.App.1983).

When, however, the harm is attributable to a defect in a mechanical device, instrument, or substance used, administered or supplied by hospital personnel, there is less agreement on the strict liability question. Plaintiffs in such cases often have attempted to rely on both strict tort liability as well as breach of implied warranty. One group of cases have involved *disposable or consumable products*. When the product supplied to the patient was not being used in the actual performance of specific medical service, a number of cases have imposed strict liability. *See* Thomas v. St. Joseph Hosp., 618 S.W.2d 791 (Tex.Civ.App.1981) (strict liability applicable to hospital that provided flammable hospital gown that severely burned the patient). A few cases have extended strict liability to hospitals for injuries caused by defective disposable products even when used during medical care. *See* Providence Hosp. v. Truly, 611 S.W.2d 127 (Tex. Civ.App.1980) (recognizing breach of implied warranty against hospital in connection with use of allegedly defective bottle of drug that allowed drug to become contaminated). Some other courts, however, refuse to apply strict liability to hospitals even for disposable or consumable items or drugs, at least when they were actually being used in conjunction with the performance of medical services. *See* Racer v. Utterman, 629 S.W.2d 387 (Mo. App.1981) (disposable surgical drape that ignited during surgery); Brackins, *Liability of Physicians, Pharmacists, and Hospitals for Adverse Drug Reactions,* 34 Def.L.J. 273 (1985).*

Courts have generally refused to apply strict liability to hospitals for harm caused by allegedly defective *reusable* devices employed in medical care. *See* Redwine v. Baptist Gen. Con., 681 P.2d 1121 (Okla.App.1984) (heart-lung machine). A few recent decisions have, however, extended strict liability to hospitals for harm caused by such reusable products. *See* Skelton v. Druid City Hosp. Bd., 459 So.2d 818 (Ala.1984) (breach of implied warranty applicable to hospital in connection with alleged defect in reusable suturing needle that broke during surgery); Grubb v. Albert Einstein Med. Center, 255 Pa.Super. 381, 387 A.2d 480 (1978) (applying strict tort liability to hospital for allegedly defective cutting machine provided by hospital and used during orthopedic surgery on the plaintiff).

Drawing a distinction between disposable products and those reused by the hospital probably represents a sensible compromise. Under this approach, a hospital should not be strictly liable under either implied warranty or strict tort theories if the patient was harmed by a reusable prod-

* The potential liability of pharmacists and retail pharmacies for prescription drugs is beyond the scope of this treatise and is not addressed here. *See* Brackins, *supra.*

uct employed in treatment and the ownership of the product was not transferred to the patient. When, however, a patient's injury was caused by a disposable or consumable product (or a reusable one the ownership of which was transferred to the patient), an argument can be made that the hospital should be subject to strict liability for harm caused by an unreasonably dangerous defect in the product.* This would create an incentive for the hospital to insist on high quality products from its suppliers. Moreover, the hospital would have a right to seek indemnity from its suppliers, assuming its record keeping practices allowed it to identify the source of the product. Similarly, a strong argument can be made that a hospital should also be subject to strict liability for disposable products consumed or used by the patient other than for treatment, such as food provided for meals. It remains to be seen, however, how far the courts will go in extending strict liability to hospitals, especially in connection with defective prescription drugs. It is also unclear whether application of strict liability to hospitals is a viable option in states with special malpractice statutes that purport to limit hospital liability to fault-based liability.

---

* Jurisdictions employ a number of formulations for strict liability. Some, for example, do not require that a defect be unreasonably dangerous. Moreover, some jurisdictions have by special statute placed specific limitations on the strict liability actions, especially for retailers. Special rules have also evolved in connection with liability of suppliers of prescription drug products. *See* Brackins, *supra*.

The liability of suppliers of blood and blood products has frequently received special attention by the courts and legislatures. Most courts have held that physicians and hospitals are not strictly liable* for blood administered in the course of patient treatment. *See* Annot., 20 A.L.R.4th 136 (1983; Supp.1984). This result is often based on a characterization of a blood transfusion as a service rather than a sale. Some courts have also refused to apply strict liability because blood was, at the time, deemed an unavoidably unsafe product with respect to some injurious ingredients. Most courts have also refused to extend strict liability to blood banks and similar entities for harm caused by blood they supplied. *See* Annot., 24 A.L.R.4th 508 (1983). A few courts, however, have distinguished blood banks from health care providers, reasoning that supplying blood is a central function of blood banks, rather than incidental to services as in the case of hospitals and physicians. *See* Belle Bonfils Memorial Blood Bank v. Hansen, 195 Colo. 529, 579 P.2d 1158 (1978) (blood bank subject to strict tort and implied warranty theories of liability). The liability of those administering and supplying blood has been affected in a number of jurisdictions by statutes classifying blood transactions as services rather than sales, at least for some purposes.

---

* Even when strict liability is not applied, those administering and supplying blood would be liable if negligent. And with new technologies for screening donors and testing blood, the potential for negligence liability is ever expanding.

CHAPTER VIII

DEFENSES AND LIMITATIONS ON LIABILITY

A. STATUTES OF LIMITATIONS

1. Limitations of Actions Generally

Statutes of limitations require that an action be commenced within a prescribed period of time following its accrual or it will be barred. There are a number of policies that underlie statutes of limitations. First, they preclude the prosecution of stale claims after a long period of time when witnesses and evidence may have disappeared and memories faded. Second, such statutes help to assure that defendants are put on notice of claims at a time when investigation will still be feasible. Third, they reduce the difficulties of individuals and insurers in anticipating liability far into the future based on past conduct. Fourth, a degree of stability and repose in human affairs and a hope of redemption with the passage of years can be promoted by barring actions after passage of a reasonable period of time. Contrary arguments are based on a fear that such statutes might foreclose some legitimate claims. It is also argued that the likelihood of a defendant being prejudiced by the unavailability of evidence due to the passage of time is reduced by the fact that the loss of evidence would usually have an even more adverse effect on the plaintiff, who must bear the burden of proof.

In addressing statutes of limitations, it is useful to focus on several questions: First, what are the applicable statutes? Second, under such statutes, when does the statutory period begin to run (or when does the action "accrue")? Third, what is that statutory period? And finally, are there any rules that might suspend the running of the statute?

2. The Applicable Statute

A majority of states have either adopted a special statute of limitations for malpractice cases or at least have expressly identified the statute of limitations that is applicable. When this has not been done, malpractice cases are usually governed by the statutes of limitations applicable to personal injury tort actions.

The special malpractice statutes of limitations that have been enacted have varied in their comprehensiveness. Some have expressly included a number of specified health care occupations. *See* Mont.Code Ann. § 27–2–205 (1983). Other statutes have employed language referring generally to health care providers. There may be a question concerning the applicable statute in actions against those professions not specifically enumerated in the special legislation. There has also been some variation in the types of malpractice included in the special statutes. Some statutes have addressed only professional negligence. Others have also included other theories of liability such as breaches of contracts promising a specific result. Still others have employed the "malpractice" terminology without guidance on the scope of that phrase.

Some of the special malpractice statutes have specifically incorporated by reference the general tort statute of limitations, and then usually have adopted a number of specific restrictions or modifications to it. Other special malpractice statutes have adopted a statute of limitations wholly independent of the general tort statute. Some malpractice statutes have also adopted special requirements for giving notice within a prescribed period after a certain event or, under some versions, prior to filing suit.

Occasionally a plaintiff will attempt to rely on the statute of limitations governing contract actions (which sometimes allow a longer period in which to bring the action) by characterizing his claim as one sounding in contract. When plaintiff's allegations are essentially that defendant failed to perform in accordance with the applicable standard of care, most courts hold that the claim is governed by a specific malpractice statute of limitations provision where applicable or, in the absence of such a provision, by the statutes applicable to personal injury tort actions generally. When, however, plaintiff seeks relief under a uniquely contractual theory, such as a contract promising a specific result, he may be able to take advantage of a contract statute of limitations unless such actions have been included within the scope of some special malpractice legislation specifying a different statute of limitations. The following discussion will concentrate on actions that are usually covered by either a special malpractice statute or by a general tort statute, since these comprise the vast majority of malpractice cases.

It should also be noted that sometimes special statutes of limitations and specific notice requirements have been adopted for claims against various governmental entities. These may be applicable to malpractice claims against such entities.

When a patient dies, rules governing the statutes of limitation applicable to wrongful death and survival actions should also be considered since they may, depending on their construction and the construction of other malpractice legislation, be relevant to malpractice claims. Special maximum cut-off limitations periods are sometimes also applied to actions against the estate of a deceased defendant.

3. Accrual of Cause of Action

a. *Traditional Rule*

Once the applicable statute, with its prescribed time period, has been identified, there remains the crucial matter of ascertaining the event that triggers the running of the statutory period. Since most statutes until recently spoke in terms of the statutory period beginning to run upon "accrual" of the cause of action without further elaboration, the question of when the limitations period began to run was largely a matter of judge-made law. The trend in recent statutes, however, has been to expressly define the accrual date.

The traditional rule was that the limitations period commences to run on the date of the *wrongful conduct* complained of. Although the "wrongful conduct" accrual date has fallen into disfavor with many courts, it has been expressly adopted by a few statutes. *See* Ind.Code Ann. § 16–9.5–3–1 (Burns Supp.1985) (for providers "qualified" under statute, two years from the alleged act, omission or neglect, subject to exceptions). The wrongful conduct accrual date has also undergone a renaissance in the form of the "hybrid" statutes adopted in many jurisdictions. *See* VIII, A, 3, b, ii.

b. *Discovery Rules*

i. Pure Discovery Rule. In the past decade, many courts have adopted the "discovery rule." This rule usually provides that an action accrues when the plaintiff discovers or reasonably should have discovered his injury. The discovery rule was based on the injustice of barring a victim's claim before he could reasonably have been expected to discover his injury.

Some courts adopted a discovery rule for medical malpractice cases generally. Others limited the rule to special factual patterns, such as situations in which a foreign object was left in an incision during surgery. In many jurisdictions where a discovery rule was judicially adopted, subsequent legislation either replaced it with a "wrongful conduct" rule or has adopted some combination of the two in the form of a hybrid rule.

ii. Hybrid Rules. In reaction to widespread judicial adoption of the discovery rule, quite a few statutes were enacted placing a limit or "cap" on the time within which the discovery rule could operate. Thus, these "hybrid" statutes have features of both the discovery rule and the wrongful conduct rule. They typically provide that the statutory period does not begin to run until the plaintiff discovers or should have discovered his injury, but after the passage of a specified outer limit period, the action would (unless covered by some exception) be barred regardless of whether the injury was or should have been discovered.

The details of the hybrid rules vary with regard to the time period in which an action must be commenced after the injury was or should have been discovered, the maximum time period for bringing suit following the wrongful conduct, and various exceptions to it. Furthermore, a few statutes contain language that, at least on its face, suggests that actual discovery is required in order to commence the running of the statute with respect to the discovery component of the hybrid rule or some exception to it.

The hybrid statutes were conceived as a compromise. A discovery rule was adopted to insure at least some protection to injured patients who might have been ignorant of facts that would lead to discovery of their injuries. On the other hand, use of a maximum cutoff period, regardless of the state of knowledge of the claimant, offers at least some repose to medical practitioners and helps to prevent the prosecution of stale claims. The problem with some hybrid statutes is that the maximum cutoff limitation may be unrealistically short because the effect of many injuries may be delayed, sometimes for many years.

iii. Nature of the Discovery Rule. Once it is determined that one of the rules employing discovery principles applies, the obvious next question is "discovery of what?" Many courts and statutes have spoken in terms of when the plaintiff discovered or (under most formulations) should have discovered the "injury." There have been at least three interpretations of the term "injury" for the purpose of the discovery rule. The most restrictive view equates injury with the harmful manifestations suffered by the patient. Under a second view, the limitations period would begin to run when plaintiff discovers or should have discovered both the harm and how it was caused. *See* DeMartino v. Albert Einstein Med. Ctr., N.D., 313 Pa.Super. 492, 460 A.2d 295 (1983). Finally, in what probably represents the trend of recent decisions, some courts require that the plaintiff knew or should have known not only that he suffered harm and its cause, but that it was caused by the wrongful conduct of another. *See* Mastro v. Brodie, 682 P.2d 1162 (Colo.1984). Some would also require that the plaintiff have or should have discovered the tortfeasor's identity.

The *Mastro* approach can be justified on a number of grounds. Even if a patient is aware of the harm suffered, he usually lacks the background to realize a connection between the harm and the treatment in question. And even if he does, he may assume that it was an "unavoidable" result. Moreover, more restrictive approaches may force patients to file a lawsuit on the mere chance that there could have been malpractice in order to prevent the statute of limitations from expiring. Finally, more restrictive rules may tempt some providers to withhold or suppress information regarding the cause of the harm. *See* Foil v. Ballinger, 601 P.2d 144 (Utah 1979) (summarizing the preceding justifications).

Under the most common formulation of the discovery rule the question is whether the plaintiff discovered *or should have discovered* the requisite facts. Thus, even under the *Mastro* approach it should not necessarily be required in every case that the plaintiff be informed by counsel that there has been "malpractice" before the statutory period begins to run, if prior to that the plaintiff *should reasonably* have concluded that there was a substantial possibility of wrongful conduct. Moreover, the potential hardship to health care providers of a broad definition of injury may be mitigated by the maximum cutoff limitation (if constitutional) to the discovery rules found in the "hybrid" statutes in many jurisdictions. *See* VIII, A, 3, b, ii.

Another question arises when an injury and its potentially negligent cause are or should have been discovered, but the full extent of the injury does not reveal itself initially, and becomes apparent only over an extended period. It must be decided whether the statute commences to run at the time of the initial manifestations of a compensable injury, or only after the injury has substantially matured. Few malpractice cases have specifically addressed this question. The prevailing view seems to be that the full extent of the injury need not have become apparent for the running of the statute to begin. In Burns v. Hartford Hosp., 192 Conn. 451, 472 A.2d 1257 (1984), the patient suffered an infection allegedly as a result of a contaminated intravenous tube. The court held that the statutory period began to run when the infection (and its alleged cause) was or should have been discovered, despite the fact that effects of the infection on the patient's leg development were not manifested until later. The court noted that "[t]he harm need not have reached its fullest manifestation before the statute begins to run."

The problem of the evolving injury is a difficult one. A rule requiring maturation of harm in order to commence the running of the statute could significantly delay the running of the statute.

Conversely, a patient with an apparently trivial injury might be time-barred before the full extent of the injury was even suspected or capable of estimation. Perhaps the most satisfactory solution would be to commence the running of a statute based on discovery rules only after the injury became sufficiently ascertainable and substantial that a reasonable person would have been motivated to seek redress. Unfairness to defendants from too long a delay in the running of the statutory period might be avoided by adoption of a reasonable maximum cutoff beyond which the discovery rule, however defined, would cease to prevent the expiration of the statutory period.

c. *Continuing Involvement or Treatment Rules*

A number of courts and a few statutes have adopted a rule whereby the running of the statute of limitations is suspended during the pendency of certain types of continuing involvement between the physician and the patient. In some states, the continuing involvement rule defines the accrual date generally for malpractice actions. *See* Noland v. Freeman, 344 N.W.2d 419 (Minn.1984) (action accrues when physician's treatment of condition ceases). In some other states, it operates as an exception to some general rule defining the accrual date. *See* N.Y.Civ.Prac.Law § 214–a (McKinney's Supp.1984) (continuous treatment exception to a general wrongful conduct accrual date, with exceptions).

There have been a number of variations of the continuing involvement rules, where recognized. Some have required that there be continuing negligence by the physician in order to toll the running of the statute. In perhaps the prevailing view in jurisdictions recognizing the rule, others have held that continuing treatment for the same condition in question is sufficient. And finally, it has occasionally been suggested that the mere continuation of the professional relationship might be sufficient to toll the statute.

For a time it appeared that the discovery rules would largely obviate the need for the continuing involvement rules. The re-emergence of the wrongful conduct rule in the form of a maximum cutoff limitation on the discovery rule embodied in the hybrid statutes may rekindle interest in the continuing involvement rules.

An important question is whether the statute should commence to run when otherwise suspended under a continuing involvement rule when the plaintiff has or reasonably should have discovered the "injury." Although there is little law on point, most courts would probably hold that actual discovery of the "injury" would begin the running of the statutory period notwithstanding continuing involvement. The courts are somewhat more divided on whether the statute should begin when the plaintiff merely *should have* discovered the injury. Perhaps when the plaintiff has something less than actual knowledge of the injury (and its wrong-

ful cause) an otherwise applicable continuing involvement rule should continue to suspend the
running of the statute. That would be more in
keeping with the policy of encouraging patient
trust in his physician. At the same time, the
physician's continuing involvement would reduce
the risk of prejudice from a "stale" claim. In any
event, an ill patient should seldom be found to
have failed to exercise due care by not discovering
his injury when he has simply placed faith in his
physician.

Continuing negligence may also have a dimension independent of any continuing involvement
rule (or any rule suspending the running of the
statutory period). If a defendant engaged in additional negligent conduct, such later acts or specific
omissions might be actionable in their own right to
the extent they cause additional harm. Thus, if
some continuing involvement rule does not prevent
the running of the statute from the outset as to the
entire harm, one might argue in the alternative
that at least the plaintiff should be able to recover
for the harm caused by later negligence that is not
yet barred.*

* Assume that a physician repeatedly examines a patient
with symptoms of tuberculosis over a period of years, but
negligently fails to order appropriate tests. A continuing involvement rule or a discovery rule, unless precluded by a
maximum cut-off provision, might suspend the running of the
statute from the first malpractice. But even if they did not, the
plaintiff might nevertheless contend that he should still be
permitted to sue for any later acts or omissions that were not

4. Possible Exceptions to General Accrual Rules

Many jurisdictions, either by case law or by statute, have adopted a variety of exceptions that may suspend the running of the statute under the general limitations rules. A common exception occurs when the defendant has fraudulently concealed the injury from the plaintiff. The weight of authority seems to require actual knowledge of the injury and its cause by the defendant-physician to sustain a fraudulent concealment claim. *See* Johnson v. Gamwell, 165 Ga.App. 425, 301 S.E.2d 492 (1983). *But see* Mont.Code Ann. § 27–2–205 (Supp. 1983) (duty to disclose act, error, or omission which defendant knew or *through reasonable diligence would have known).* The rule requiring actual knowledge appears to be the better-reasoned approach. Failure by the physician to discover the nature and source of plaintiff's condition may be negligent, but it is hardly fraudulent.

A second question is whether affirmative acts of mispresentation or concealment are required, or whether conscious nondisclosure is sufficient. While some cases have required more than mere

yet barred under the general accrual rules, and at least to recover for the harm attributable to that later conduct.

* A few courts have also recognized a related "estoppel" rule. A physician may be estopped from relying on the statute of limitations when the plaintiff reasonably relies on the representations of the defendant in forbearing suit even when those representations are unintentional and without knowledge of the mistake. *See* Witherell v. Weimer, 85 Ill.2d 146, 52 Ill.Dec. 6, 421 N.E.2d 869 (1981).

nondisclosure, a number of recent cases have recognized an affirmative duty *to disclose. See* Borderlon v. Peck, 661 S.W.2d 907 (Tex.1983).

It is stated in some cases and statutes that fraudulent concealment rules cease to operate once the plaintiff has discovered or should have discovered the "injury" (however defined). *See* Borderlon, *supra.* This rule is sensible when plaintiff has actually discovered his injury since at that moment the concealment ceases to have any effect. When, however, a defendant had knowledge of the plaintiff's injury and failed to disclose it to the plaintiff, or worse, actively misled the plaintiff, a good argument can be made that the mere fact that the plaintiff *should have* discovered his wrongful injury should not nullify the fraudulent concealment rule. The intentional fault of the defendant in deliberately concealing the injury clearly outweighs any lack of diligence on the part of the plaintiff in failing to discover it.

Some statements of the rule refer to the defendant's concealment of the "injury," without defining the term. Others speak of the "act, error, or omission." A good argument can be made that a defendant should be required to disclose only the nature of the injury and its cause, but that he should not be required to characterize his conduct as negligent or speculate about legal liability since such matters often are not resolved until trial. Moreover, the plaintiff will often be protected to some extent by a broader definition of injury under the various discovery rules (*see* VIII, A, 3, b, iii) even if application of the fraudulent concealment rule is to some extent limited by a narrower definition of injury for the purposes of determining what the defendant must disclose to avoid the fraudulent concealment rule.

A number of states have adopted a special exception for situations in which a foreign object has been left inside a patient. Typically these rules create an exception to a general wrongful conduct accrual date or to the wrongful conduct maximum cutoff period under a hybrid statute. Once the patient discovers or, under most views, should have discovered the foreign object, a specified period begins to run.

A number of other rules suspending to varying degrees the running of the statute have been recognized in some jurisdictions. For example, a number of provisions suspend the running of the limitations period, usually until the disability is removed, when the plaintiff is a minor, or sometimes of unsound mind or an inmate at a correctional institution at the time the cause of action accrues.* In addition, some states have provisions tolling the statute under some circumstances while the defendant is outside the jurisdiction, at least if he is not subject to service of process. A few states may also suspend the running of the statute, at

---

* Some states have modified those rules by placing a limit on the length of time that minority alone, for example, may suspend the statute.

least for a time and for some purposes, for a claim asserted as a counterclaim in an action commenced under certain circumstances by another.

The foregoing rules may apply to medical malpractice actions unless the statute of limitations governing malpractice is construed to exclude malpractice actions from the reach of such rules or provisions.

The running of the statute is also typically suspended for a time in those jurisdictions with the type of review board procedure that specifically requires that a claim be submitted to the board *prior to* the institution of the action.

5.   Reform of Statutes of Limitations

Limitations of actions for malpractice claims have become overburdened with complex rules and exceptions.   This has introduced considerable uncertainty into an area of the law designed expressly to alleviate uncertainty.   Specific statutory definitions of "accrual date," "discovery," "injury," "fraudulent concealment," and other concepts are needed in many jurisdictions.   Questions of the applicability of general limitations provisions and doctrines to medical malpractice cases should also be clarified.   Detailed and comprehensive legislation would appear to be the most suitable means of addressing these shortcomings.

The hybrid statutes, with their combination of a discovery rule subject to a maximum cutoff running from the date of the wrongful conduct, represent a step in the right direction. A finite cutoff is probably necessary at some point regardless of the state of the patient's knowledge if the policy considerations underlying the statutes of limitations are to be vindicated. But such a cutoff should be long enough (I would suggest at least seven years) to allow a reasonable opportunity for the injury (including its wrongful cause) to manifest itself and be discovered. Further, the cutoff period should not apply to cases of fraudulent concealment.

B. DEFENSES BASED ON PLAINTIFF'S CONDUCT

A person may be barred from recovering for negligence when his own carelessness ("contributory negligence") proximately contributes to his injury. The alternate doctrine of "comparative negligence," adopted to varying degrees by many states, would reduce plaintiff's damages to reflect the comparative negligence of the parties rather than bar the action completely. An action may also be barred when the plaintiff voluntarily encounters or "assumes" the risk of another's negligence, or perhaps damages reduced for at least some types of assumption of risk under some comparative negligence approaches.

In order for contributory negligence and related doctrines to be relevant, both the defendant's and the plaintiff's negligence must have been causes in fact and proximate causes of the harm.

Generally a competent adult may be contributorily negligent when his conduct falls short of that degree of care that society expects a reasonable person to exercise for his own safety. For the standard applicable to children and mentally-impaired, see Prosser at 178–82.

There are a number of possible limitations on these defenses in the malpractice setting. First, some courts have held that the doctrine does not apply when the patient's negligence contributed only to the injury necessitating the medical intervention, such as a fall, but in no way contributed to the failure of treatment, such as the alleged failure to diagnose a fracture.* Second, since the patient is expected to place trust in his physician, he will rarely be charged with contributory negligence for a failure to question his physician's judgment. Third, some courts have held that the patient's conduct must be evaluated in terms of a reasonable person suffering from the same physical and mental conditions as the plaintiff. *See* Weinstock v. Ott, 444 N.E.2d 1227 (Ind.App.1983). Accordingly, a patient is required to exercise that degree of care expected of a reasonable person *under similar circumstances,* and the effects of disease, injuries,

* *See* Overstreet v. Nickelsen, 170 Ga.App. 539, 317 S.E.2d 583 (1984). The court did not explain its reasoning. The result could be explained under an application of the last clear chance principle under which contributory negligence may not apply when the defendant had a later opportunity to prevent the harm. *See* Restatement § 479.

disabilities, anesthesia, and medication should all be considered as relevant circumstances.

Circumstances in which contributory negligence is most frequently asserted involve conduct taken against medical advice, such as the patient's leaving the hospital, failing to return for follow-up, or failing to follow other medical instructions. A patient may also be negligent in providing his medical history to the physician, although the courts are unclear to what extent the patient must reasonably do more than respond to the physician's questions. *Compare* Fall v. White, 449 N.E.2d 628 (Ind.App.1983), *with,* Hynes v. Hoffman, 164 Ga. App. 236, 296 S.E.2d 216 (1982).

In some situations, the defendant may have negligently contributed to or failed to prevent suicide or other self-inflicted harm by the patient. Courts seem to have focused primarily on whether the defendant was negligent and, to a lesser extent, whether the defendant's conduct constituted a superseding cause (thus precluding defendant's conduct from being a "proximate" cause). *See* V, C, 2, e. Although it is conceivable that contributory negligence or assumption of risk could apply in such cases, most courts would probably take the patient's mental condition into account in deciding his reasonableness, and as a result such defenses would seldom operate to deny recovery. *See generally* Prosser, at 1075.

When the patient's negligence contributes to the *gravity* of the resulting harm rather than to the *occurrence* of the malpractice-induced injury, the action is not barred, but under the doctrine of "avoidable consequences," plaintiff's damages may be appropriately reduced. *See* Quinones v. Public Adm'r of County of Kings, 49 A.D.2d 889, 373 N.Y.S.2d 224 (1975). The defendant has the burden of proving that plaintiff unreasonably failed to mitigate damages. When it is argued that plaintiff had a duty to undergo further treatment to mitigate damages from the malpractice, factors to be considered in evaluating his reasonableness include the risks, probability of success, costs, inconvenience, and pain anticipated in the proposed therapy. Hansen v. Bussman, 274 Or. 757, 549 P.2d 1265 (1976).

C. RELEASES AND RELATED MATTERS

1. In General

A patient may settle a claim with a physician and release the physician from liability to him in connection with the injury in question. Such releases generally present no serious problems. However, the use of releases has raised serious questions in several other types of situations in the malpractice setting. These are discussed in the subsections that follow.

2. Releases of Other Tortfeasors

The conduct of another tortfeasor may be a contributing cause of the same harm that was also caused by the health care provider. Sometimes the tortious conduct operates concurrently, as when two physicians both misdiagnose a patient's condition. In another possible scenario, a prior tortfeasor may cause an initial injury requiring medical attention which in turn produces further harm. The first tortfeasor would ordinarily be liable not only for the immediate injuries he causes but also for the harm caused by the foreseeable negligence of the physician. These situations raise the question whether the release of the claim against the other tortfeasor will operate to release from liability to the victim a physician whose negligence was also a contributing cause of all or some of the plaintiff's harm.

The courts have been divided on the question whether a release of one joint tortfeasor releases the others. The traditional view had been that a release of one joint tortfeasor normally released the other. Some courts recognized an exception to this rule when a "covenant not to sue" rather than a release was used. Under the modern trend, many statutes now provide that the release of one joint tortfeasor does not release the others unless its terms so provide.* *See* Uniform Contribution Among Tortfeasors Act, § 4, 12 U.L.A. 98 (1975); Restatement § 885. A somewhat similar rule has been followed by some courts, holding that the release of one joint tortfeasor is presumed not to

* Some courts otherwise following the modern rule have refused to apply it where one person is released and the liability of the other is solely vicarious based on his relationship to the person released.

release the other in the absence of evidence to the contrary. *See* McCullough v. Bethany Med. Ctr., 235 Kan. 732, 683 P.2d 1258 (1984).

Historically, the courts have also been divided on the question of the effect of a release of a prior tortfeasor on the liability of a physician who negligently treats the original injury and causes part of the total harm suffered. *See* Annot., 39 A.L.R.3d 260 (1971; Supp.1985). The sensible trend of the cases has been to hold that the release of the original tortfeasor does not without more release a physician who later treats the victim. Some courts recognized a presumption, rebuttable by express language in the release evidencing an intent to release the physician, that a general release of the original tortfeasor does not release a malpractice claim against a physician.

Regardless of what rule is adopted concerning the effect of a release, if the plaintiff has received full compensation for his entire harm (including any additional harm caused by the physician while treating the original injury), he may not receive further redress from the physician. Moreover, damages recovered from another tortfeasor may reduce the liability of the physician to the extent that recovery is sought for the same injury that was redressed in the prior action. However, when the negligence of two or more physicians or providers were causes of the same harm, they might be subject to claims *inter se* for contribution. Although courts have sometimes been unwilling to regard the one causing an initial injury and the physician who subsequently treated the injury as joint tortfeasors so as to allow contribution, some cases have allowed the original tortfeasor to seek indemnity against a physician for aggravation of the original injury or infliction of additional harm. *See* Annot., 8 A.L.R.3d 639 (1966; Supp.1984).

3. Exculpatory Releases Prior to Injury

Occasionally physicians and hospitals have, prior to the infliction of an injury, entered into an exculpatory agreement with the patient purporting to release the physician or hospital from liability for future negligently-inflicted injuries. Courts usually hold such agreements invalid as against public policy. *See* Olsen v. Molzen, 558 S.W.2d 429 (Tenn. 1977). *See also* Ill.Ann.Stat. ch. 111, 4478 (Smith-Hurd Supp.1985). *But cf.* Shorter v. Drury, 103 Wn.2d 645, 695 P.2d 116 (1985) (while neither the pre- nor post-operative refusal to accept transfusions nor a release for consequences of such refusal released the physician for alleged surgical negligence, they did reduce some damages in connection with harm avoidable with transfusions).

In *Olsen,* the court noted characteristics of such an agreement: (1) it concerns a business suitable for public regulation; (2) the service is of great importance; (3) the defendant generally holds himself out as willing to perform services for any member of the public who seeks them; (4) as a result of the essential nature of the services, the defendant possesses a decisive advantage in bargaining power; (5) defendant employs a standard-ized contract with no provision for obtaining pro-tection against negligence; and, (6) the plaintiff is, as a result of the transaction, subjected to the risk of defendant's negligence. The court held that an agreement need only fulfill some of these charac-teristics to be invalid.

4. Arbitration Agreements

Sometimes the patient and health care provider have agreed to submit malpractice disputes to binding arbitration instead of to the traditional judicial process. There is a great deal of diversity among the states with respect to agreements to arbitrate. Some states have no statutes governing arbitration. Others have general arbitration stat-utes. And still others have statutes specifically designed for agreements to submit medical mal-practice controversies to arbitration.

The validity of arbitration agreements has been challenged, with varying degrees of success, on constitutional and public policy grounds, and un-der the terms of the legislation, if any, authorizing arbitration. Questions involving construction of the statute and agreement include whether such agreements may cover future medical services, whether they are subject to revocation and under what circumstances, and whether they may be binding on non-patients, such as next of kin.

D. POSSIBLE IMMUNITIES

1. In General

There are a number of rules that may render some defendants immune from tort liability under certain circumstances. Some *individual* defendants who are governmental employees may be entitled to claim official immunity. Some *institutional* defendants, such as hospitals, may be entitled to either governmental immunity if operated by a governmental entity or charitable immunity if run by a charitable organization.

2. Official and Statutory Immunity of Individuals

Governmental employees or those serving in an official capacity may be afforded varying degrees of official immunity. Such immunity may be expressly created by statute or may be of common law origin. Usually a person must have been acting within the scope of his employment before he may invoke official immunity. It is sometimes also required, especially for non-statutory immunities, that the employee have been engaged in a discretionary function. There may also be a number of additional prerequisites in some situations.

Some statutes confer immunity on employees generally of a governmental entity for many torts, sometimes by making claims against the government the exclusive remedy for such torts. Other statutes confer special immunity on certain classes of employees. For example, statutes grant immunity or other protection to certain medical personnel of the federal government (including military) for many tort claims in connection with medical services by making an action against the federal government the exclusive remedy* for some claims or by authorizing insurance or other protection through hold harmless arrangements for other claims. *See* 1 L. Jayson, *Handling Fed.Tort Claims* § 175.04 (1985).**

Official immunity is sometimes absolute and is sometimes qualified, in the latter case meaning that it is subject to loss under certain circumstances.***

---

* Claims by certain classes of plaintiffs against the federal government may sometimes be precluded. *See* VIII, D, 3.

** Even independent of such statutes, cases have often held military medical personnel acting within the scope of their employment immune from claims by other military personnel for tortious injuries at least when incident to their service. *See* 1 L. Jayson, *supra,* § 155.02, n. 10. Moreover, statutes provide that torts settlement with or judgment against the federal government releases the employee whose conduct gave rise to the claim. *See id.* §§ 229.01; 310.

*** A number of grounds have sometimes been held to destroy a qualified immunity. These have included "malice," bad faith, or improper purpose, or in some circumstances, unreasonableness. In the case of violations of constitutional or statutory rights, a qualified immunity may be lost if a reasonable person would have recognized that such rights would be violated. *See* Prosser, at 1059–60.

3. Institutional Immunities

a. *Governmental Immunity*

The concept of governmental immunity holds essentially that the government cannot be sued without its consent. It finds its roots in the common law, to a limited extent in the Eleventh Amendment, and in some state statutes and constitutional provisions. Governmental immunity seems to have been based on a premise that the sovereign can do no wrong. In truth, the immunity was probably inspired by a fear that civil liability might unduly drain the public coffers and perhaps inhibit the vigorous exercise of governmental functions. There is also a concern that abrogation of governmental immunity might vest too much control in the judiciary over the allocation of governmental resources—typically a legislative function—thereby subverting the separation of powers.

Because of the sheer number of government-affiliated medical institutions at the national, state, and local levels, and health care providers employed by some governments, the question of governmental immunity plays an important role in many malpractice actions. As a result of the particularized manner in which various federal, state, and local governmental entities have dealt with the question, it is difficult to generalize about the current state of the law.

The federal government adopted the Federal Torts Claims Act in 1946, waiving its immunity

subject to a number of exceptions.*   Many federal
employees and members of the armed services are
often, however, precluded from suing the federal
government in tort for employment and service
connected injuries. *See* 1 L. Jayson, *Handling Fed.
Torts Claims* §§ 153–155 (1985). This has reduced
the frequency of medical malpractice claims
against the federal government.**   Military and
federal employees may, however, be entitled to
various administrative benefits.

The immunity of state-run hospitals is undergoing a process of gradual erosion. In some states,
the courts have abrogated the state's immunity.
Abrogation of that immunity has frequently been
in the form of legislation. Typically, such legislative abrogation has often been subject to a variety
of procedural requirements and limitations on recovery, with immunity expressly preserved except
as specifically abrogated.

The immunity of hospitals operated by local governmental entities has probably undergone the
most rapid erosion. There has been a trend for
legislatures to enact a comprehensive scheme that
details the extent of liability and then reaffirms or
reinstates the immunity except as so abrogated.

* *See generally* 1–3 L. Jayson, *supra.*

** The availability of malpractice claims by civilian employees against the federal government for employment-connected
injuries may depend on whether the court adopts the "dual
capacity" doctrine. *See id.* §§ 153–154; VIII, E, *infra.*

When governmental immunity has been abandoned, such abandonment to varying degrees often takes one or more of the following forms: by an outright acceptance of liability subject to specific limitations or exceptions; by adoption of a "governmental-proprietary" distinction, waiving immunity for the latter; by imposing liability to the extent of liability insurance coverage; by distinguishing between gratuitous and billed services; by waiving immunity for specified theories of liability; and, by waiving immunity for only certain levels of government. *See generally* IIA Hospital Law Manual, *Immunities From Liability*, ¶¶ 1–8 to 1–13 (Aspen Sys.Corp.1983).

b. Charitable Immunity

The doctrine of charitable immunity, to the extent still recognized, may relieve charitable institutions, including charitable hospitals, from liability. The doctrine has a common law origin for the most part. Its defenders argue that charities are committed to a public service that should not be undermined by the threat of liability, that donors might be discouraged if their contributions were subject to torts claims, and that recipients of charitable largess should not have standing to complain of incidental injuries. The answer to these arguments is a simple one. Is it not consistent with charitable objectives to redress negligently-inflicted injuries? And are not beneficiaries of gratuitous services most in need of monetary redress for devasting personal injuries? As one court remarked, "[a] charitable institution should be just before being charitable or generous." Nicholson v. Good Samaritan Hosp., 145 Fla. 360, 199 So. 344, 348 (1940).

The doctrine of charitable immunity is clearly on the decline with a decided majority of jurisdictions rejecting it outright. Even where the doctrine is retained, it is often riddled with exceptions that allow, for example, a claimant to proceed against non-trust assets or when there is insurance coverage.

E. OTHER POTENTIAL LIMITATIONS ON LIABILITY

A number of more specific rules derived from both statutory and case law may also limit a physician's liability. Most states have enacted so-called "Good Samaritan" statutes that operate to limit a physician's liability for medical care rendered at an emergency. The language of such statutes varies widely. Their applicability is commonly subject to one or more qualifications. Some statutes protect ordinary negligence and may not apply in cases of more aggravated conduct. Immunity is usually limited to medical services rendered at the scene of an accident or emergency and usually does not extend to emergency services at a hospital or physician's office. A minority of statutes expressly cover emergency care at a hospital or are construed to do so, at least when the physician in question was not specifically assigned to emergency cases nor an attending physician. Some statutes require that the services be gratuitous. Moreover, the physician must generally have acted in good faith. Some statutes also apply to other individuals, such as nurses, who render aid at an emergency.

A physician's liability may be affected in some circumstances by workers' compensation acts. In many states workers' compensation is not only the exclusive remedy for covered employees against employers for most work-related injuries, but also protects co-employees acting within the course of their employment from some types of tort liability for many work-related harms suffered by other co-employees. A physician-employee might accordingly be protected from a malpractice claim by a co-employee if the harm he causes to a co-employee occurs in the course of employment, is subject to the compensation statute, and the jurisdiction applies the exclusive remedy rule to physician-employees under the circumstances involved. *See generally* 2 Larson, *Workmen's Comp.* §§ 72.20, 72.60 (Desk ed. 1984). An employer-physician or hospital employer or other employer may also be protected from malpractice actions brought by their employees when the injury was covered by workers' compensation, unless the court disregards the employer status because of the "dual capacity" of the employer. *See generally id.* §§ 65–69, 72.63, 72.80. Statutes generally allow a malpractice action against a defendant who is not a protected co-employee or protected employer of the plaintiff for negligently contributing to an injury covered by workers' compensation, and most do not require an election of one remedy.

CHAPTER IX

HOSPITAL LIABILITY

A. IN GENERAL

Many of the legal concepts governing the liability of individual physicians are applicable to hospitals as well. *See* Shilkret v. Annapolis Emergency Hosp. Ass'n, 276 Md. 187, 349 A.2d 245 (1975). When the law relating to hospital liability has played a dominant role in the law of malpractice generally, as in the "duty-to-treat" materials (*see* II, B) and governmental and institutional immunities, an effort has been made to integrate relevant hospital authorities into other sections of this book. *See also* VII, B, 2. The present chapter highlights some other aspects of malpractice law that are particularly germane to hospital liability.

As a general rule, except perhaps in some situations involving defective devices or substances (*see* VII, B, 2), a hospital is not subject to strict liability. Neither it nor its employees or agents impliedly guarantee the health or safety of its patients. Rather, a hospital is required to exercise reasonable care in accordance with sound hospital practice to protect the health and safety of its patients. Since a hospital is merely the sum of numerous individuals participating in a common enterprise, it is not surprising that the primary source of hospital liability is vicarious, arising from the individual actions of specific hospital employees who injure a patient. *See* IX, B. There has also been a trend in recent years to impose so-called "corporate liability" on the hospital for acts or omissions of its employees, administrators, and staff acting collectively on behalf of the corporation. *See* IX, C.

B. VICARIOUS LIABILITY

1. For Torts of Physicians

A hospital is generally not *vicariously* liable for the negligence of non-employee physicians who merely exercise hospital or so-called "staff privileges."* *See* Cooper v. Curry, 92 N.M. 417, 589 P.2d 201 (1978). It may under certain circumstances be *directly* liable under corporate negligence principles for harm caused by such physicians. *See* IX, C, 1 & 2, d & e. When, however, there is a direct economic relationship between the hospital and physician, vicarious liability becomes a much more credible prospect. Some decisions, especially older ones, refused to find a master-

* The fact that a physician exercises so-called "staff privileges" or is a member of the hospital staff does not necessarily mean that he is an "employee" of the hospital. In fact, most physicians holding staff privileges are not employed by the hospital. Rather, they are entitled to use hospital facilities for their patients and may work with the governing board and administrators of the hospital in setting and implementing certain policies. Thus, in most hospitals there are two classes of physician staff members—those merely holding staff privileges and those who are actual employees of the hospital. Interns and residents are among the more common examples of the latter.

servant relationship even in such cases, concluding that the physician was an independent contractor. However, more recent decisions have accepted the idea of vicarious liability of a hospital for injuries caused by a physician when a master-servant relationship, typically an actual employment relationship, existed between the hospital and physician. *See* Johnson v. St. Bernard Hosp., 79 Ill.App.3d 709, 35 Ill.Dec. 364, 399 N.E.2d 198 (1979); Suhor v. Medina, 421 So.2d 271 (La.App.1982). Thus, for example, when a physician is a regular salaried employee of the hospital, such as a resident pursuing advanced study in a specialty, or a paid director of a hospital clinic, the trend is to hold that the hospital may be vicariously liable for the injuries caused by the physician while acting within the scope of his employment.* The requisite "control" over such physician-employees would largely be implied from the existence of a formal employment relationship.

In some situations the physician shares an economic relationship with the hospital but cannot

---

* A few courts have permitted physicians to become "borrowed servants" of other physicians whom they are assisting, although the trend is not to apply the borrowed servant status to assisting physicians. *See* VI, E, 4. When a physician-employee (such as an intern or resident) of a hospital does become a borrowed servant of another physician, some cases might hold that the hospital ceases to be vicariously liable for his actions. Recent decisions, however, have shown a tendency to continue to hold hospital-employers liable in borrowed servant situations even when the borrowing physician is also held vicariously liable. *See* VI, E, 5.

fairly be characterized as a salaried employee. These cases typically involve physicians who have agreed to provide support services to the hospital through radiology, pathology, anesthesiology, emergency room, or other departments. In some of these situations, such physicians may bill the patient directly. In others, the patient pays the hospital, which in turn pays the physician (or professional corporation in which the physician is a shareholder or employee). The courts are divided on the question of whether such physicians are independent contractors (for whose conduct the hospital would not be vicariously liable) or servants (for whom the hospital might be held vicariously liable). Some courts, apparently impressed by the relative independence of the physician to exercise professional judgment and by the contractual arrangements that seem to place the physician in the role of an independent contractor, have refused to hold the hospital vicariously liable. *See* Pogue v. Hosp. Auth. of DeKalb County, 120 Ga. App. 230, 170 S.E.2d 53 (1969) (emergency room services); Dickinson v. Mailliard, 175 N.W.2d 588 (Iowa, 1970) (X-ray services).

There have, however, been an increasing number of cases that have recognized that physicians providing support services, especially emergency room services, to patients coming to the hospital may be found to be employees of the hospital. *See* Willoughby v. Kenneth W. Wilkins, M.D.P.A., 65 N.C. App. 626, 310 S.E.2d 90 (1983); Smith v. St. Francis Hosp., Inc., 676 P.2d 279 (Okl.App.1983). In *Smith,* the court emphasized that emergency room physicians had to meet the hospital's quality control standards; that the hospital billed the patients; that support staff, facilities, and supplies were provided by the hospital at no cost to emergency room physicians; and that physicians' fees were based on rates set by the hospital. Other courts have emphasized that their designation as "independent contractors" in the contract with the hospital was not necessarily conclusive. *See Willoughby, supra.*

Hospitals have also sometimes been held vicariously liable for the conduct of physicians under an "ostensible agency" analysis irrespective of whether the hospital-physician relationship would otherwise support vicarious liability. *See* Paintsville Hosp. Co. v. Rose, 683 S.W.2d 255 (Ky.1985); Restatement (Second) of Agency § 269 (1958). The ostensible agency rule holds that when a hospital causes a patient to justifiably assume that a physician is a hospital employee, the hospital may be vicariously liable for the physician's conduct. The court in *Rose* noted that an express representation of an employment relationship was not required, but could be implied from the circumstances. The court also suggested that the doctrine was unavailable if the patient (or his surrogate) knew or reasonably should have known that the treating physician was not a hospital employee.

It is occasionally suggested that a hospital might have a sufficiently close non-economic relationship with a physician who was not an employee* that it could be subject to vicarious liability without invoking the ostensible agency rule. Some physicians provide gratuitous services, such as assisting in the training of interns and residents employed by the hospital. Here the control by the hospital over the conduct of such physicians engaged in training new doctors may be more significant, the incentive for quality control measures more necessary, and the justification for holding the hospital vicariously liable for the supervising physician perhaps more defensible.

2. For Non-Physicians

A hospital will often be vicariously liable for the wrongful conduct of nurses and other medical personnel who are employees of the hospital. A potential exception to this rule may occur when a hospital employee assisting a physician in the treatment of the patient is found to be a "borrowed servant." Until recently, it was usually assumed that if a person were the borrowed servant of the

* In one case, the court held that a jury question was presented whether a non-salaried psychiatrist serving as chairman of the department of psychiatry of a psychiatric hospital was a hospital employee. *See* Simmons v. St. Clair Mem. Hosp., 332 Pa.Super. 444, 481 A.2d 870 (1984). The psychiatrist's responsibilities allegedly included the physical facilities in the unit and problems that developed with patient care. The court did concede, however, that the evidence of a sufficient relationship on which to base vicarious liability was "tenuous."

physician, the hospital was thereby relieved of vicarious liability. However, a number of recent decisions have rejected that view, holding that both the "borrowing" physician *and* the hospital may be held vicariously liable. *See* VI, E, 5.

C. CORPORATE RESPONSIBILITY FOR PATIENT CARE

1. Corporate Liability in General

Hospitals historically contributed little more than bed and board in patient care. Any meaningful patient care came from the attending physician. Today circumstances have changed dramatically. The hospital not only provides food and lodging, but a host of support functions including skilled nursing care, specialized diagnostic and therapeutic procedures, pre- and post-operative care, and numerous other services. Hospitals are increasingly involved in overseeing the total health care of the patient. Not only does this raise the possibility of vicarious liability for the tortious conduct of hospital servants individually, but also the possibility of what has come to be known as "corporate liability."

Obviously, a corporate entity can act only through the individuals that comprise the corporate amalgam. Even in cases of so-called "corporate liability," at some point one or more individuals acting on behalf of the hospital entity must have committed a wrongful act or omission. Thus, corporate liability, stripped of its gloss, in reality

seems to be merely an expression of special applications of a number of traditional tort concepts.
In some situations, corporate liability may merely
be an application of vicarious liability in which a
number of employees, directors, or officers—perhaps some not even identified—were involved in an
act or omission or in formulating a policy that
caused injury.* Or, the injury may have been
caused by one or more hospital employees whose
specific identity is unknown but whose acts or
omissions were proven to be the hospital's responsibility. Thus, many cases decided on corporate
liability grounds could probably be rationalized in
terms of vicarious liability,** often in conjunction
with *res ipsa loquitur* and rules of circumstantial
evidence.

* Some courts have narrowly conceptualized corporate negligence to include only a failure of the officers or directors to
maintain the required standards, leaving situations involving
the personal negligence of ordinary employees to be addressed
under traditional vicarious liability. *See* Buckley v. Lovallo, 2
Conn.App. 579, 481 A.2d 1286 (1984). For the purpose of this
treatise, corporate liability is used in a broader sense to em-
brace all of the types of situations described in the accompanying text. As defined, it may to some extent overlap with
traditional vicarious liability theories.

** Thus, in Newhall v. Central Vt. Hosp., Inc., 133 Vt. 572,
349 A.2d 890 (1975), plaintiff suffered a fall after the "hospital"
failed to respond to her light. In upholding a jury verdict for
the plaintiff, the court suggested that a finding of negligence
might have rested on a failure to respond to the light in the
absence of an explanation of why no response was reasonably
possible. Individual hospital employees were never identified,
thus emphasizing the notion of collective failure that typifies
corporate liability.

In other situations, although the negligent acts may have been by non-employees, corporate liability may be based on a conclusion that such individuals were acting on behalf of the hospital and were performing essentially non-delegable duties, the negligent performance of which rendered the hospital liable. Thus, even though hospitals are not normally held vicariously liable for the individual professional negligence of non-employee physicians with staff privileges, to the extent that those non-employee professional staff members assumed responsibility for making decisions on behalf of the hospital that affect patient well-being, the hospital may be charged with corporate responsibility for their failures. Accordingly, while the hospital may not be *vicariously* liable for the negligence of a surgeon in performing an appendectomy, the hospital may be subject to *direct corporate liability* for its general failure through its governing board, employee and non-employee professional staff (including perhaps this surgeon), administrative personnel, and regular employees, to adopt and implement reasonable policies, for example, to prevent the spread of hospital-borne infections or to identify incompetent practitioners and suspend their staff privileges.

Except for a split of authority on the strict liability of hospitals for defective products (*see* VII, B, 2), the liability of hospitals for injuries suffered by patients in connection with medical care ordinarily requires a finding of fault. Most courts (and some statutes) seem to give professional standards of hospitals conclusive weight and require expert proof (or perhaps an acceptable substitute) to support a finding of negligence involving technical expertise. *See Buckley, supra.* A number of states apply national standards, whereas others continue to apply some version of locality rule. *See generally* II, C, 3, d. A few courts, however, have rejected the conclusiveness of professional standards of hospitals at least when based on custom. Since the standard of care for hospitals often encompasses routine matters comprehensible to laymen, the common knowledge doctrine probably has broader application in the hospital context than in the case of individual physicians. *See Newhall, supra.*

Five basic obligations have most commonly been relied upon, with varying degrees of success, to support a claim founded on the corporate liability of a hospital in connection with the delivery of medical services. These are discussed in the next subsection.

2. Nature of Corporate Responsibility

a. *Hospital Equipment, Supplies, Medication, and Food*

A hospital must take reasonable steps to provide adequate and safe equipment, supplies, medication, and food for its patients. Hospitals have historically not been held strictly liable under either torts or warranty theories for defects in hospital equipment, materials, or drugs used in connection with patient care, although there now appears to be a split of authority on the question, especially for some types of products. *See* VII, B, 2.

Apart from a few applications of strict liability for some defective products, a hospital is generally only required to exercise reasonable care to furnish safe equipment. That does not mean that every hospital must possess the latest models or types of equipment. The costs of such a requirement would be prohibitive and would not represent an optimal allocation of resources. Rather, a "hospital is required to furnish equipment which is reasonably suited for the purpose for which it is intended." Starnes v. Charlotte-Mecklenberg Hosp. Auth., 28 N.C.App. 418, 221 S.E.2d 733, 736 (1976). A hospital is also required to take appropriate measures to insure proper maintenance and selection of supplies. For example, in Revenis v. Detroit Gen. Hosp., 63 Mich.App. 79, 234 N.W.2d 411 (1975), a hospital was charged with negligence in the selection of an eye donor for a cornea transplant. The court held that a jury could find that the hospital was negligent in failing to establish a procedure whereby the individual responsible for determining the suitability of the cornea for transplant would have access to all relevant medical records of the proposed donor.

A hospital might also be held liable in negligence for injuries caused by the improper feeding of a patient. A patient may, for example, be fed an unsuitable diet or negligently prepared food, or may be fed too soon before or after a specific medical procedure, such as surgery. Most of the reported cases appear to have been decided on negligence grounds. *See* Annot., 42 A.L.R.3d 736 (1972). However, there is probably no good reason why strict liability (under either a tort or a warranty theory) should not also be available when the patient is provided *defective* food. The fact that the providing of food is often divorced from the purely medical services perhaps militates even more strongly in favor of strict liability. *See generally* VII, B, 2.

There are various statutes, such as food, drug and cosmetic acts, that may affect liability for defective food and products. Some of these statutes could conceivably be relevant to the liability of hospitals, though there does not appear to be much case law directly on point. *See generally* II, D, 2, D & f.

b. *Hospital Environment*

The hospital must exercise reasonable care to maintain safe premises. It must not only take reasonable steps (such as warnings, repairs, and safety measures, depending on the circumstances) to protect the patient from known dangers, but also inspect the premises in order to discover and appropriately deal with other risks. The unique infirmities of patients should be taken into account when evaluating the adequacy of the care exercised by the hospital.

c. Safety Procedures

The hospital must adopt and follow procedures that are reasonably calculated to protect its patients and others. Thus, appropriate steps must be taken to prevent the exposure of patients to contagious diseases. *See* Kapuschinsky v. United States, 248 F.Supp. 732 (D.S.C.1966). Likewise, suitable measures should be employed to prevent a patient or other person from being attacked or otherwise injured by another person (including another hospitalized patient), and to prevent the escape of institutionalized insane patients. *See* II, B, 6. Reasonable steps should also be taken to prevent unauthorized access to or disclosure of patient's medical records. Policies must be adopted and followed to assure that patients are reasonably cared for given their condition. Thus, monitoring of all patients should be adequate. A patient's signal for assistance should meet with a reasonable response. Appropriate physicians should be notified about relevant changes in the patient's condition.

A number of decisions have found that hospitals, even general hospitals, have a duty to exercise reasonable care to prevent a patient's suicide or self-inflicted injury. *See* Pisel v. Stamford Hosp., 180 Conn. 314, 430 A.2d 1 (1980) (patient in psychiatric unit of hospital). *See generally,* Annot., 36 A.L.R.4th 117 (1985). Thus, in No. Miami Gen. Hosp. v. Krakower, 393 So.2d 57 (Fla.App.1981), a hospital was held liable for allegedly failing to adequately implement the emergency room's "suicidal precautions" notation to prevent the patient from leaping from the fire escape. The most important factor in determining liability for alleged violations of such duties is "whether the hospital authorities in the circumstances could reasonably have anticipated that the patient might harm himself." Bornmann v. Great S.W. Gen. Hosp., Inc., 453 F.2d 616, 621 (5th Cir. 1971) (affirming verdicts for defendants on various grounds).* Issues of causation, proximate cause, and contributory negligence and related defenses may also be raised in such cases. V, C, 2, e; VIII, B.

d. Selection and Retention of Employees and Conferral of Staff Privileges

In addition to vicarious liability, a hospital may be held directly liable for a failure to exercise reasonable care in the selection and retention of employees. Due care by the hospital is also required in the conferral and continuation of staff privileges to physicians who may not be hospital employees. *See* Johnson v. Misericodia Com. Hosp., 99 Wis.2d 708, 301 N.W.2d 156 (Wis.1981) (conferral of staff privileges); Purcell v. Zimbelman, 18 Ariz.App. 75, 500 P.2d 335 (1972) (continuation of staff privileges).

---

* Some courts have stated the duty, at least with respect to general hospitals, in terms of the reasonable care that the patient's *known* condition requires. *See id.;* Johnson v. Grant Hosp., 32 Ohio St.2d 169, 291 N.E.2d 440, 61 Ohio Op.2d 413 (1972). The hospital's responsibilities should also extend to those conditions that it should reasonably be expected to discover.

By way of illustration, in *Johnson,* the alleged negligence of a physician with orthopedic surgery staff privileges at the defendant-hospital injured a patient's nerve and artery during surgery causing a permanent paralytic condition to the patient's thigh. There was evidence that had the hospital investigated the physician's background with due diligence, it would have discovered evidence that one hospital had revoked some of the physician's orthopedic privileges and required a consultation before any open surgical procedure two months before he applied for privileges at defendant hospital, that the physician was at least for a number of years neither board certified nor board eligible in orthopedics, that in 1973 some of his peers believed he was not qualified by training or demonstration as an orthopedic surgeon, and that seven malpractice claims had been filed against him. Thus, the court concluded that there was credible evidence that a hospital exercising ordinary care would not have granted orthopedic staff privileges to the physician.

When it is alleged that the hospital's employees, governing board, or administrators negligently fail to properly screen or evaluate physicians seeking or holding staff privileges, hospital liability could probably be supported on either a theory of vicarious liability or corporate liability. When members of the non-employee professional staff (physicians merely holding "staff privileges") who also participated in evaluating those seeking staff privileges were negligent in doing so, liability is usually based on corporate negligence principles. Such a result could perhaps also be explained in terms of more traditional concepts, reasoning that the hospital owed the patient a non-delegable duty and thus could be charged with the failure of even non-employees acting on its behalf in conferring staff privileges.* *See* Joiner v. Mitchell County Hosp. Auth., 125 Ga.App. 1, 186 S.E.2d 307 (1972). *See also* Restatement, Second, Agency § 251 (1958).

In order to prevail under a theory of negligent conferral or continuation of staff privileges, most courts would probably require that the plaintiff establish that the physician in question negligently caused the injury; that the injury was the result of his lack of competence to perform such medical procedures;** that the hospital (including its governing administrative personnel, employees, and non-employee professional staff acting on its behalf) failed to exercise reasonable care to discover such lack of competence; and, that had such an investigation been conducted, staff privileges would

---

* Some courts have also allowed the plaintiff to sue the non-employee professional medical staff itself in addition to the hospital for that staff's alleged negligence in connection with allowing the exercise of staff privileges in question. *See* Corleto v. Shore Mem. Hosp., 138 N.J.Super. 302, 350 A.2d 534 (1975).

** The *Johnson* case, *supra,* has clouded this point, making it unclear whether proof is required that the physician was in fact not competent to perform the procedure in question. *See* 301 N.W.2d at 171–72. It is difficult to imagine, however, how such an element could be omitted consistent with this theory of liability.

have been denied, revoked, or restricted so that the medical procedure would not have been performed by the physician. Expert testimony will usually be required to prove that the hospital was negligent under such circumstances. *See Johnson, supra,* (identifying certain "minimum" requirements that should be followed). The hospital would be charged with acquiring and evaluating the knowledge that would have been acquired had it exercised reasonable care in investigating its medical staff applicants.* In addition to any facts that should have been discovered by the hospital employees and its non-employee staff assisting in conferral of privileges, any actual knowledge of these individuals would usually be imputed to the hospitals. *See* Fridena v. Evans, 127 Ariz. 516, 622 P.2d 463 (1980).

So far the courts have been reluctant to extend the corporate liability of hospitals to cover harm caused by conduct of non-employee physicians holding staff privileges when such conduct occurred entirely outside the hospital. *See* Pedroza v. Bryant, 101 Wash.2d 226, 677 P.2d 166 (1984). Such conduct might, however, be relevant to the question of whether the hospital would be liable for

---

* The *Johnson* court at times used language suggesting that the hospital's decision would be based on facts that it knew or "had reason to know." However, the opinion taken as a whole seems to suggest a duty to conduct a *reasonable investigation* into the applicant's background, suggesting more of a test based on what the hospital reasonably *should have known.* On the difference between a "reason to know" and "should know" formulation see generally Restatement § 12.

allowing such physicians to exercise staff privileges on the hospital's premises.

e. *Responsibilities for Supervision of Patient Care*

One of the most difficult questions concerning a hospital's potential corporate liability is whether or to what extent the hospital (acting through its administration, employees, and non-employee professional staff) must supervise the care administered by non-employee physicians holding hospital staff privileges.

In the seminal case of Darling v. Charleston Community Mem. Hosp., 33 Ill.2d 326, 211 N.E.2d 253 (1965), a patient suffering from a broken leg was treated at the emergency room of the defendant hospital by the physician on call. A cast was applied and the patient was admitted to the hospital. Thereafter, notwithstanding allegedly obvious danger signals and the progressive worsening of the patient's circulation over the next two weeks, no doctors other than the attending physician were consulted until the leg had become gangrenous. Amputation was ultimately required. The Illinois Supreme Court held that the jury's verdict against the hospital was supportable on either of two grounds. First, the jury could have found that the hospital had negligently failed to have a sufficient number of trained nurses who were capable of recognizing and calling to staff attention a progressively worsening gangrenous condition. Second, the jury could have concluded that the hospital negligently failed to review the treatment rendered to the patient by the attending physician and to require appropriate consultation or examination by other physicians.*

Although this theory will often overlap with duties to exercise reasonable care to assure that staff privileges are conferred on competent physicians, the two theories are different. Whether a hospital acted reasonably in conferring or continuing staff privileges depends primarily on review of the physician's background prior to the allegedly negligent treatment of the patient. On the other hand, responsibilities for supervising the care of the patient will focus primarily on the current care and condition of the patient in question.

A number of decisions have endorsed the imposition of a duty on hospitals to supervise the quality of care administered by a patient's attending physician. *See* Poor Sisters of St. Francis v. Catron, 435 N.E.2d 305 (Ind.App.1982); Annot., 12 A.L.R.4th 57 (1982; Supp.1985).

* Some later decisions have narrowly construed *Darling,* sometimes assuming that the attending physician was a hospital employee. The opinion is unclear on this point. Other cases, however, have viewed *Darling* as endorsing a broad concept of hospital responsibility for overseeing the quality of care rendered to hospital patients by non-employee physicians. If the physician were a hospital employee, that would have provided a basis for simply holding the hospital vicariously liable for the attending physician. However, the thrust of the court's holding was apparently based on the *direct corporate liability* of the hospital based on its responsibilities for supervising the quality of care administered by those exercising staff privileges.

Once a duty to supervise the care rendered by attending physicians has been recognized, there remains the question of the nature of that duty. Most courts recognizing such a duty have suggested that the hospital would not be liable unless it (presumably through its administration, employees, and responsible non-employee staff) knew or "had reason to know" that its intervention was necessary to protect the health of the patient. *See* Tucson Med. Ctr., Inc. v. Misevch, 113 Ariz. 34, 545 P.2d 958 (1976). Although courts sometimes use the "reason to know" and "should know" language interchangeably, technically they have different meanings. "Reason to know" has been generally defined to mean that a person has information that would cause him to infer that the fact in question exists, or that he should govern his conduct as though it did. Restatement § 12 (1965). "Should know" means that one is under a general duty to exercise reasonable care to find out even if not put on notice. *Id.*

In the context of the hospital's duty to supervise the care administered by the attending physicians, the "reason to know" formulation, so defined, probably represents a sound rule. Such a formulation probably requires that before a hospital would have a duty to intervene, the appropriate personnel (administrative, employees, or non-employees staff physicians acting on behalf of the hospital) should at least have been aware of facts which should reasonably have led them to infer the existence of a danger to a patient at the hands of the attending physician. Thus, in Pickle v. Curns, 106 Ill.App.3d 734, 62 Ill.Dec. 79, 435 N.E.2d 877 (1982), plaintiff alleged that the hospital negligently allowed a physician to administer electroconvulsive therapy without first examining the patient or giving a muscle relaxant. In affirming dismissal of the action, the court of appeals relied on the absence of allegations that the hospital knew or had reason to know that the alleged malpractice would occur.* The court noted pointedly that it did not recognize a duty of hospitals "to insure that each of its [non-employees] staff physicians will always perform his duty of due care to his patient." 435 N.E.2d at 881.

Assuming that the hospital has reason to know that conduct by a non-employee physician poses an unreasonable risk of harm, complex issues remain about what the hospital should reasonably be expected to do to protect the patient. Obviously, it should, after informing the patient, seek the concurrence of the attending physician in corrective actions. If that proves impossible, the patient or, if he is not competent, his surrogate, should be informed of the danger and given the option of selecting a new physician. If the patient nevertheless insists on pursuing a dangerous course with his attending physician, consideration might be given to seeking judicial intervention.

* Although the court used both the "reason to know" and "should know" language, the opinion taken as a whole seems more consistent with the former.

CHAPTER X

CURRENT PERSPECTIVES AND FUTURE PROSPECTS

A. AN OVERVIEW OF RECENT STATUTORY CHANGES

About two decades ago the courts began to make far-reaching changes in the law of medical malpractice. These changes generally had the effect of expanding liability. The strict locality rules and the wrongful act accrual date for statutes of limitations were significantly modified or abandoned in many instances. The primacy of professional standards in defining the standard of care was occasionally challenged directly and was eroded indirectly by expansion of concepts such as the common knowledge doctrine. Theories such as informed consent evolved. These are but a few of the numerous changes in the law of malpractice.

A number of socio-economic developments also fostered an increase in malpractice claims.*

* They include: (1) the breakdown of physician-patient rapport; (2) the impersonalization of health care; (3) quantitative increases in the demand for and delivery of health care; (4) a negative public image of medical professionals; (5) an inadequate supply of medical personnel and resources; (6) the emerging consumerism among patients; (7) the growing litigiousness of society generally; (8) an increased public understanding of medical facts; (9) unrealistic public expectations regarding medical treatment; (10) the increasing complexity and extensive-

As a result of these changes in the legal and social environment the number and magnitude of malpractice claims mushroomed dramatically. In some jurisdictions the number of claims doubled within a few years. Verdicts exceeding a million dollars became common. Liability insurance rates skyrocketed. Some insurors stopped offering liability insurance, at least in some jurisdictions. And the epiphenomenon of "defensive medicine"* reared its head.

The preceding developments appeared, at least to some observers, to reach crisis proportions about ten years ago. This in turn inspired an unprecedented level of legislative activity. Some statutory provisions seemed to spring from a perception that the increase in malpractice claims was basically a problem calling for changes in the law calculated to reduce damages. Thus, some statutes provided for ceilings or limitations on damages, a decremental scale for contingent attorney's fees, limita-

ness of medical procedures and techniques; (11) a growing public reluctance to accept the inevitability of pain and death; and (12) a tendency to regard good health as a matter of right. *See* King, *In Search of a Standard Care for the Medical Profession: The "Accepted Practice" Formula,* 28 Vand.L.Rev. 1213, 1217 n. 11 (1975).

* The practice of defensive medicine is essentially the management of a patient's care not only with an eye for the patient's welfare, but also in an effort to preemptively fashion an unassailable record in anticipation of possible future malpractice litigation. Excessive diagnostic tests and X-rays, unnecessary surgery, and inordinate use of antibiotics are, to name a few, the expensive and potentially dangerous manifestations of defensive medicine. *See* King, *supra,* at 1216 n. 10.

tions with respect to *ad damnum* clauses in pleadings, and changes in the collateral source rule.

A second group of statutory provisions attempted to restrict liability. While many recent statutes of limitations have codified the discovery rule, they have often also incorporated a maximum cut-off period. The standard of care for negligent treatment and diagnosis and the standard of disclosure for informed consent cases have also been addressed by many statutes. They often adopt or reaffirm professional standards as well as requirements for expert testimony.

A third type of statutory provision has focused on the forum in which malpractice cases are heard. Some statutes have provided for the creation of review boards or screening panels to hear a case before the case is tried before the court. Some provide for hearings prior to commencement of the action while others provide for such hearings after the action has been commenced. The right to a *de novo* jury trial on the merits is usually preserved. The board's conclusions are admissible at trial in some states, but not conclusive. Thus, these provisions typically supplement but do not replace the traditional judicial trial. Other statutes have adopted provisions recognizing, subject to numerous qualifications, agreements to arbitrate malpractice disputes. The results of such arbitrations may, depending on the relevant statute and agreement, be binding on the parties.

A fourth group of statutory provisions have sought to help guarantee that liability insurance will be available at affordable rates by authorizing the creation of state-run or physician-owned companies.

Finally, the federal government has shown signs of becoming increasingly involved in the malpractice sphere. In addition to laws affecting the liability of the federal government and various employees (*see* VIII, D, 2, 3), some federal statutes and regulations may also affect the liability of private parties. *See* II, C, 3, e. In addition, there have been a number of proposals before Congress providing for fundamental changes in the law.

The preceding statutory developments have thus far not stemmed the flood of malpractice claims. Many of the statutory changes were simply ineffective. Moreover, some of the more effective provisions met with vigorous constitutional challenges that, with varying degrees of success, resulted in some of them being declared invalid.

Constitutional challenges have been based on provisions of both federal and state constitutions. The success of constitutional challenges has tended to vary not only from state to state but also according to the type of provision under attack. Generalization is difficult because of the variety of provisions involved and bases for constitutional challenge. Although questions of constitutionality are beyond the scope of this book, the following overview* may at least give a sense of recent trends.

Provisions dealing with the substantive elements and proof of malpractice have seldom been challenged. But when they have, the courts have been divided.

The courts have also been divided on the constitutionality of pre-trial review and screening provisions. Constitutional arguments have been based on the right to jury trial, equal protection, usurpation of judicial power, and access to the courts. A majority of courts addressing the question have upheld such provisions.

Although the courts are divided, a majority of provisions changing the statute of limitations dealing with medical malpractice in general have been upheld. Application of such provisions to minors has received a more mixed reception. Constitutional arguments have typically invoked rights based on equal protection, due process, and access to the courts.

Statutory provisions limiting damages have engendered the strongest constitutional challenges, although the courts here are also divided. The more indirect changes such as those involving the collateral source rule and attorney's fees have generally fared better than provisions that attempt to

* The following summary is derived in part from Professional Liability in the '80's, A.M.A. Special Task Force on Prof. Liability Ins. 1984–85 (Report 2, Nov. 1984) (hereinafter cited as Professional Liability Report).

limit total damages or place restrictions on certain types of damages such as non-economic losses. Even with respect to the latter provisions, the courts have been divided.

Constitutional and statutory construction questions have also arisen in connection with whether or to what extent various statutory reforms, especially statutes of limitations, should or constitutionally could be given retroactive effect.

In general, the most common constitutional challenge has been based on an equal protection argument. Essentially, the courts have been asked to decide whether special restrictions and limitations on malpractice claims can be justified as bearing a reasonable relationship to valid state interests served by the legislative reforms. These interests have included reducing the enormous costs of malpractice claims and assuring the availability of liability insurance.

B. NEED FOR LAW REFORM

The total claims against insured physicians alone for 1983 may exceed 32,000, as compared with about 14,000 during the height of the so-called crisis during a 12 month period in 1975–76. Professional Liability Report No. 1, at 10. According to reports from physician-owned insurance companies, there was an annual claims frequency of approximately 12–14 claims per 100 insureds in 1979, but claims frequency increased to 20–25 claims per 100 physicians annually four years later. *Id.* at 13–14. The average paid loss by physician owned companies showed a 254% increase from 1979–83. *Id.* at 17.

The costs of the unabated explosion in malpractice claims are difficult to quantify. Malpractice insurance premiums alone were estimated at $1.75 billion in 1983. *Id.* at 14. Defensive medicine adds an estimated $15 billion dollars annually to the costs of health care. *Id.* at 16. The threat of malpractice claims has also produced many early retirements or changes in the type of practice. Time lost at conferences, depositions, and trials in connection with malpractice claims must also be considered. As impressive as these costs are, they may be overshadowed in their effect by the intangible costs of provider dysfunction, nihilism, seige mentality, and isolation that the pervasive threat of malpractice liability has caused.

The traditional fault-based system for allocating losses arising from medical accidents is beset with inefficiency and irrationality. Malpractice cases are complex, time-consuming, and expensive, so much so that it is economically feasible to prosecute only the more serious injuries, leaving many other claims unredressed. Fees for the plaintiff's and defendant's counsel and the costs of administering liability insurance together may take as much as two-thirds or more of each dollar paid for medical malpractice insurance. This is a poor return on the investment that the public makes through the higher medical charges imposed to defray such costs. This is especially true considering the other ways in which our society's increasingly scarce resources could be allocated.

With the growing complexity of modern medicine, there is also a real question whether lay jurors, even with the help of some expert testimony, can consistently render informed and objective decisions in malpractice cases. There is also a question of societal governance—whether jurors should be repeatedly vested with such broad discretion to decide how millions of dollars should be allocated. Some have also questioned the efficacy of the threat of malpractice liability as a deterrent, citing the fact that liability insurance protection undermines the deterrent effect of the threat of potential liability. The incrimination that accompanies allegations and findings of "malpractice" is often disproportionate to the gravity of defendant's conduct, especially given the inherent imponderables in medical practice and in determinations of substandard performance. Finally, the traditional fault-based system fails to help many persons suffering medical accidents. In most instances, there simply was no "fault" in the quality of care, or at least none that can be proven. Or, the potential damages simply are not large enough to justify a case.

C. FUTURE DIRECTIONS

Any rational approach to law reform should consider three questions: first, what legislative changes are desirable; second, which of those reforms stand a reasonable chance of being enacted into law; and, third, how might such reforms be formulated to afford the best chance of surviving constitutional challenges? Reforms may be made within the existing fault-based system of tort liability, or that system might be replaced in whole or in part with some other form of loss allocation such as a no-fault system. These possibilities are examined below.

The traditional tort action fulfills a number of objectives. First, it deters substandard conduct by the threat of civil liability. Even with insurance, there remains the ever present threat that one's liability might exceed his policy limits or result in higher premiums or even loss of insurance. Litigation is also very time consuming. The adverse publicity of a malpractice lawsuit as well as its emotional costs are also strong deterrents. Since the medical profession, like most professions, has so far not consistently policed itself, reforms should ideally include some mechanism to help assure quality care.

Tort actions also compensate the victim. This softens the potentially devastating effects of some medical accidents on individuals by spreading the loss to all those who pay for medical services. Since the costs of such claims are ultimately passed on to consumers, those costs become part of the cost of providing medical services or products. This may contribute to a better allocation of resources by helping to inform consumers of the true costs of the goods and services that compete for their limited dollars.

Reforms within the tort system should not only attempt to eliminate or reduce the adverse effects identified in the preceding subsection, but should also attempt to do so without subverting the general deterrence and loss-allocative function of tort law. One way to preserve most of the benefits of the present system, while at the same time mitigating some of its more oppressive features, would be to place some real limits on damages. Perhaps recovery of all of past and future economic losses and medical expenses could be allowed, but a limit could be placed on damages for pain and suffering. Damages for pain and suffering are extremely subjective, unpredictable, and difficult to control. They are also subject to abuse. There is also a question whether something as intangible as pain can even rationally be quantified.

A clear but reasonable outer limit should also be placed on the time during which a person may bring an action. Perhaps plaintiff could be given one year from when he discovers or should have discovered his injury, but subject to a seven-year maximum cutoff from the date of the alleged wrongful conduct except when there has been fraudulent concealment.

Legislation could also make it clear that professional standards should be conclusive on complex issues of professional competence. Also, the extent of a physician's duty to non-patient third parties should be clearly defined and circumscribed. Other reforms might include effective restrictions on informed consent actions by adopting specific informational guidelines for various medical procedures. Restrictions might also be placed on actions alleging guarantees of a specific therapeutic result. Physician's vicarious liability for the acts of non-employees who are not partners should be abandoned.

Reforms will also have to be able to pass constitutional muster. The likelihood that statutory changes will be invalidated by some courts might be reduced by making the reforms broadly applicable to all personal injury torts cases, but not applicable to conduct occurring before the effective date of the statutes.

There have also been proposals for more fundamental systemic changes. Most of these would in one way or another replace the present fault system with a model that does not depend on fault as a precondition to recovery. Despite surface appeal, these proposals raise serious questions. First the extent to which abandonment of fault as an element of liability would simplify loss allocation and produce administrative savings is debatable. If a pure no-fault approach were adopted under which all iatrogenic (therapy-produced) injuries were compensable, serious problems would remain in charting the bounds of iatrogenicity. Many patients are seriously ill before they receive medical intervention. As a result, determining precisely whether therapy "caused" an injury would remain a complex task even if proof of fault were no longer required. If a strict liability requiring "defective" services (but not fault) were adopted, matters would even be more complicated. Arriving at a functional definition of "defective medical services" would be an elusive goal. One suspects that such a test would, as in some of the "defect in design" cases in the products liability sphere, come to depend in part on traditional negligence principles.

Second, the overall costs of a no-fault or strict liability system for medical injuries could be staggering. It is estimated that a large percentage of the population has had a health-impairing experience with medical care, though not necessarily one involving malpractice. Iatrogenic injuries sustained by hospital patients alone probably number in the millions each year. These figures dwarf the number of malpractice claims.

Third, a no-fault system for medical accidents could raise questions about its fairness. Individualized damages that seek to return each claimant to his own pre-injury condition can perhaps be justified under a fault system where the tortfeasor, as we are told, must take his victim as he finds him. When fault is not required, however, individualization of economic recoveries may be questioned for preserving and reinforcing (at the expense of health care consumers generally) inequities in individual socio-economic circumstances that antedate the injury. To base one's right to compensation on the fortuity of having received the injury at the hands of a physician rather than from some other source would seem difficult to justify. *See* Keeton, *Compensation for Medical Accidents*, 121 U.Pa.L. Rev. 590, 609 (1973).

Fourth, because of uncertainty about the means of accident avoidance (apart from avoiding negligence) and difficulties in organizing for research and information distribution, the imposition of strict liability upon medical practitioners would probably not enhance risk avoidance through collective action. 84 Yale L.J. 1141, 1156–57 (1975).

Fifth, if individual health care providers continued to have a financial stake in the loss for which they were responsible even if not at fault, treatment of the more high risk patients and some medical procedures might be discouraged.* This could distort the objective of basing health care decisions on the cost-benefit considerations of the medical procedure contemplated.

At the very least, some substantial ceilings or damages would be necessary under a no-fault approach to make such a system economically feasible and fair.

* This might occur where, for example, a system of loss allocation (such as strict liability) was financed through insurance held by individual providers, and insurance premiums were based on the accident record of the insured as well as the risks inherent in the provider's specialty or type of practice.

From this concededly oversimplified discussion, it is apparent that there are no easy solutions to the malpractice problem. Perhaps enactment of a national health insurance plan for financing health care for serious illness might create an environment in which meaningful reform of malpractice law might occur. Such a plan, based on a social security model, could foster a more conservative and faithful administration of the fault system by affording those stricken with misfortune a sure source of medical care apart from damages from malpractice litigation. Courts and legislatures might then be less constrained to press forward with needed law reform within the fault system, especially effective ceilings on damages. The prospect for a no-fault system probably depends on whether some of the conceptual and practical obstacles to such a system can be overcome and an effective mechanism developed to replace the role of the traditional malpractice action in assuring real accountability in the medical professions.

Ultimately, something must be done to end the unpredictability and virtually limitless liability exposure of health care professionals that has so undermined and poisoned the physician-patient relationship and has consumed such a large share of our society's increasingly scarce resources.

INDEX

References are to Pages

ABANDONMENT
    See also, Duty, Professional relationship
Breach of contract, 259
Termination of professional relationship, 23

ABUSE OF PROCESS
See Commitment

ASSAULT
Liability for, 180

ASSUMPTION OF RISK
See Defenses and Limitations

AVOIDABLE CONSEQUENCES
See Defenses and Limitations

BATTERY
Liability for, 180

BORROWED SERVANT
See Vicarious Liability

CAUSATION
    See also, Proximate Cause
Burden of proof, 209
Expert testimony requirement, 200
Informed consent, 164
Multiple causes, 202
Preexisting conditions, 203

333

CAUSATION—Continued
Proof of causation, 200
Tests of causation, 199

CIRCUMSTANTIAL EVIDENCE
See *Res Ipsa Loquitur*

COMMITMENT
Liability for wrongful, 181

COMPARATIVE NEGLIGENCE
See Defenses and Limitations

CONFIDENTIAL INFORMATION
See Unauthorized Disclosures

CONSENT
　　See also, Informational Needs of Patient; Informed Consent
Forms of consent,
　　Consent by patient, 131
　　Implied consent, 137
　　Scope of consent, 137
　　Standard for consent, 152
　　Substituted consent, 143
Requirement of consent, 131
Right to refuse treatment, 143

CONTRACT ACTIONS
　　See also, Abandonment; Malpractice; Legal Theories
Failure to perform, 259
Procedural features, 6, 254, 269
Promises of specific results, 254
Statute of limitations, 269

CONTRIBUTORY NEGLIGENCE
See Defenses and Limitations

CRISIS
Malpractice, 320

DAMAGES
　　See also, Causation; Proximate Cause

DAMAGES—Continued
Birth as an injury,
    Defective child, 224
    Normal child, 220
Compensatory, 229
Contract, 254
Law reform, 328
Punitive, 230
Statutory changes, 320
Torts, 229

DEFAMATION
See Unauthorized Disclosures

DEFENSES AND LIMITATIONS
    See also, Unauthorized Disclosures, Privileges to disclose
Arbitration agreements, 290
Assumption of risk, 283
Avoidable consequences, 285
Charitable immunity, 295
Comparative negligence, 283
Contributory negligence, 283
Good Samaritan laws, 296
Governmental immunity, 293
Official immunities, 291
Releases,
    Exculpatory releases, 289
    Other tortfeasors, 286
Statutes of limitations, see Statutes of Limitations
Statutory, 296
Workers' compensation, 297

DEFENSIVE MEDICINE
Costs of, 325
Definition, 320

DISCOVERY RULE
See Statutes of Limitations, Accrual

DUTY
Multiple health care providers, 22

DUTY—Continued
"No duty" rule,
    Hospitals, 12
    Individual practitioners, 10
Non-traditional duties,
    Assisting in claims, 214
    Disposition of human tissue, 217
    Non-patients, 34
    Non-therapeutic examinations, 30
    Peer review, 216
Professional relationship,
    Duration, 23
    Limitations on practice, 29
    Non-therapeutic, 30
    Sources of professional duty, 15
    Traditional relationship, 15
Proximate cause, 211
Scope of duty, 29
Sources of duty,
    Consensual relationship, 15
    Contracts with non-patients, 21
    Undertaking, 16

EXPERT TESTIMONY
See Causation; Proof of Negligence; Standard of Care

FALSE IMPRISONMENT
Liability for, 181

GOOD SAMARITAN STATUTES
Limitations on liability, 296

HISTORICAL PERSPECTIVES
Emergence of malpractice action, 1
Legal Theories, 6

HOSPITAL LIABILITY
Corporate liability,
    Equipment, 307
    Food, 307
    General principles, 304

HOSPITAL LIABILITY—Continued
Medication, 307
Premises, 309
Safety procedures, 310
Staff privileges, 311
Supervision of patient care, 315
Supplies, 307
General principles, 298
Immunities,
Charitable, 295
Governmental, 293
Vicarious liability,
Non-physicians, 303
Ostensible agency, 302
Physicians, 299

INFLICTION OF MENTAL DISTRESS
Liability for, 193

INFORMATIONAL NEEDS OF PATIENT
See also, Consent; Informed Consent
Misrepresentation, concealment, and nondisclosure, 175
Subsequently-discovered dangers, 175

INFORMED CONSENT
See also, Consent; Informational Needs of Patient
Battery or negligence, 155
Causation, 164
General principles, 154
Informed refusal, 173
Privileges to withhold information, 168
Professional standards, weight of, 156
Standard of disclosure, 156
Who must disclose, 170

INTENTIONAL TORTS
See also, Assault; Battery; Commitment; Defamation;
False Imprisonment; Infliction of Mental Distress;
Invasion of Privacy; Unauthorized Disclosures
Malpractice actions generally, 179

INVASION OF PRIVACY
Intrusion, 193
Types, 184
Unauthorized disclosures, 185

LAW REFORM
Future directions, 326
Need for, 324
Recent statutory changes, 319

LEGAL THEORIES
Tort or contract, 6

LEGISLATION
Current prospects, 326
Recent developments, 320

LIBEL
See Defamation; Unauthorized Disclosures

LIMITATIONS OF ACTIONS
See Statutes of Limitations

LOCALITY RULES
Competency of experts, 81
Standard of care, 58

MALICIOUS PROSECUTION
See Commitment

MALPRACTICE
Definition, 3
Increase in claims,
    Causes, 319
    Magnitude, 320, 324
Legal theories, 6
Nature of medical malpractice, 5

MISREPRESENTATION AND NONDISCLOSURE
    See also, Statutes of Limitations, Fraudulent concealment
        rules
Informed consent, see Informed Consent

MISREPRESENTATION AND NONDISCLOSURE—Continued
Liability for, 175

NEGLIGENCE
Defenses, see Defenses and Limitations
Duty, see Duty
Elements, 9
Proof of, see Proof of Negligence
Standard of care, see Standard of Care

NO–FAULT
See also, Strict Liability
Opposing arguments, 325, 329

PRIVILEGE
Defense, 188
Meanings of term, 187
Privileged disclosures, see Unauthorized Disclosures
Testimonial privilege, see Unauthorized Disclosures
Therapeutic privilege, see Informed Consent

PROOF OF NEGLIGENCE
Circumstantial evidence, see *Res Ipsa Loquitur*
Exceptions to expert witness requirement,
    Admissions, 86
    Common knowledge, 84
    Court-appointed experts, 110
    Defendants' statements, 86
    Guidelines of professional organizations, 106
    Institutional rules, 106
    Manufacturers' instructions and information, 89
    Medical literature, 98
    Violation of regulation, 102
    Violation of statute, 102
Expert testimony,
    Competency, 77
    Geographic competency, 81
    Professional competency, 78
    Requirement, 52
    Securing, 76

PROXIMATE CAUSE
See also, Causation; Duty
Birth as an injury, 219
General principles, 211
Self-inflicted injury, 227

RES IPSA LOQUITUR
Applicability to malpractice, 112
Causation and circumstantial evidence, 113
Elements,
    Conduct of plaintiff, 123
    Exclusive control, 119
    General principles, 114
    Inference of negligence, 116
    Plaintiff's knowledge and proof, 124
General principles, 111
Procedural effect, 126
Reform, 129

RESPONDEAT SUPERIOR
See Vicarious Liability

SELF-DETERMINATION, RIGHT OF
See Consent; Informational Needs of Patient; Informed Consent

SLANDER
See Dafamation; Unauthorized Disclosures

STANDARD OF CARE
See also, Proof of Negligence
Acceptable practice, 43
Average practitioner, 75
"Best judgment" rule, 72
Customary practice, 43
"Error in judgment" rule, 69
Expert testimony requirement, see Proof of Negligence
Frames of reference,
    Defendant's situation, 55
    Geographic, 58
    Peer review and utilization controls, 63

STANDARD OF CARE—Continued
Professional, 55
Time of act or omission, 55
General principles, 39
Professional Standard Review Organizations, 63
Professional standards,
Definition of, 43
Weight of, 47
"Respectable minority" rule, 65
Schools of medicine, 55
Specialists, 57

STATUTES OF LIMITATIONS
Accrual, 270
Applicable statute, 268
Continuing involvement rules, 276
Disabilities, 281
Discovery rules, 271
Fraudulent concealment rules, 279
General principles, 267
Hybrid rules, 272
Possible exceptions, 279
Reform, 282
Traditional rule, 270

STRICT LIABILITY
See also, Contract Actions; Vicarious Liability
Future prospects, 329
Hospitals, 262
Physicians, 260

UNAUTHORIZED DISCLOSURES
Confidential information, 185
Defamation, 183
Invasion of privacy, see Invasion of Privacy
Privileges to disclosure, 188
Testimonial privilege, 187

VICARIOUS LIABILITY
See also, Hospital Liability

VICARIOUS LIABILITY—Continued
Borrowed servant,
    Absent physicians, 241
    Hospital liability, 250
    Present physicians,
        In general, 243
        Assumed or exercised control, 245
        Other physicians, 248
        Right to control, 244
    Reappraisal, 250
    Theory of, 239
Employees' torts, 233
General principles, 231
Other physicians, 234
Partners and partnership, 236
Professional corporations, 237

†